Manche

The Mercer-Allison Years

MANCHESTER CITY'S first home game of 1964-65 was a resounding success – a 6-0 win over Leyton Orient. But by the time Swindon Town arrived at Maine Road in January 1965, City's fortunes had taken an alarming tumble. They had been knocked out of both Cup competitions – each time by a Third Division team – and had lost 11 times in the old Second Division. Not surprisingly attendances had dropped and an all-time low of 8,015, less than ten per cent of the club's record gate, bothered to turn up to watch City play Swindon.

At Easter, manager George Poyser resigned and the rest of the season City were managerless as they finished 11th. In July 1965, City announced their new man: Joe Mercer, former England, Everton and Arsenal wing-half who had been out of the game for 12 months after suffering a stroke while managing Aston Villa.

Mercer needed a younger man to work with the players on the training pitch and he chose Malcolm Allison, the former West Ham defender who had himself suffered bad health, his playing career ended when he lost a lung to TB.

No-one in their wildest dreams could imagine the success these two would bring to Maine Road. Within 12 months City had won the championship of the Second Division. Two years later they were League champions of England and by 1971 had added the FA Cup, League Cup and European Cup-winners' Cup . And for good measure they had at last overcome the always looming shadow of Manchester United.

This, then, is the story of the most successful period in Manchester City's history. With the personal recollections of skipper Tony Book, prolific scorer Neil Young and Malcolm Allison himself, the events of that remarkable period are retold here. Events which not only gave City supporters such wonderful times but which also endeared the team to football fans up and down the country as they wondered at the style of play created by Genial Joe and Big Mal.

IAN PENNEY had his first glimpse of Maine Road on 18 May 1966, a couple of months before England's World Cup glory. Taken by his late father (the only Red in the family until he gave up), Ian saw no goals against Southampton but he did see the Second Division trophy paraded. It was the first success of the legendary Mercer-Allison partnership and it began the author's love affair with Manchester City, and in the 40-odd years since it has shown no signs of diminishing despite the events of the mid to late 1990s.

In 1973, Ian began working at the famous Manchester bookshop, Sherratt & Hughes in St Ann's Square. He moved to the Stockport branch in the 1980s before returning as manager of the now-rebadged Waterstones in 1993. Made redundant by the IRA bomb blast in June 1996, Ian was for nearly ten years manager of the Stationery Office Bookshop in Albert Square, the proverbial 'stone's throw' from the steps of Manchester Town Hall, the scene of many a triumphant parade during City's glory years.

His first book *The Maine Road Encylopaedia* was published in 1995, followed by *Blue Heaven* 12 months later. He has also contributed articles to both the club's match day programme and monthly magazine as well as to the fanzine *King of the Kippax*. His other books include *The Essential History of Manchester City*, *The Legends of Manchester City*, *England's Football Legends* and *Maine Road Favourites: Where are they now?*

Manchester City
The Mercer-Allison Years

Ian Penney with
Malcolm Allison, Tony Book and Neil Young

Foreword by Norah Mercer

First published in Great Britain in 2001 by

The Breedon Books Publishing Company Limited

Breedon House, 3 The Parker Centre, Derby, DE21 4SZ.

Paperback edition 2008

This edition published in Great Britain in 2012 by The Derby Books Publishing Company Limited,

3 The Parker Centre, Derby, DE21 4SZ.

ISBN 978-1-78091-239-4

Printed and bound by Copytech (UK) Limited, Peterborough.

Contents

Dedication

To my wife Sheila, for once again supporting me,
despite the mess!

Acknowledgements

To my cousin, Neil Woodhead, for continuing the work started
by my late father in instilling in me all things Manchester City,
and for the meticulous scrapbooks he kept during
these halcyon days.

To Mrs Norah Mercer, firstly for consenting to let her late
husband take on the job at Maine Road back in 1965, and
secondly for her kind words in the foreword.

To anyone and everyone who was involved either on or off the
pitch between 1965 and 1972 for making the period a fabulous
one for those who followed the fortunes of Manchester City
Football Club.

And finally, thanks also are due sincerely to Malcolm Allison,
Tony Book and Neil Young, whose personal recollections form a
major part of this work.

If there is one sad fact in the completion of this book it is that
my good friend, the late John Maddocks, is no longer around to
see the finished article. At least we all know now, that the Blue
Half is well represented in Heaven.

Ian Penney,

June 2008.

Foreword

by Norah Mercer

MY HUSBAND'S time as manager of City from 1965 through to the early 1970s was one of the most enjoyable periods of his life. He loved the club, the supporters, the players, the hope and the atmosphere of that period. As did I.

Joe's partnership with Malcolm Allison brought great success to the club, and Joe used to joke that the only thing City didn't win during his time was the Grand National! It was a great time for us all, and yet it very nearly didn't happen at all. Joe had been unwell and forced out of the game at Aston Villa. He wasn't supposed to return to football, but Joe couldn't help himself. He'd spent his life in the game and, to be truthful, he needed it.

He joined City in July 1965; picked up Malcolm Allison as his assistant, signed a couple of players – including Mike Summerbee – and the journey along the road to future success commenced. Within five years they'd won promotion, the League, the FA Cup, the League Cup and the European Cup-winners' Cup, with Joe becoming the first man to win both the FA Cup and the League as a player and a manager.

This book aims to cover those years of success, and I wish the author Ian Penney well. I first met Ian in December 1993 at the launch of *Football With a Smile* – Gary James' excellent biography of Joe – and it is clear he is passionate about City. That night I met so many supporters who were keen to tell me how much Joe's time at Maine Road meant to them. It was a very enjoyable evening, and I have made many trips to Maine Road and the City of Manchester Stadium since then to support City.

Finally if this book is as good as City's successes during this period, or as strong as Ian's passion for the Blues, then it will prove to be an excellent read.

Thank you

A Fall From Grace

IT HAS become part of footballing folklore: a German-born former prisoner of war breaking his neck diving at the feet of an onrushing centre-forward in a Wembley FA Cup Final. The goalkeeper's name was Bert Trautmann; the year was 1956 and his victorious team was Manchester City.

Just eight years later, one of the most famous teams in the country had suffered relegation to the Second Division, and on three occasions had been supported by miserly crowds of less than 9,000 for home games. The game against Swindon Town on 16 January 1965 is still a club record for the lowest home attendance when only 8,015 managed to drag themselves down to Moss Side. It is less than ten per cent of the club's highest ever attendance.

The early days of the 1960s were undoubtedly dark times for Manchester City Football Club. In his book Manchester City; Meredith to Mercer and the FA Cup, the respected journalist Eric Thornton wrote: "Over the years, I had gone to the ground in many moods. None so dismal as those of that period. The depression began to settle on you even in town. For there were no queues for public transport. Or for taxis. The days when the crowds had to struggle for both had gone. They stopped running the relief service from the side of the Town Hall. They trimmed the 'specials' from Piccadilly until one Saturday it looked as if the match had suddenly been called off because nobody seemed to be going to Maine Road."

Referring specifically to that Swindon game, he went on to say: "With half-an-hour to go the ground was practically empty. A few thousand trickled into it within the next 15 minutes. Somebody said to me as I came down the corridor after checking the programme in Walter Griffiths' office: "They're starting to come in now." I nipped up into the Press Box, and knew the information was wrong. For there didn't seem many more than 5,000 in that vast bowl. There were acres and acres of empty seats in the main stand. The Platt Lane stand was also almost empty. You could have driven a fleet of buses along the terraces without any danger of touching anybody. It was a terrible sight.

Some more came later. But even at the final count there were only just over 8,000. Such a poor figure I felt shocking asking the secretary for it so I could announce it generally to all the other newspaper boys.

One of the players said to me afterwards: "I've never felt so depressed in all the time I've been a professional footballer. It was ghastly playing a first-team match in front of all those vacant spaces.""

So incensed were the fans after the game that some of them staged an angry protest outside the ground and at one point bricks were hurled at the main stand windows.

Depressing reading indeed and although obviously not acceptable for a club of City's stature, perhaps more understandable when looked at purely from a statistical point of view.

Despite City's FA Cup success back in 1956, their average home attendance of 32,256 dropped by 2,500 the following year, a fact in itself interesting. There then followed two seasons of highly respectable averages of more than 32,500, culminating in a 35,637 average for the 1959-60 campaign. This figure was helped by the arrival of Denis Law towards the end, and when Lancashire neighbours Burnley clinched the First Division Championship in the very last game with a 2-1 victory, just short of 66,000 were crammed into Maine Road to witness the game.

Fred Eyre, nowadays one of the most sort after (and best) speakers on the after dinner circuit, was a schoolboy footballer at Maine Road during the early 1960s. "I joined City around the same time as Neil Young back in 1959. I'd known him for a while as we'd both played together in the same Manchester Boys team. Youngie had always been an outside-left, with me playing right or left-half. To quote the old joke: 'I could play badly on either side'. I know these days I constantly make fun of my apparent lack of ability, but back then I was actually (and without the joke or getting too big-headed) quite a good player. City offered us both amateur forms in the close season, with me a place on the groundstaff in November. I think Youngie joined the groundstaff the following February, on his 16th birthday.

I stayed until 1963 when I moved to Lincoln, but as I came home to Manchester every weekend, and kept in almost weekly touch with most of the other lads, I was pretty much up to date with the events going on at City.

Obviously things weren't great at the club during this time, although as schoolkids, none of us had any great experience of things elsewhere and were therefore unable to make any real comparisons with other clubs. Playing regularly in the 'A' and 'B' teams we would play the same sides up to six times a season and as a result we got to know some of the opposition players quite well. I became close friends with Tommy Smith of Liverpool and after games we'd spend half an hour so together waiting for the team buses to turn up. He'd start telling stories about 'Shanks did this', 'Shanks said this' type of stuff, and I used to think, 'Bloody hell, our manager never even speaks to us at all apart from an occasional nod in the corridor.'

Smith used to tell us about Shanks playing five-a-side with the youngsters in the car-park at Anfield ('We had to let him win otherwise we'd have all be there 'til midnight') and we'd think it was a miracle if our manager put his overcoat on and watched a training session for two seconds. Liverpool at the time were still in the Second Division and some of the things Smith told us began to make us think that maybe things were different at other places. When Liverpool won promotion they played City at Anfield on a Wednesday night and I remember Smith rang me at home and asked if I was going to the game. He suggested we spent the afternoon in New Brighton and then went to the game in the evening. He arranged for me to stand in the boys' pen, right next to the touchline, along with the Liverpool reserves to watch the match. At this point I thought: 'Hello, things are happening here.' As far as I could see, they weren't happening at Maine Road."

The new decade saw crowds drop every single season, with the lowest being the desperate 1964-65 season when the average was less than 14,800.

The man in charge of team matters during the last two seasons was George Poyser. A former player with, amongst others, Wolves and Brentford, Poyser had been manager at Notts. County before becoming assistant manager to Les McDowall at Maine Road in 1957. Two weeks after McDowall moved to Oldham in June 1963, the club favoured the experienced and familiar Poyser as the new man to take over the reigns. Without being too critical of Poyser, and with the greatest player of all, hindsight, perhaps then was the time to bring in new blood. Not only did Poyser have to try to sort things out on the pitch, he also had to battle against the successes of Manchester United and their developing Old Trafford stadium. It was indeed, extremely difficult to 'keep the faith' during this period.

To his credit, Poyser attempted to improve things as the purchases of Derek Kevan, Jimmy Murray and Johnny Crossan showed, but his two seasons in charge were really a case of 'one step forwards and two back'. Homegrown youngsters such as Alan Oakes and Glyn Pardoe were also by now establishing themselves in the first team and Neil Young had become an almost permanent fixture. Arguably the major factor in all this though was a lack of confidence, something which struggling sides always find difficult to regain. Another youngster at the time just breaking through was Mike Doyle who described the club as "a ship without a rudder". Fred Eyre: "I remember Mike Doyle's very first day at City; he got into a scrap with Bobby McAlinden. I was foreman of the groundstaff by then, the 'boss' groundstaff boy. I had no problem with the fight but straight after training, Jimmy Meadows, the trainer, sent for me and gave me a real bollocking in his office for not stopping it. As if I could stop Doylie! As if I'd even want to try!"

At Easter 1965, Poyser resigned as manager. His trainer, former player Jimmy Meadows, left with him. Defeats in the Cup competitions by Shrewsbury and Mansfield (both of the Third Division) were perhaps the final straws as City finished a disappointing season in 11th position in Division Two. It was clear something had to be done to resurrect the club back to greatness. Chairman Albert Alexander was more than aware of the situation but was not going to rush into any hasty decisions. He waited until July before making his announcement.

Neil Young remembers

I was born in Fallowfield, less than half a mile from Maine Road; in fact you could actually see the ground from my bedroom window. The whole family were big City fans and from a very early age I would go down regularly in all weather to watch the team play.

I didn't really have one particular hero; I suppose because the side was so good in the mid 1950s that they were all heroes to me. Little could I know that when I stood as a youngster shivering on the terraces, one day I would be on that very same pitch playing alongside such names as Dave Ewing, Bill Leivers, Wembley scorer Joe Hayes and the legendary Bert Trautmann. Bert (or Mr Trautmann as we groundstaff boys had to call him) was a magnificent goalkeeper. So good in fact that we soon discovered the only way to beat him with a shot in training was to mishit it!

At school I played regularly and made the Manchester Boys' Under 15 side when I was still only 13. Although two years difference can be quite a gap at that age, I was always tall and fortunately for me this balanced things out. We played annually against London Boys and I remember one occasion playing in a game at White Hart Lane. Although we lost 7-2 the experience for me was fantastic. The following year we gained revenge with a 4-1 win at home in Manchester. It was the first time I had played at Maine Road.

Harry Godwin was scouting for City at the time and had taken an interest in me. He'd watch me regularly and would talk with my mum, always leaving either a bag of mints or sweets at our house whenever he'd leave. Harry was really a lovely man whose keen eye for talent brought many a young player to Maine Road over the years.

Through Harry I signed for the club in May 1959 with a starting salary of £6 a week. Just before I'd signed, United's Johnny Aston also offered me a deal to join them but I turned it down. Being asked to play for 'your team' has to be the realisation of a dream for any football-mad youngster. There was a rota system in force at the time that all groundstaff boys had to adhere to. The duties included sweeping the terraces and gyms and cleaning up to 40 pairs of boots. I always hated the boots as they'd have to be absolutely immaculate, especially those of the first team, and it was a task I always tried to get out of. I can still remember players such as Ken Barnes saying to me: "Have you done my boots yet Neil?"

As time progressed, I began to play outside-left for the club's 'A' team. In one particular game – against Blackburn Rovers – I remember taking a corner-kick and just collapsing in a heap as I kicked the ball. I'd strained ligaments in my left knee and it swelled up like a balloon. So much so in fact that I had to have my trousers cut in order to get them on and was walking around with the help of a crutch. The club doctor said he'd have to drain the fluid off the knee and he did this with a huge needle, stopping every so often to empty it. In all he took one and a half pints, and all with no anaesthetic! To say it was unpleasant would be an understatement! Although I was out of action for something like ten weeks, it was touch and go as to whether I'd actually play again.

Despite this setback I was desperate to get back to playing again. Even the misfortunes of the first team at the time didn't detract me. When you're young, you don't think about what's going on all around you; you just want to play. The fact that there were four other players all capable of playing outside-left in the first team didn't deter me either. I figured that with both Clive Colbridge and Ray Sambrook being 'old' (I think they were both about 28!) and David Connor being at home almost anywhere on the pitch, the only real competition for me was David Wagstaffe who was about 12 months older.

With 'Waggy' playing outside-left for the reserves, I was given the opportunity to play at outside-right, the theory being that I could cut inside and have a shot with my better left foot. This paid off and I began to score quite a few goals for the reserves, sometimes playing against former first-team opposition full-backs who were making their way back after injuries.

Manager Les McDowall – a man we youth and reserve players saw very infrequently

– obviously liked what he saw with me at number seven and he gave me my first-team debut at Villa Park in November 1961 when I was just 17. I borrowed a pair of boots from Bert Trautmann for my first game. They were absolutely beautiful; so soft, they were the best pair of boots I'd ever seen. They were so comfortable I kept them for about three years, repairing them constantly with sticking plaster along the way. Although we lost the game 2-1 I managed to keep my place and never missed a League game for the rest of the season. I scored my first goal for City the following month against Ipswich just before Christmas, finishing the season with ten goals from 24 games.

The following season, 1962-63, ended with a 6-1 thrashing at West Ham and City were relegated. The defeat at West Ham and the ensuing consequences made it probably the worst moment in my entire career at Maine Road. On a personal note I'd played in 31 of the 42 League games and scored five times. Alex Harley was miles in front of everyone but the fact that we let in more than a hundred was the real reason we went down. Les McDowall left the club at the end of the season and his assistant George Poyser took over. George was a really decent fellow but his footballing thinking was on exactly the same plane as McDowall's and so consequently nothing changed. Looking back, the club needed to make a clean break and bring in fresh faces and new ideas when McDowall left.

Having said that though Poyser could quite easily have won promotion in his very first season had it not been for an injury to the free-scoring Jimmy Murray in January. Murray came back after an absence of six weeks by which time we'd lost any real chance of promotion and finished sixth.

Things worsened in 1964-65. This was the year of the Swindon 8,000 crowd and City finished 11th in the Second Division. Certain sections of the fans began to give the players some considerable stick – fair enough, they pay their money and they're entitled to voice their opinion – and I can remember players walking across the pitch and leaving the ground through the Kippax stand rather than face the angry fans outside the main stand. Being a younger player, I escaped the harsher criticism aimed at some of the older players, but sometimes fans don't seem to realise that players don't play badly on purpose and it's on these occasions when the players need the fans behind them not against them.

We lost in both cup competitions to Third Division sides and George Poyser left at Easter leaving Johnny Hart to look after team matters until the end of the season. Perhaps, in the end, it was the best thing for the club. The arrival of a new manager from the outside always puts the players on their toes and generally improves things all round. Little did anyone know how much things would be improved.

1965-66
Will Anyone Come?

ON 13 JULY 1965, Manchester City made one of their greatest ever signings when Joe Mercer, the former Everton, Arsenal and England player, and ex-Sheffield United and Aston Villa boss, was unveiled as their new manager.

Highly respected in the game, Mercer had been forced to leave his post at Villa Park in July 1964 after suffering a stroke. The Midlands newspapers of the time said Mercer and Villa had parted 'by mutual consent', although Joe himself felt badly treated, still thinking he was capable of offering something to the game. How ironic then that the next few years would see an apparently ailing manager transform the fortunes of an apparently ailing football club.

It was a brave decision by both Mercer and City. Speaking several years later, Mercer commented: "Football could live without Joe Mercer but Joe Mercer couldn't live without football." His wife Norah, worried about endangering his life again, remained unconvinced, wanting him to wait another 12 months and certainly to find a less stressful position. However when he got a call from City secretary Walter Griffiths in July 1965, Mercer's love of the game proved too strong and he leapt at the chance.

Despite his abundant enthusiasm for the game, Mercer was also intelligent enough to realise that he would have to change his ways. No longer was he able to don the tracksuit and take the strenuous training sessions as in previous years. He knew he needed a strong, right-hand man. Fortunately for Mercer, and Manchester City, one such man was also available.

Malcolm Allison was appointed Mercer's number two on 21 July. Mercer recalled later: "I 'phoned an extrovert, ebullient but brilliant coach called Malcolm Allison. Like me he was out of work – sacked by Plymouth Argyle. It took me two days to find him, but he said he would join me if I took the job. Secretly I met the Manchester board and accepted the job, telling them of my plans for Malcolm."

Allison had already built himself a reputation at Lilleshall for being a coach with a big future. Fascinated by tactics and psychology, he'd got into coaching earlier than he would have liked when the loss of a lung through tuberculosis curtailed his playing days at West Ham. Allison claims to have always had a 'soft spot' for City after listening to their FA Cup Final defeat at the hands of Everton back in 1933. Never one to dodge a challenge, as well as having a preference for the underdog, Mercer's offer to Allison was just too good to turn down. Both men felt they had points to prove and were determined to make the detractors eat their words.

The new management team had inherited a playing squad of just 21, a far cry for the apparently endless squads of today's game, and was a mixture of both seasoned 'pros' and largely untried youngsters. In order to evaluate this 'inheritance' the club arranged three pre-

Malcolm Allison remembers

Around Easter time that year I'd left my position with Plymouth following ongoing disputes about team selection. Perhaps the final straw came when I wanted Noel Dwyer in goal for one game and the board wanted reserve team 'keeper John Leiper. In my usual forthright manner I asked: "Who's picking this team?" When I realised it wasn't me, I left.

During my time out of work I had three 'phone calls. The first from Stanley Matthews at Port Vale, the second from Raich Carter at Middlesbrough and the third from Joe Mercer at Manchester City. I think they were all in a matter of days during July. All three were legends in the game and I felt privileged to have been contacted by one of them let alone three. They all knew of my work over the previous ten or so years at Lilleshall, indeed Stanley Matthews had actually been in the same class as me along with his Blackpool teammate Stan Mortensen. Joe had seen me in action at Lilleshall but I'm not certain if Raich Carter had. He'd probably found out about me through the footballing grapevine and I arranged to travel up to Middlesbrough to see him on a Tuesday.

Joe Mercer rang me over the weekend prior to my trip to Middlesbrough and I explained that Raich Carter was thinking of offering me the coaching job. Joe said: "Malcolm, come and see me first." So I went up to Manchester on the Monday to see him. I met Joe and we had a chat in his office and I never got to Middlesbrough. I knew straight away this was the job for me, especially as I still had a liking for the club since that FA Cup Final on the wireless back in the 1930s. A couple of weeks later I got a message saying had I spoken to Stanley Matthews at Port Vale? I said I hadn't but of course by then it was too late. To this day I still don't know where that message had got to.

The salary at Maine Road was £40 a week, although Joe did say: "If we're doing alright at Christmas I'll see you get a rise." I was on £30 a week at Bath City and £40 a week at Plymouth so it certainly wasn't the money I was interested in. I suppose, in a way we both needed each other as we both had something to prove. Joe had been written off as a manager because of his so-called failures and his illness and me because I was too outspoken and arrogant. He hated to lose at anything and like many other great players he wasn't used to, and therefore couldn't handle, criticism. If you look at some of the great post-war English players, very few have actually had any sort of success as managers. Stanley Matthews, Tommy Lawton and Bobby Charlton are examples, whereas Jack Charlton, universally acknowledged as the lesser player, had considerable managerial success at both club and international level. Alf Ramsey is of course the exception to this rule, and he was ultimately successful when he devised a new playing formation.

Joe and myself had the full backing of the chairman, Albert Alexander, who was City through and through and whose family had been involved with the club for something like 70 years. The secretary Walter Griffiths was different though. Like many other secretaries he thought he could run the club and we clashed on many occasions during the early part of our working relationship.

When I first came to Manchester – I actually signed on 21 July 1965, just eight days after Joe had – I remember seeing kids playing football on the fields and there'd be 21 red shirts and one blue one. Then there was all the chanting at the schools: "United, United." Everywhere I went all I could see was United. Looking back, maybe this was the major factor in me wanting to succeed. It certainly made me more determined.

Not long afterwards, Joe and I were invited by United's captain Noel Cantwell to a celebration dinner in honour of their Championship success. Noel was a good friend of mine from the West Ham days and I actually stayed with him for a while when I first took the job at City. Amongst all the celebratory speeches I said to Matt Busby's son Sandy: "You've had a 20-year start, but we'll catch you in three." Pat Crerand decided to try out my gambling side when he wagered £10 we'd never get 30,000 inside Maine Road again. Needless to say I had no hesitation in accepting his bet. Call it bravado if you like but these were examples of the type of thing I had to do to try to remove the inferiority complex that had built up around the City players. Even Mike Doyle, a long-serving Blue and much publicised United 'hater' described the Maine Road set-up at the time as "slapdash." The confidence of the players was very low.

Because of Joe's health problems he told me almost from day one that he would leave the training side of things to me. This was exactly what I wanted to hear although one day during pre-season training I was the bearer of bad news. I said to him: "Joe, we're going to have to get rid of five or six of these players." I told him bluntly that they were all cheating in training. I used to play forwards against defence, and unknown to the players I would create situations. Situations like this are much more noticeable in training than they are in a full match. I would knock balls through the gaps and no one would run after them. One of these players was Derek Kevan who had been leading goalscorer the previous season. He was on his way to Crystal Palace fairly quickly and another one was Dave Bacuzzi, although it did take a bit longer for me to dispense with his services.

On the positive side though we did have about seven or eight young players who had ability. We had two good goalkeepers in Harry Dowd and Alan Ogley, and Ogley was in fact the first person that I ever saw who wore contact lenses whilst playing. We had Alan Oakes, Glyn Pardoe, Mike Doyle and Neil Young and I tried to get these players a little extra money. Neil Young in particular had some debts. I think at the time he owed the milkman £2!

We played a pre-season friendly at Maine Road against Dundee and I remember walking down the tunnel prior to kick-off to check if anyone had turned up to watch. We lost 2-1 and were awful. We hadn't quite got the team sorted out properly at that time despite trying a few different things. I said to Joe: "We're going to struggle but we've got to go ten games without getting beat. We've got to play defensively, be tight at the back and not give anything away. If we can manage to do that then at least we'll put some confidence back into the side." We lost one of our first 15 League games, the defeat coming in the eighth game when we lost 4-3 at Cardiff. This was the game that convinced me about Dave Bacuzzi's future as a Manchester City player.

The first game of that season was a 1-1 draw at Ayresome Park, Middlesbrough, a game which also saw substitutes for the first time in England. Ironically, if things had been different, I could have been on their bench that day instead of City's.

season friendlies, a home game with Dundee, and then away trips to both Walsall and Tranmere. Defeat at home followed by a draw at Walsall and victory at Tranmere did little to inspire confidence for the obvious rigours to come. Ralph Brand, a proven goalscorer north of the border, was a new face at Maine Road on 11 August and was Mercer's first signing for City.

After those poor showings, particularly against Dundee, a performance which angered even the most placid Mercer, travelling City fans saw a much-improved effort a fortnight later in the opening League game at Middlesbrough. Mercer and Allison both knew this was a crucial game, as it would give an indication of the club's standing in the division. The ensuing 1-1 draw provided the versatile Wythenshawe-born Dave Connor with his first taste of man to man marking (on 'Boro's Ian Gibson) and it gave Jimmy Murray the opportunity to score the first goal under the new regime. Roy Cheetham played centre-half in that game and he remembers Allison's training methods were "shorter and faster, with more emphasis on ball work" and "they undoubtedly rekindled the dormant spirit within the club". Just 24 hours before kick-off at Ayresome Park, City had paid £35,000 to Swindon Town for the services of Mike Summerbee, a man who'd scored the winning goal at Maine Road in the '8,000 game' a little over six months earlier. A direct and aggressive right-winger or centre-forward, Summerbee made his debut at Middlesbrough and would not miss a single game all season. Little could anyone predict then, just what a great signing this would be. The day after the Middlesbrough game, Michael Summerbee (as he was called in the very polite *Daily Telegraph*) was injured in a car crash near Stafford where he was taken to hospital and treated for shock and cuts. The speed of recent events had meant Summerbee was short on wardrobe and he was travelling back to the West Country to collect his clothes. It had been a hectic three days for 'Buzzer' and, unknown to him, a further visit to a Black Country doctor was lying in wait in the not too distant future.

More than 25,500 were at Maine Road when the recently relegated Wolves visited on the following Wednesday. It was a less than inspiring performance by the Blues and although they won 2-1, the opposition provided both goals. In a game highlighted only by "magnificent" performances from Oakes and Connor, Wolves' George Miller and Bobby Thomson kindly donated efforts to the City cause. Thomson's own goal with just five minutes left seemed to inspire Wolves more, who, in the words of one newspaper, proceeded to "batter the City goal", and when the highly-talented 19-year-old Peter Knowles scored in the 88th minute it looked as though the visitors might get something from the game after all.

Another own goal came from the generosity of the Bristol City defence in the third game of the season. After Cheetham's slip let in John Atyeo mid-way through the first half, Mike Doyle deflected a shot past Dowd to send City in at the break two goals down. Harsh words were obviously said in the changing rooms as within 30 seconds of the restart Brand's header pulled one back for the Blues. It proved to be exactly half of his City tally over the next two seasons. Eight minutes later Gibson in the Bristol goal punched Crossan's centre into his own net for the equaliser. Still obviously angered by the events of the first half, Allison was spoken to by the referee late on in the game for "shouting and gesticulating" from the touchline.

Neil Young remembers

Probably the biggest changes Joe and Malcolm brought to the club were the training methods and the way they instilled confidence in the players. Malcolm was especially good on the psychology; he used to make each of us think we were the best in world let alone the club.

I first came across him when we played a Second Division game at Plymouth, a place no one liked travelling to back then purely because it was so far away.

They scored an obviously pre-worked penalty and Malcolm leapt from the dug-out and threw his hat high into the air. I thought: "Look at him", as it was unusual to see any manager jumping about like that.

Under the previous regimes, the training sessions were basically run, run, run. There was no variation and we hardly saw a ball until the next game. Now we still ran – usually at Wythenshawe Park – but there was much more emphasis on ballwork. This provided the opportunities for the players to show they could actually play instead of being simply good runners. The contrast couldn't have been more different.

Neither could the personalities of Joe and Malcolm. Malcolm would be constantly working with the players, bellowing out his instructions, always trying to get that little bit of extra out of all of us. Twice a week we'd actually train on the pitch itself and Joe would walk around, taking every little detail in, but never saying a word. Later the two would get together in Joe's office and Joe would say: "Why don't you try that?" or "What about this?" kind of thing. Although he left all the training to Malcolm, Joe knew exactly what was going on; he never missed a trick. He was a very shrewd man. I never once saw them disagree about anything. If they did, then they must have done so in the office, away from the players. That is the sign of good management. If the management shows any disharmony then it only rubs off on the players or staff. Joe really was like a father figure to us all. At any time, any one of us could go and see Joe with a problem, whether it was to do with football or not. Nothing was ever too much trouble.

I remember we'd go up to either Blackpool or Southport for a couple of days for a bit of relaxation. The players would go to a club, have a few drinks and get to bed about two o'clock in the morning. More often than not Malcolm would be with us but he'd be up at seven banging on bedroom doors shouting: "Come on, get up. We're off to the beach for a run." We all thought: "Bloody hell, if he can do it with one good lung, we can do it with two." More often than not we all felt awful but we all got up! It was a great bit of psychology.

Joe and Malcolm both encouraged me to shoot more often than I had been doing. They both said I had a good left foot and for a while I was given almost a free role on the pitch. Eventually I'd have shot from any angle, the theory being that goalkeepers were used to saving shots only from certain areas and anywhere else could cause them problems.

Another thing we'd do in training was head tennis. I partnered Mike Doyle and I remember once taking part in an FA organised tournament in Leeds which we actually won against teams like Arsenal and Chelsea.

Some of the things Malcolm would get us to do only confirmed that, at the time, he was one of the top three coaches in the world. I think he was probably about 20 years ahead of his time. Nowadays when I coach youngsters I try to think back to the way Malcolm taught us. That way, I know I won't be going far wrong.

The season had started on a solid footing and Allison's plan of "going ten games without getting beat" was still holding up. On the negative side though the team was struggling to find the net of its own accord and some long-suffering and cynical supporters (and who could blame them after the events of the previous few seasons?) began to query the apparent quick removal of last season's top-scorer Derek Kevan from the ranks.

City travelled to Molineux for the return game against Wolves just five days after the Maine Road encounter. Amazingly for the third successive game, the opposition (now it was the turn of full-back Gerry Harris) assisted the Blues with their goalscoring endeavours. This time though Mike Doyle, Johnny Crossan and ex-Wolves' player Jimmy Murray also found the back of the net as the Blues ran out 4-2 winners. All this after former Blue David Wagstaffe had given the home side the lead in the fifth minute. Three minutes later, City led 2-1. Joe Mercer, himself a wing-half during his playing days gave Doyle a backhanded compliment for his last-minute goal when he told him: "You took that goal well– but you left us wide open at the back!" Other notable events in this game included Allison receiving another touchline lecture from a referee (apparently this time for coaching) and Summerbee being unceremoniously bundled into the second row of the Molineux stands by centre-half David Woodfield. For his trouble, Woodfield received his marching orders whilst Summerbee was concussed and carried off on a stretcher, later having 18 stitches in a head wound.

Neil Young played his first game of the season, away at Coventry, and was immediately on target. His brace were supplemented by another effort from Murray in the 3-3 draw. Hard to believe that a game of six goals could be described by one newspaper as "a dour struggle", nevertheless it was watched by the fifth highest crowd of the day anywhere in the country. The point gained at Highfield Road kept City in sixth place, one place ahead of their hosts, albeit on goal average. The fast-becoming prolific Young would eventually finish the season as leading goalscorer with 17 in all competitions.

Neil Young remembers

I travelled with the team up to Middlesbrough on the morning of the first game of the new season. Suddenly out of nowhere I developed a temperature of 104. Nobody knew what it was so they sent me home and I spent a few days in bed. I went to the ground on the following Tuesday expecting to play against Wolves at home the next night and the same thing happened again. I went back home and felt all right for a couple of days but it flared up yet again when we travelled to Wolves the following Wednesday. I think

I'd got so far as to putting my boots on in the dressing room!

I saw the club doctor, Mr Rose, and he was completely baffled. In the end he sent me to see a specialist, saying it could be something to do with my adenoids. I went to see the specialist and he told me that I needed both my adenoids and tonsils out. After the operation I spent a week in the Private Patients' Hospital in Whalley Range and I was great after that. I got back into the team at Coventry and scored twice so if anyone is looking to score a few goals then 'get your tonsils out'. It worked for me!

At just 15 years and 314 days old, Glyn Pardoe had been given his first-team debut by manager Les McDowall back in April 1962. He could almost be classed as a 'veteran' when Carlisle United lost 2-1 at Maine Road thanks to Pardoe's two goals on 11 September 1965. Six games into the season and still unbeaten. Allison's plan was still holding up.

On 14 September, the Blues once again entered the transfer market when they signed Everton's reserve-half George Heslop for £20,000. The same month also saw the arrival of battling wing-half Stan Horne from Mercer's former club Aston Villa. With the nucleus of the side still being the same (but by now increasingly more confident and fitter) players from last season, Mercer and Allison's 'fine tuning' was beginning to show results. Six became seven following a 3-3 draw away at Norwich, with Pardoe again scoring twice, this time aided and abetted by his captain Crossan. However all good things must come to an end and a trip to Cardiff proved fruitless in the eighth game. Despite scoring three times themselves (Pardoe and Murray again, and the only goal of the season for Matt Gray who'd come on as a substitute for Crossan) City conceded four at the other end, the winner coming from Cardiff's Terry Hankin just five minutes from the end. In true Manchester City style, this game ended a run of four successive defeats for the Welsh side who'd also made eight changes to the team that played the previous week.

It was to be a minor setback. The Blues remained unbeaten for the next seven games until losing by the only goal at Plymouth on 6 November. Pride and confidence had been restored to a club that had been so low just a few months ago. Not only did they top the division for a spell, but, forced to take notice once again, the crowds began to flood back. More than 34,000 witnessed the return goalless draw with Norwich on a Wednesday night in October. Amazingly this was nearly 1,500 more than First Division Champions Manchester United's home game with Fulham the previous Saturday. Just two months into the season, a joyous Allison gleefully collected his £10 winnings from the bitterly disappointed Crerand.

Neil Young remembers

The side had only lost a couple of games up until December. I think the main difference in the side from last year was confidence. As soon as you win two games your confidence goes sky-high. You get that feeling that if we can win again that's three on the run and then players say: "Come on, let's make it four". Then all of a sudden you think you're never going to lose. Whereas when you lose, the attitude changes to: "Oh no, we don't want to lose this one as well". Confidence is a massive thing in football. I'd even go the same way to the ground until we lost; then I'd go a different way. Footballers are a superstitious lot! We also started to get a lot more of the ball in training. We played a lot of five-a-side games and attack against defence. I'm sure that helped us enormously.

The Blues had also made a good start in the League Cup, a competition only too familiar to Mercer from his days at Aston Villa where he'd been to two finals, successful on one occasion, empty-handed on the other. Despite being forced to play six reserves owing to a glut of injuries, Mercer's men triumphed over First Division Leicester City by a 3-1 scoreline at Maine Road on 22 September, thanks to goals from Murray and Pardoe, and remarkably, yet another own goal! The unlucky player this time was Bobby Roberts although he partly redeemed himself later in the game when he converted a penalty after Oakes had handled the ball in City's area. It proved to be the first of many cup meetings with the Midlands side over the next few seasons. Their reward in round three was another home tie, this time against Coventry, a team like City, aiming for promotion to the First Division. Pardoe and Crossan scored for the Blues, who lost the game 3-2, this time being on the receiving end of an own goal when the unfortunate Alan Oakes provided the winner for the visitors.

December 1965 provided the players with a few extra days off when bad weather forced both games with Rotherham United to be postponed. The rearranged away fixture would prove to be highly significant when eventually played four months later. Top Russian side Moscow Dynamo were also visitors to Maine Road that month. On their first UK visit for 20 years, the Russians ran into what was by now a City team brimming with confidence and lost 2-0. It was a fine scalp for an emerging and confident side, with Doyle and the "outstanding" Crossan getting the goals.

Meanwhile, back in the League, the number one priority for Mercer and Allison, City's attack was beginning to find its' feet, a point confirmed when Leyton Orient were soundly beaten 5-0 at Maine Road, with Summerbee, Crossan and a Neil Young hat-trick providing the goals. Heslop's arrival had tightened things up considerably at the back and City remained in the top three thanks largely to conceding just eight goals in a run of 14 games leading up to the New Year. On New Year's Day itself, a crowd of 47,171 saw City beat a Huddersfield Town side (with the meanest defence in the division – only 18 conceded – and currently top) 2-0 with the ever-inspirational captain Crossan, this time from the penalty spot, and Doyle getting their names on the scoresheet. In a highly competitive game, Huddersfield's centre-forward Tony Leighton struck the bar with a penalty kick and it was only when Doyle headed home after 67 minutes that City were safe. The two hard-earned points moved the Blues to within one of Huddersfield and second-placed Coventry with a game in hand on both. Two weeks later, in icy conditions at Maine Road, City played out a goalless draw with Preston to go top.

Neil Young remembers

Some say the hat-trick I got against Leyton Orient was my only one for City but I remember scoring three against Arsenal some years earlier. That game was memorable because someone gave me an engraved lighter as a memento, although some newspapers did credit Arsenal's Dave Bacuzzi (later of course to join City) with the last touch on the third when my shot hit a post.

Malcolm used to say to me: "If you want the ball just go and get it". It didn't matter where I was on the field, he knew I wouldn't give the ball away. He said I was a really good passer and if I ever got into any difficulties then I should just switch the play across the field to Mike over on the right. He had a lot of confidence in the players and would always encourage me to have a shot. When I did find the net, after the game he'd say: "See, I told you so." He was that sort of coach.

Around this time Mike Doyle began to score a few goals as well. 'Tommy' was especially good in the air and would always create problems for the opposition's defence. We'd always send him up for set-pieces knowing full well that there was a good chance he'd get his head on it.

When we beat Huddersfield on New Years' Day the crowd was fabulous. I hear some managers even today saying: "I hope the players don't react to this big crowd". We couldn't wait to get out in front of a big crowd. There's nothing worse than playing at a ground where there's no atmosphere.

On 5 February, the Blues drew 1-1 at Bristol City, a game shown on BBC Television's Match of the Day. It was City's first showing on the programme, which had started its life back in August 1964. Some grainy black and white footage still exists on a BBC compilation video and shows Neil Young crashing in a (for him at least) rare thundering right-foot shot off the underside of the bar. It also shows an inability to clear a corner from Ray Savino successfully, which led to Brian Clark equalising for the home side. Despite close rivals Huddersfield winning 3-1 at Middlesbrough, City still remained top of the division by a single point. Football supporters from outside of Manchester were by now paying more than lip service to the events taking place at Maine Road. A terrific FA Cup run would only confirm this even more.

Malcolm Allison remembers

Ralph Brand had recently joined us from Rangers, bringing with him some good pace and fine scoring records for both club and country. I have to credit Joe for this signing because in all honesty I'd never heard of him. Unfortunately he wasn't as successful at City, scoring just a couple of goals before we sold him to Sunderland two years later.

Mike Summerbee was the next player Joe brought in and this proved to be a great signing for Manchester City. Joe had seen him play for Swindon and the paperwork was almost completed just prior to the Ralph Brand deal going through. When I saw Summerbee playing in practice matches he was playing too deeply for an outside-right and I encouraged him to play further forward. He later switched to centre-forward for us where he did equally as well, because he was good enough, and strong enough, to hold the ball up for others.

George Heslop came in from Everton in September for £20,000 although because the money was so tight at the time we had to pay for him on the instalment plan of about £1,000 a month. Heslop was understudy to the England centre-half of the time Brian Labone, and we thought if that's the only reason he's not in the side then he's certainly worth looking at. He did a good job for us at the back where he provided much needed physical presence and pace as well as being a good organiser. Joe brought in one of his former Aston Villa players Stan Horne in the same month as Heslop's arrival but the bulk of the side was made up from last season's players. We were lucky to have David Connor available then because he was such a good utility player and played anywhere we asked him to. Neil Young came into the side and did really well for us. He started off as a left-winger, was a lovely crosser of the ball and had a terrific left foot. Johnny Crossan was a good, experienced professional who captained the side from midfield although I do remember my training methods weren't too popular with him! The new training and playing methods at City were revolutionary only inasmuch as they'd had none previously! All we did was change them from a losing side to a winning one.

In the third round City were drawn away to First Division Blackpool and came away with a respectable 1-1 draw thanks to Connor's man-marking of Alan Ball and a superb 30-yarder from Pardoe. In the replay two days later, Crossan headed in Young's cross in the 19th minute and City were on their way to a 3-1 victory. It was a night of headers all round as Summerbee made it 2-0 following a fumble by Tony Waiters in the Blackpool goal before Ray Charnley pulled a headed goal back for the visitors. Doyle completed the headers with City's third goal nine minutes from time. The same player suffered two heavy falls during the game and was later x-rayed for a possible fractured shin. Fortunately the x-ray revealed only serious bruising and Doyle was able to take his place in the line-up for the 3-1 League victory over Middlesbrough the following weekend. The Blackpool game was watched by a crowd of 52,661, the largest at Maine Road since Burnley's Championship decider back in May 1960 with the gate receipts totalling more than £11,000.

The seemingly ever-present own goal (thanks to left-half Ron Cockerill) supplemented Mike Summerbee's effort as Grimsby Town were beaten 2-0 in round four, the result setting up another cup meeting with Leicester. As with Blackpool, again the tie took two games to decide a victor. Neil Young scored twice in the 2-2 draw at Maine Road on 5 March in front of another huge crowd; the 56,787 surpassing the Blackpool gate by some 4,000. In the replay at Filbert Street the following week, a rare error by the legendary England goalkeeper Gordon Banks gave Young the opportunity to score the only goal of the game. The quarter-final tie with Everton assumed epic proportions as the teams were so closely matched it took three games to separate them. The first game at Maine Road (on Grand National Day) provided no goals but yet another 'bumper' crowd as 63,034 swelled the club's slowly increasing bank balance. The scoreline was the same for the replay at Goodison Park with 60,349 watching the action. Molineux was decided as the neutral venue for the second replay on 5 April. Despite a tremendous team spirit and self-belief, City found this game just one too many and lost 2-0, Derek Temple and Fred Pickering scoring either side of the half-time break for 'The Toffees'. Everton went on to defeat

Manchester United in the semi-final and then Sheffield Wednesday at Wembley (3-2 after being 2-0 down). It was scant consolation for City to be knocked out by the eventual winners, but such a stirring cup run only gave the Blues confidence to maintain their good League form as they pushed for promotion in the final weeks of the season.

Neil Young remembers

Those three games with Everton in the Cup were all very, very close. Although we lost out in the end, we thought we'd acquitted ourselves well in all three games against what was a class Everton side. There wasn't much difference in the side that beat us to the one that would win the First Division Championship a couple of years later.

After the final game Malcolm came into the changing rooms and said: "Well, they're a top First Division side and you're a Second Division side. But, you're as good as them." I suppose that was the point when we all thought we could win the division. Looking back those games really inspired us on to better things and we only lost once more all the season. In the end we sort of ran away with that division.

At the beginning of the season City had signed a future Maine Road legend in the shape of Mike Summerbee. On 16 March 1966, the eve of the transfer deadline, they signed another player, one destined to become arguably the best ever to wear the famous sky-blue shirt. Colin Bell was a shy, 20-year-old playing at nearby Bury. He'd been watched several times by Allison who's apparent criticism of the player was aimed directly at putting off scouts from the many other clubs on Bell's trail. In the end Bell's choice was between City and Blackpool. Years later Bell commented: "Blackpool were in the First Division but at the wrong end and looked as though they could be relegated. City on the other hand were top of the Second and looked odds-on for promotion. I wanted to play First Division football so I looked at both clubs – there was no choice really."

Bell's fee was £45,000 and despite the increasing gate money, cash was still relatively thin on the ground at Maine Road. Allison was desperate to sign him: "Somehow we 'found' the money although when Joe first saw him he wondered just what he'd spent this fortune on!" On 19 March, Colin Bell took to the field at The Baseball Ground, Derby, for his first game in Manchester City's colours. City won 2-1 with Bell himself scoring along with Young. Although it was Bell's first goal for City it can hardly be described as his best as Derby full-back Ron Webster's clearance struck him in the small of the back and flew into the net. An example of things seemingly always going right for teams at the top, and wrong for those at the bottom.

Neil Young remembers

The arrival of Colin Bell was tremendous for both the side and for me personally. Colin was the sort of player who could make 20, 30, 40-yard runs and defenders couldn't pick him up. If I had the ball on the left-hand side of the goal, just outside the penalty-area, Colin would make his run knowing that I'd put the ball in front of him for him to run on to. It was really easy for me to find him and I'm sure he scored loads of goals by just doing that. It was just the same from the right-wing as well with Mike Summerbee. We both knew that once Colin 'got on his bike' all we had to do was to put a nice ball over the defence and it would finish up in the back of the net. That's exactly what happened at Rotherham. Colin had so much stamina it was unbelievably easy for him.

After the visit to Derby, City suffered just one defeat in the next six games (2-1 ironically at Bury), arriving at Rotherham for the rearranged fixture on the evening of Wednesday, 4 May. Neil Young's cross from the left was headed in by Bell for the only goal of the game. That solitary goal was enough to guarantee promotion. Bell: "Malcolm had been carrying the champagne around for ages ready for the promotion celebration. The changing rooms at Rotherham were very small – just a wooden hut – but we still managed to drink it. I'd never seen champagne before; I didn't know what it was!"

A 2-2 draw followed at Leyton Orient with Bell and the almost by now expected, own goal (Dennis Sorrell deflecting Summerbee's cross) again on the scoresheet. In a "patchy" game full of "uneven tempers" Summerbee, Bell and the splendidly named Richard 'Flip' Le Flem from Orient, were cautioned although contemporary reports suggest that they were a little unfortunate as "most of the others could have gone the same way". City's defence (Dowd, Kennedy, Horne, Pardoe, Heslop and Oakes) were also described as "overweight and cumbersome" in one article; something which would have surely angered not only Mercer and Allison but also the players themselves. Being unfit was something no one could say about any City side of this era.

On 13 May, City travelled to Charlton and led comfortably 3-0 to place one hand firmly on the Second Division trophy. Oakes, Crossan and Connor looked to have made the game safe, but in true Manchester City style, they then managed to concede two to make the game almost too close for comfort. Despite Charlton's sterling efforts City held on, and, still with one game left in the season, had won the Second Division Championship.

The runners-up spot was still to be decided though, with Coventry City, Huddersfield Town and Southampton all vying for second position in these days prior to the play-offs. In the end Southampton won through and it would be that same side that provided the opposition for City's last game of a memorable season on Wednesday, 18 May. If City beat The Saints 6-0 then Coventry would have been promoted. In the end (and perhaps not too surprisingly) both teams were more than happy with their end of season positions and played out a less than memorable goalless draw. Only Colin Bell's header against a post came near to breaking the deadlock.

The supporters of Manchester City cared 'not one jot'. They had seen their side improve immeasurably in one season and were back in the First Division. Mounted police were called for in order to keep the jubilant fans in check as Football League President Joe Richards presented the Second Division Championship trophy along with the winners' medals. Fans of legal drinking age (and many more not) partied long into the night. It was the first of many parties over the coming years.

Malcolm Allison remembers

As the transfer deadline approached I was interested in two more players although I knew we only (just) had the money for one. Wyn Davies was one of these players but the one I really wanted was a young lad from Bury called Colin Bell. I used to drive Joe and the directors mad talking about him all the time saying: "We've got to sign Colin Bell. We must have him." I'd seen Colin play at Plymouth when he was 17, and Paul Doherty who worked on City's programme, lived in Bury and saw them often, agreed with me saying: "Malcolm, you've got to buy Colin Bell." I said: "I know, I know." Apart from the money side of things, I also knew that Blackpool were interested in Colin but I was determined to get him. I remember sitting in a board meeting at Maine Road one Wednesday afternoon and Bury had a game at Gigg Lane that night. I excused myself from the meeting saying I wanted to go to see this game and Colin Bell in particular. One of the directors asked if he could come along with me and we took off for the game in my battered old German car. This was in November and it was a bitterly cold night and on the way to Bury the director said to me: "Malcolm, could you close that window?" I said: "I'd love to only it was stolen the other night!" These were the days long before the luxuries of club cars!

I'd been tracking Colin long before we actually signed him and I would go to games regularly and sit in the directors' box where I knew others were also watching him. I used to shout things like: "He can't head it. He can't pass it; he's no good on his left foot. He's hopeless!" All these comments were aimed at trying to put the others off and fortunately they worked. I would have been furious if he hadn't signed for us.

When we played at Rotherham in the first week of May, Colin scored the only goal of the game and it clinched us a place back in the First Division for the following season. It's a goal still remembered by many City fans even today. Somebody even wrote a song about it. The other thing I remember about that game was the state of the dressing rooms. They had the boilers banging away in the middle of them and overall they were awful, perhaps the worst I'd ever been in. I really had a go at their chairman about the conditions but it was no use.

Colin played that game with a heavily strapped ankle although it looked far worse than it was. Like many top athletes, he was a bit of a hypochondriac. Any little ache or pain going around Colin would pick up, and I would have to use a bit of psychology to try and talk him out of it. I used to put my arm around his shoulder and say: "You're looking good, doing great." Just words of encouragement really. However if there was anything that I thought would have affected him or been bad for him, then there was no way I would have risked it or played him in a game. I knew it was just a psychological thing with him and so I used to nurse him through it. I'd give him a fitness test and say: "Cor, you're flying!" He just needed those few little words. Colin Bell was the best player I ever worked with. His all-round ability was phenomenal.

When we won 3-2 at my old stomping ground at Charlton nine days after that Rotherham game the prize of the Second Division Championship was ours. We paraded the trophy to the Maine Road fans the following week in the last game of the season against Southampton, the team that would be joining us in the First Division. At a party afterwards in Manchester's Town Hall, Alan Oakes came over to me and said: "Malcolm, that was the hardest season I've ever had. The training was so hard." I looked at him and said: "It'll be even harder next year when we're in the First Division." He went white and said: "What?" I said: "We've really got to work at it now." He was only 23 at the time but he was a good trainer and I knew he could do it. The wonderful thing about the team was the discipline they showed in training. They were a very young side and all good athletes.

At the end of that tremendous first season the chairman, Albert Alexander, came to see me. He said: "Malcolm, well done, well done. I'm going to give you a bonus. I'm giving you £400. I'm giving Joe £600, you £400 and the secretary Walter Griffiths £400." My reply was somewhat brief. I said: "The secretary deserves it. He booked us into some fucking good hotels!"

1966-67
Establishing a Foothold

"...IT IS NOW." Three little words spoken by Kenneth Wolstenholme at the end of the 1966 World Cup Final. 1966, a year that saw England crowned World Champions, and Manchester City (wearing striking sky-blue, white and maroon hooped socks) playing First Division football again after an absence of three seasons. It was also a year quoted later by comedian Bernard Manning as: "The year Colin Bell signed for City, and United won **** all!" in parody of a well-known advertising slogan at the time in vogue. After the World Cup Final, football supporters, especially those of Manchester City, couldn't wait for the new season to begin.

Before the campaign started, Mercer and Allison both knew that the team would need to be strengthened, particularly at the back. On 20 July, Allison finally persuaded Mercer to agree to the signature of right-back Tony Book from Plymouth Argyle. Allison had worked with Book in previous years, and despite his age (he was two months short of his 32nd birthday), knew that Book possessed both the fitness and qualities required for Manchester City. A fee of £17,000 was agreed between the clubs, which prompted Book to comment: "I had no hesitation in once again working with this brilliant coach. This time though there was really big money at stake and I felt I had to justify that money to a club who had just won the Second Division Championship and were attempting to consolidate in the top flight." As with Summerbee and Bell, this signing too would prove to be a highly significant one in the history of the club.

Malcolm Allison remembers

Both Joe and myself knew this was going to have to be a year of consolidation, although as we'd done so well against First Division opposition in the FA Cup the previous season, we also knew we could play a bit. When I came to Maine Road 12 months earlier, people from the press to the boardroom used to ask me: "How are we going to do this year Malcolm?" My reply was: "We're going to win the Second Division Championship!" I used to say things like that just off the top of my head, but I was always a confident person. That particular quote could have backfired on me quite easily because at the time I'd not seen a single player! This time though I made no such quotes. My aim was just to get a place in the division – somewhere in the middle – and stay there. I had no ambitions of winning the title that season.

We had some good, young players but I knew we were still weak in one particular area. That was at right-back and I knew exactly who I wanted to bring in to fill that gap.

Tony Book was the man I wanted and he was an amazing player. I'd worked with Tony at both Bath City and Plymouth and so I was well aware of his capabilities. I spent £3,000 to bring him to Plymouth from Bath and I remember when the deal was signed, the Bath chairman started laughing at me. I said: "What's so funny?" He said to me: "You know how old he is don't you? And you've just spent £3,000." I knew exactly how old he was and it didn't bother me one bit. I never once looked at a player's age, whether it be 'young' or 'old'; I just looked for ability. I had enough problems with players being able to play without thinking about what his age was. His age though was a problem initially for Joe.

I'd spent some time looking for a right-back, I even watched about three or four international ones, and I didn't fancy any of them. I thought long and hard about it and then said to Joe: "There's a boy playing at Plymouth; he's better than all these." When I told him who it was he didn't really pass comment. Whenever I told Joe anything like this, about a particular player or whatever, he used to go away and ring all his old mates such as Stan Matthews and Tommy Lawton. He used to ask them what they knew and what their opinions were. I knew what his reply would be the following day: "Malcolm, this fella Book is 31!" "I know Joe, I know," I replied. "How old were you when you went from Everton to Arsenal?" I continued: "You were 32 but it didn't stop you, did it?" Joe couldn't argue with that!

Book's debut came in the opening game on 20 August, ironically against the side that had gained promotion with them, Southampton. In a line-up showing just two changes from the game at Maine Road three months earlier, Book replaced Stan Horne, with Jimmy Murray standing in for Crossan who had been injured in the summer in a road traffic accident. The game finished 1-1 with Summerbee scoring for the Blues. A much sterner test followed the following Wednesday when reigning champions Liverpool provided the opposition at a Maine Road packed with 50,320 spectators. Many thought it would be an easy two points for the visitors. Many went home shocked as a terrific City performance ensured they ran out 2-1 winners thanks to goals by Murray and Bell. Two more points were secured three days later when Alan Oakes scored the only goal of the game as Sunderland were beaten at Maine Road.

Tony Book remembers

Football has always been a major influence in my life, even from an early age. My dad was in the army, serving in India, and I moved out there with him when I was three. I stayed there until I was 11 and that's really where I learned the game, a lot of the time in bare feet.

Back in England I played at school, and later with both Bath Boys and Somerset Boys, in those days as an inside-forward. It was only in the army that I became a full-back. Like everything else in the military (I was in the Royal Army Medical Corps) you didn't get much of a choice, I was just told: "That's your position, just get on with it". The army team was made up of six pros and five amateurs and a fella by the name of Frank Blunstone was in our team. Frank played more than 300 games for Chelsea and he arranged to get me a trial at Stamford Bridge. When I was demobbed, I got a letter from the Chelsea manager, Ted Drake, saying he didn't think I would be good enough but did say I might make the grade lower down the leagues.

After the army I went back to the West Country and played for Peasedown Miners as an amateur and then for Frome Town as a part-timer. Frome was the first time I ever got paid for playing; I think it was about £2 10 shillings a week! It was whilst I was playing at Frome that I first got involved in the building trade. We got knocked out of one of the preliminary rounds of the FA Cup and the players each got a letter saying the finances were bad and the club was prepared to let us go. I showed this letter to a pal of mine who I was working with on the building site who was also a player with Bath City. He in turn showed it the boss of the construction company – Arthur Mortimore – who also happened to be the chairman of Bath City. Next thing I knew I was a Bath player and I stayed for 11 years.

Bath was no different to any other part-time or amateur club. We used to train two nights a week and then play the games on a Saturday. Until Malcolm Allison arrived. Then two nights became four and in the summer we'd train on Sundays as well. We did well under Malcolm and narrowly lost a game after a replay to Bolton Wanderers in the FA Cup when Francis Lee scored a penalty. I think Malcolm saw something in me because he asked me to go to Canada with him for a summer season. He was in charge of Toronto City and I had a great time playing against some top Italians and we ended up winning the double.

After Canada Malcolm moved on to Plymouth and I returned to Bath and more bricklaying. But Malcolm had remembered me and offered Bath £3,000. I was nearly 30 at the time and Malcolm told me to 'doctor' my birth certificate so I could make the move. Twelve months after Malcolm had gone to City he bought me again, this time for £17,500, which to me was a big fee at the time. Even though I was just a couple of months off my 32nd birthday, I had no hesitation in accepting his offer. I'd been playing part-time football for so long and played with so many players and seen them come out of the leagues, I always thought I had a little bit of a shout if someone would just give me a chance. One of the strengths I had as a player was the way I trained and the fitness I had. I went to City hoping that if I could stay for two years I'd be very happy.

When I first got to Maine Road I'm sure some of the players wondered why they'd signed this old fella, which, to be fair, they had. But then your ability comes into and they make up their minds about you; it was as simple as that. I had no problem settling in. I was lucky to have some really good lads around me. Johnny Crossan especially was first class towards me. He was married and would invite me and Mike Summerbee round to his house all the time after training. He was as good as gold.

It was a start, which, in all honesty, not even the most ardent City follower could have predicted. However things began to take a turn for the worse as City travelled to Anfield for the return fixture on 30 August. Murray scored his second goal in a week, and although Gray was also on target, City lost 3-2 to a Roger Hunt-inspired Liverpool side. This defeat started a run of five games in 18 days in which the Blues scored four goals, but, and indeed more disconcerting, collected just one point. A 3-0 defeat at Aston Villa was followed shortly afterwards by a 4-1 home defeat at the hands of West Ham when Colin Bell provided the only cheer of a hugely disappointing day.

The 'slide' was temporarily halted in the next game, against Arsenal at Maine Road on 10 September when Glyn Pardoe (playing centre-forward) scored City's goal in the 1-1 draw. Respite from the trials and tribulations of the League (the Blues had taken just six points from seven games) came four days later as City met Second Division Bolton Wanderers in the second round of the League Cup. A crowd of just over 9,000 at Maine Road saw Bell, Murray and Pardoe score in a 3-1 win. Future City favourites Francis Lee (who not surprisingly scored) and Freddie Hill played for the visitors, and a third, Wyn Davies, found his name in the programme but missed the game through injury.

And so to Old Trafford for the first 'derby' since May 1963. At last a chance to see not only how far Mercer and Allison's side had progressed, but also to finally knock the seemingly always high-flying Reds off their perch. Alas it was not be, as City 'froze' and a sometimes fraught game was decided by a single goal as former Blue Denis Law rounded Harry Dowd and slid the ball into an empty net. So fraught was the game that at one point the normally passive Oakes had to be pulled away from a clash with Law by no less a person than Summerbee. Surely a case of role reversal!

Malcolm Allison remembers

We started the season with a draw at Southampton and then beat Liverpool in front of a crowd of 50,000 at Maine Road. No more worries about an empty ground! Sunderland were then beaten 1-0 and with five points from the first six we couldn't have asked for a better start. The team was exceptionally fit and very, very confident but I knew that it would still be a very difficult year for us.

This proved to be the case as we lost our next three games, conceding ten goals into the bargain. A draw with Arsenal stopped the slide and our next game was at Old Trafford. We lost the game 1-0 thanks to a goal from Denis Law, but gave such a poor performance it left a sour taste in my mouth for days. That game made me determined from then on that my team would not be afraid of anybody. The players didn't want to go on the pitch before the game and I had to accept the situation although it was killing me. I went mad at them in the dressing room afterwards calling them "a load of fucking cowards" and saying to them: "How dare you be afraid of Manchester United." They'd lost the game in their heads even before the kick-off and I made the decision there and then that mentally at least, a Manchester City side would never lose again to Manchester United. I seem to remember we did a bit better in future clashes!

Undoubtedly disheartened by the events at Old Trafford, City won their next game thanks to a Johnny Crossan goal at Blackpool. Unfortunately though, October turned out to be as bad as September. Three consecutive defeats (at the hands of Chelsea, 1-4, Tottenham, 1-2, and Newcastle 0-2) forced Mercer and Allison to rethink their defensive formations. Mercer commented later about the defeat by Chelsea: "They took us apart on our own ground. They exposed our weaknesses." Tony Book was moved from his right-back position to one of sweeper with Mercer admitting: "It was insurance against further good hidings". The attacking philosophy of the previous season was put on hold as the Blues temporarily concentrated their efforts purely on survival. It would come back with a vengeance later, but at least for the time being, it took second place to staying in the First Division.

The problem of conceding goals in the League also spread to the League Cup. For the third time in a month, City conceded four goals in a game as West Bromwich Albion knocked them out in round three. Despite goals from Young and Summerbee, Albion won the game 4-2 and would go all the way to the final, where, unfortunately for them, Queen's Park Rangers and Rodney Marsh were lying in wait for them.

Malcolm Allison remembers

In an attempt to improve results we decided to move Tony Book from an orthodox right-back position to sweeper, a position up until then hardly ever used in England. I'd played Tony there on occasion whilst at Plymouth and I knew he was capable of doing a job for us. I remember Plymouth playing Bury in the League Cup one year and Plymouth won 1-0. Bob Stokoe was manager at Bury and after the game he came over to me and said: "It's not fair, playing that fella at the back like that!" It was just so new to him although not to me because I'd seen it used years ago when I was in the army in Austria. The people who have been really successful in the game are the ones with vision, the ones who make the changes by playing different formations. Herbert Chapman at Arsenal invented the 'WM' formation, which went unchanged for over 20 years. When Don Revie implemented the Hungarian approach of a deep lying centre-forward to Manchester City they immediately won the FA Cup. Alf Ramsey went one step better when he played without traditional wingers. He of course carried off the greatest prize of all in soccer.

In order to improve what was already a very high level of fitness, it was around this time that we began to take the players to Salford University and brought in top England athlete Derek Ibbotson. Derek put the players through some very gruelling sessions and was very complimentary about the abilities of some. He told me with a bit of guidance, Colin Bell in particular could make the grade as a top-class athlete.

Following that defeat at Newcastle (on 15 October) the new formation appeared to be doing some good as City won three and drew one of their next four games to move slowly away from the relegation zone. Crossan with two and Bell secured a 3-2 win at Burnley whilst Neil Young's goal was enough to share the points with Newcastle in the return game at Maine Road. Thanks to Summerbee's fourth goal of the season, City then won 1-0 at Stoke a week before what turned out to be a controversial home clash with Everton. Much was said in the press prior to the game about the abilities of the two outstanding midfielders on show, Colin Bell and Alan Ball. In the end though, the talk was more about a disallowed goal by Everton's Jimmy Gabriel (not mention plenty of aggressive tackles) rather than the two individuals. Bell had the last laugh for City by scoring the only goal of the game mid-way through the second-half although he did suffer some damage to a knee for his troubles.

Neil Young remembers

I think it's fair to say that everyone knew it would be a hard season for us. For a start we were up against a better standard of players, a lot of who were internationals. It was a big step up for us; there is a big difference between Second and First as it was then or Championship and Premiership as it is now. It can take at least half a season for a side to get into the swing of things in a new division.

You'll normally find that a promoted side will start the new season really well and can win four or five of the first seven or so games. Only then will the established sides find out what they are like. The new boys will then have a slump of about six or seven weeks when they won't win a game. That's more or less what happened with us.

When Tony Book came at the start of the season, understandably, the players didn't know what to expect. At first people said: "What the bloody hell has Malcolm done?" But when you work closely with Malcolm you get to know him inside and out; what his likes and dislikes are. But we all thought well, he must know something, and after three or four games we all knew. Not many players got the better of Tony Book.

Apart from a 4-1 defeat at Fulham, on the pitch at least, November had been quite a good month. Malcolm Allison could only witness the events from a seat in the stands as he was serving a 28-day FA imposed ban for 'expressing his feelings' in the media. December on the other hand proved very disappointing. By Christmas, City were in 15th place; indeed they were to win just one of their next nine League games following that victory over Everton. Although a 3-0 win against West Bromwich Albion helped matters (Pardoe, Jones and Crossan), the biggest problem for the Blues at the time was a sheer lack of goals.

Youngster Chris Jones had been brought into the side as a replacement for the injured Mike Summerbee at centre-forward, but in those nine games, City only managed to find the net on seven occasions. These seven included the three against West Bromwich and a Nobby Stiles own goal in a 1-1 'derby' draw at Maine Road. Bill Foulkes had given the Reds the lead, heading in a corner with 15 minutes left, and it looked all over for the Blues, until, in the 89th minute, Stiles headed Bell's cross past Stepney for a spectacular equaliser. Despite the inconsistencies of the season so far (City were 19th out of 22), 62,983 watched the game with United on 21 January. Not surprisingly, it was City's highest home gate of the season.

Just to prove that last season's tremendous run in the FA Cup had been no fluke, City began another campaign that would see them yet again reach the quarter-final stages. Like last year, the Blues found themselves drawn against Leicester, but whereas then it took two games to decide a winner, this time just one was needed; goals from Doyle and Pardoe clinching the tie at 2-1. The draw with Manchester United and the victory over Leicester seemed to 'kick-start' City's season. Those two games began an unbeaten run of 11 in both League and Cup, making it easily the best run of the season.

Tony Book remembers

After making my debut against Southampton at the start of the season, I missed just one game in two seasons. I injured a shoulder at Leicester and got a lift back to Manchester – along with Alan Oakes and Glyn Pardoe if memory serves, who were also injured – with Sidney Rose the club doctor. I passed out during the x-ray when I was told to hold a weight with my bad arm; the pain was just unbearable.

City had some good, young, local players at the club who were just coming into their own and I was lucky enough to sign at just that time. Joe was the father figure at the club. He was the one who'd put his arm around your shoulder, have a chat with you and a walk around the ground. You never saw him too much on the training ground; that was Malcolm's territory. Malcolm was the one who did all the training and Joe was the PR man; the one who kept everything right. That was the partnership. Malcolm was doing things back then that people are doing today. He really was 20 years ahead of his time. The first time around there was nobody to touch him.

The first season was really a bedding-in one for me, and I suppose, the team. Joe and Malcolm used to change the formation around – they even played me as a sweeper for a while – but it wasn't until we played two full-backs, three half-backs and five forwards that we started to come into ourselves really.

The run included League victories against Blackpool and Burnley (identical scorelines and scorers; 1-0, Bell) and Cup wins against Cardiff City and Ipswich Town, both ties requiring replays. Also during this period, a niggling, bad-tempered game at Stamford Bridge finished goalless (City played a nine-man defence with only Doyle and Summerbee left up front) after 106 minutes play owing to the referee adding on more than a quarter of an hour of injury time. The game had started seven minutes late as well when City were ordered to change their white socks as they clashed with those of the home side. When Colin Bell scored a late winner at Burnley, it took City's run of unbeaten League and Cup games to eight and effectively cleared any worries of relegation. If relegation was no longer a worry, goalscoring certainly was. City had now scored just 27 goals in 29 League games; only Newcastle United had scored less. On the same day as Bell was scoring at Turf Moor, future City record-signing Rodney Marsh was at Wembley, inspiring his Third Division Queen's Park Rangers side to victory over First Division West Bromwich Albion in the League Cup Final.

On 16 March, Malcolm Allison used his powers of persuasion once again as Tony Coleman arrived at Maine Road. Coleman's reputation as a 'rebel' preceded him, and Joe Mercer required considerable cajoling before being convinced that "a skin-head covered in tattoos" would do a good job for the side. In the end Joe was convinced and Coleman (after making his debut two days later in a goalless draw at Leeds) did indeed 'do a good job' on the left-wing for the next two-and-a-half years. The Coleman signing confirmed the 'teamwork' of Mercer and Allison. Both would back each other to the hilt if they were adamant about a particular decision.

Old cup adversaries Leicester put paid to winning ways with a 3-1 win at Maine Road on Good Friday; a seemingly out-of-touch and lacklustre Johnny Crossan providing little consolation. One newspaper reported that City's performance was so poor all it did was "ease the traffic problem at the end of the game as so many fans left early". Twenty-four hours later, also at home, a young, fresh-faced Paul Hince (later to become a journalist with the *Manchester Evening News*) scored twice on his debut as four goals, and two points, were shared with West Bromwich Albion. On Easter Monday, the Blues lined up once again against Leicester. There appeared little difficulty in beating them in Cup games, but things proved different in League games as Chris Jones' goal proved inadequate with the Foxes scoring twice at the other end.

A 1-0 reverse at Sheffield United preceded a sixth-round FA Cup clash with Don Revie's mighty Leeds United at Elland Road. City threw the formbook out of the window and having reverted to an all-out attacking formation, were desperately unlucky to lose to a hotly-disputed Jack Charlton header five minutes into the second half. No less a newspaper than *The Sunday Times* described the Yorkshire side as "lucky, lucky Leeds."

Malcolm Allison remembers

The new formation helped to some degree although we still had no real consistency in the League after that defeat at Old Trafford. In January, once again we found ourselves drawn against Leicester in the FA Cup, and again, like last year, we would go on to reach the quarter-final stages. Two attempts were needed to dispose of both Cardiff and Ipswich and then the sixth round took us to Elland Road. Joe was quoted in the newspapers at the time as saying Leeds were "robot-like" and nearly everybody in the game expected us to defend in the hope we could get them back to Maine Road for a replay. Nothing could be further from the truth as we played 4-2-4 and attacked them with everything we had.

In the end the gods were against us and we went out 1-0 to a hotly disputed goal from Jack Charlton. Everybody in the ground – with the exception of the one who counts, the referee – knew Charlton had impeded our goalkeeper Harry Dowd as he bundled in Eddie Gray's corner. All the newspapers said the wrong team had gone through to the semis and Don Revie admitted it had been their hardest game of the season. On the positive side of things, we'd had two excellent FA Cup runs in the last two years and had gone out to two of the country's top sides.

About a fortnight before that Leeds game I'd talked Joe into signing a left-winger with somewhat of a reputation as being a bit of a troublemaker. Tony Coleman had been given a free transfer by Stoke City, described as "unmanageable" by Preston and had punched a referee whilst playing for Doncaster. Despite all that, I still wanted him. I knew if we played him wide on the left and brought Neil Young inside, it would improve the balance of the side. Joe's first thoughts were even more negative than with Tony Book: "No, no, no. We can't have him. Isn't he the lad who threw a bed out of a window at Lilleshall?"

After Preston, Tony had played some non-League football with Bangor; a side managed then by T.G. 'Tommy' Jones, an old playing pal of Joe's from his Everton days. As usual Joe got on the 'phone to make his enquiries. At Bangor I knew if we offered

£3,000 we could get him but he then moved to Doncaster and of course the price went up. I saw him dominate one particular game and went back to Joe to try and persuade him. In the end he agreed – this was just one example of us backing each other up – and we managed to knock Doncaster down from their asking price of £17,000 to just over £12,000. I was quoted at the time as saying Coleman's signing was "like the nightmare of a delirious probation officer" but he went on to provide great service from the wing for the next couple of seasons. Admittedly I did have the occasional difficult moment with him, but I still claim he was a good signing for Manchester City although I do sometimes wonder whether I failed somewhat with him in the long run.

Neil Young remembers

We used to have some cracking games with Leeds. Actually the same could also be said about Liverpool, Arsenal and Everton as well. Back then there were seven or eight sides that could have won the division, so nearly every week produced a big game.

I remember we'd just had lunch at the hotel in Leeds prior to the game and the lads all gathered round the television to watch Grandstand. Don Revie came on and I think it was Kenneth Wolstenholme who asked him: "Have you prepared for City this afternoon?" And Revie's reply was a huge compliment for me when he said: "Yes, we've prepared for Neil Young. He is of one those players you must keep a grip on for the whole 90 minutes." I just sat back in my seat and thought: "You'll do for me!"

Francis Lee told me that the Leeds players who were on international duty with him were also complimentary about me saying that there was always a chance I could score a goal. After I'd retired I sat down and worked out my goalscoring ratio and it was something like one in every three and three quarter games so it wasn't too bad.

The performance at Leeds inspired the Blues to remain unbeaten in their next four League games. A seven-minute Colin Bell hat-trick was enough to beat Stoke at Maine Road on a Wednesday night in April, followed by more than respectable 1-1 draws with both Aston Villa (home) and Everton (away) with an easy 3-0 victory against Fulham sandwiched in the middle; Oakes, Crossan and Bell's 13th of the season putting paid to Johnny Haynes' side. Those six points gave the Blues a cushion from others teams engaged in the struggle at the bottom. Blackpool had already 'given up the ghost' but any one of Fulham, Newcastle, Aston Villa and Southampton were still possibilities for the drop. In the end it would be Aston Villa who missed out; four points behind Newcastle.

City entered the last month of the season with a 2-0 defeat at Nottingham Forest. It proved to be their last as the remaining three games provided 1-1 draws against both Sheffield United (Crossan) and West Ham (Bell), and a 2-1 'revenge' against Leeds (Crossan and Young) in the penultimate match. A fine end to the season with just one League defeat in the last eight games had ensured City's survival. The final table shows they finished in a commendable 15th position with, in the end, a huge safety net of ten points more than relegated Aston Villa.

Interestingly enough the leading scorer from last season (with 17 in all competitions) had managed just four this time, despite playing one game more. Neil Young modestly refuses to put his efforts in direct context to that of the team although statistics prove that the more Young scored, the more successful the team was. Peter Gardner once wrote a piece claiming: "When Pat Crerand plays well, so do United. The same could be said about Neil Young and City."

Sometime prior to the start of the 1967-68 season, Young found his best ever 'scoring boots'. After all, statistics don't lie.

Malcolm Allison remembers

The team was now really coming together as we wanted and although we had a good, solid goalkeeper in Harry Dowd, I was still on the lookout for a proven international in such a crucial position. The best in the world became available when Gordon Banks' position at Leicester looked in jeopardy because of the emergence of a young Peter Shilton. I told Joe: "Get the money, we must have him." Leicester wanted offers in the region of £50,000. I left the dealings up to Joe as I took a weekend break and came back to the ground first thing Monday morning. "Did you get him?" I asked. "No," came the reply. "I offered £45,000 but they turned it down," Joe told me. I said: "Joe, you know they wanted £50,000. Why did you bid less?" I think it was a combination of Joe's thrifty, working-class roots and the fact that the club still had no real money to speak of, but anyway we lost out and Banks signed for Stoke. This was one of just two serious arguments I had with Joe in a working relationship lasting nearly seven years. That £5,000 proved very costly a few years later when Banks' performance for Stoke in a League game at Maine Road effectively stopped us winning the Championship.

We finished the 1966-67 season in 15th position, ten points and six places away from the relegation places. Admittedly we hadn't pulled up too many trees along the way but we had achieved the number one priority for the season, namely establishing a foothold in the top division. Meanwhile Manchester United had once again carried off the title, four points clear of Nottingham Forest and Spurs and the small matter of 21 ahead of us. I wasn't too concerned. I knew our day was coming.

1967-68
K2 and Everest

AS A prelude to a season beyond the dreams of even the most optimistic – including Malcolm Allison – City played two friendlies in the space of four days at the beginning of August. A convincing 4–0 victory against Borussia Dortmund at Maine Road on the 11th followed the successful 2–0 trip to Portsmouth. At the same time of these friendlies, supporters were invited to join 'The City Set' in a special 60-page magazine produced by the club at a cost of half-a-crown. The idea of the magazine was (in the words of chairman Albert Alexander) to "keep the fans in the picture concerning the policies being carried out at Maine Road". It contained features on all the current first team players, articles by both Joe and Malcolm as well as some of the backroom staff and a good luck message to Roy Cheetham who'd agreed a move to American side Detroit Cougars at the beginning of January. All in all, excellent value for 'two and a tanner'.

Another player to leave Maine Road – considerably earlier than Cheetham – on 23 August to be exact – was Johnny Crossan, the inspirational Irishman who had captained the Blues to Second Division success some 15 months earlier. Since his car crash shortly after that triumph, Crossan had appeared on occasion to be out of sorts; with both knee and appendix trouble, he had fallen out of favour with certain sections of the crowd. Come August-time, he'd fallen out of favour with the management as well and joined Middlesbrough for a fee of £34,500.

Tony Book remembers

I think that any doubts anyone had about my ability had been squashed in that first season. They knew now I could cope and when Johnny Crossan left in the summer I was delighted to be asked to take over the captaincy. I had no hesitation in accepting the job as I'd had previous experience at both Bath and Plymouth.

As for Malcolm's training methods, some of them I'd seen before although because he was now meeting people on a bigger stage, he was trying out different things. He got to know people at Salford University and we started to use special diets, treadmills and the like. He would always consider anything that he thought would benefit the lads. We didn't have the weight machines like they have today. Back then Malcolm would have to lift the weights on to the players backs himself, and sometimes there could be upwards of 15 players. It makes me smile sometimes to read nowadays about coaches and managers trying out this and that because it's all been done before as far as I'm concerned. Nothing is really that different; it's just a different way of putting it over I suppose.

With Tony Book named as the new captain, the season started in earnest on 19 August and was in marked contrast to the events of 12 months ago. Last season started with five points from a possible six; this one started with just one from the first three games. Interestingly enough the fixture-list produced exactly the same start as last time in the first two games, albeit in reverse. This time more than 49,000 watched the goalless opener with Liverpool at Maine Road, with the second game being a 3-2 setback at Southampton four days later despite goals from Coleman and Bell. Worse was to follow next as the Blues succumbed 3-0 at The Victoria Ground, Stoke. This was perhaps City's worst performance of the season and was described later by Allison as "disgraceful".

When Southampton travelled north for the fourth game, they witnessed first hand the kind of dynamic, attacking play that was to win so many admirers (not to mention trophies) over the next few years. Only 22,000 turned up for this particular Wednesday night clash, but they saw Bell and Young both score twice in a 4-2 win. It began a run of five consecutive wins, with 16 goals scored – and only four conceded – into the bargain. Allison's training methods, especially the fitness side of things, was certainly paying off as opposition teams were simply overrun. After Southampton, Nottingham Forest were beaten 2-0 thanks to Coleman and Summerbee's efforts, followed by a similar scoreline against Newcastle; Hince and Young on target this time. Summerbee would later describe the game against Forest as his best performance of the season, adding: "I had the better of their centre-half McKinlay all day, and to cap it off I got one of my special headers – from three yards!"

Malcolm Allison remembers

The season began slowly to say the least as we lost two of our first three games. Alan Ogley kept goal in the first two games and Harry Dowd in the third but I was still on the lookout for another goalkeeper.

Game four saw us beat Southampton 4-2 at Maine Road and so begin a run of five straight wins. During this run we gave a young Manchester lad – one of many at the club then thanks to some excellent scouting work – by the name of Paul Hince, his second League outing. He has since made his mark in the journalistic world, but back then was an outside-right who played against Nottingham Forest. He was up against John Winfield, a left back of some considerable experience who had been educated in the 'hard but fair' school of defending. On this day Hince ran him ragged and Winfield's patience eventually snapped forcing the referee to issue a stern lecture. I too was less than impressed with some of Winfield's challenges, suggesting to the referee he shouldn't still be on the pitch. Hince's youth and obvious enthusiasm forced him to call out: "Don't send him off ref. He's easy. I'm enjoying it." That 2-0 victory over Forest was perhaps the first time I really thought we had a chance of doing something in the top division.

Hince continued both his and City's good run of form, scoring against Newcastle and then another three days later in a 3-0 away win at Coventry. Not content with scoring, Hince also laid on a goal for Summerbee at Coventry as the Blues moved to fifth position, just two points behind the leaders Liverpool.

The League Cup-tie on 13 September saw City yet again paired with Leicester, as well as the introduction of another local youngster given a chance in the first team. Coming on as a half-time substitute for a 'flu ridden Neil Young, Stan Bowles scored twice (accompanying Book and Young) as the Blues progressed easily to the next round by a 4-0 scoreline. His hat-trick was denied when a brilliant header missed by inches.

Things got even better for the Collyhurst-born Bowles as he made his League debut in the next game against Sheffield United at Maine Road. This time he replaced the injured Tony Coleman on the left-wing with the fit again Young being restored to his customary number ten shirt. Bowles had played outside-left for Manchester Boys but had at first been considered 'too slight' for this position by City, he himself thinking his future with the club lay at left-half. His fairy tale continued. Sheffield United were humbled 5-2 and he scored two more. Summerbee, Bell and Young were the other, more familiar, names on the scoresheet. To celebrate his elevation to the first team – and a rise in pay to £20 a week – Bowles celebrated by buying himself a new suit!

Malcolm Allison remembers

Stan was a skilful, left-sided player with a good instinct for goals. This proved the case when he scored four times in his first one and a half games for us. Off the field was another matter for Stan however and we clashed on more than one occasion. Two incidents in nightclubs for instance ended in blows being thrown – and caught – but perhaps the most famous Stan Bowles story concerns him missing a 'plane.

City had arranged to play a pre-season friendly against Ajax in Amsterdam and everyone arrived on time for the flight except Stan. Not surprisingly, and probably not for the first or last time, he'd overslept. Realising he couldn't get to the airport in time for the flight, he never even bothered to try to get there too late. When the flight was delayed by four hours it gave Joe and me ample time to try to track him down but it was all to no avail. Stan was hiding in a friend's wardrobe. To say I wasn't delighted with his behaviour would be an understatement! We sold him to Bury not long after one of our nightclub disagreements but in all honesty Bowles did go on to become a good First Division player who would eventually play for England.

Despite this great start of four goals in 135 minutes, Bowles found himself back down to earth when Coleman returned for the 1-0 defeat at Highbury and he wasn't even named substitute. Mercer and Allison both told the press (and probably wisely) that they didn't want to rush things with the player and they were 'still grooming' him. However he was selected for the game on 30 September, the Maine Road 'derby' and for the third successive time, Bowles got his name in the papers. This time though it was for actions with his hands rather than his feet.

The game against United (which was also Ken Mulhearn's debut in the City goal) couldn't have started better for the Blues when Colin Bell opened the scoring after just five minutes

Neil Young remembers

When Stan Bowles came into the team on the left-hand side some people thought my place could be in jeopardy. However Malcolm told me – even though Stan started like a house on fire – that I was safe. He told me that even if Stan did well he could put me wide out on the left or alternatively put him out wide and bring me back into midfield.

Stan was a really good player who had terrific balance. He was tremendous on the ball, could perform brilliant shimmies and was great at dragging the ball back. He was a great asset to have in the team. Perhaps his only downside was he was a little on the light side but he did have a good career.

A few weeks after Stan's debut, Joe and Malcolm went out and signed Francis Lee from Bolton. We'd tried Mike Summerbee at centre-forward but he'll tell you himself, he was never really a goalscorer. What he was, was a tremendously brave and strong winger. The side just needed that final, cutting edge and Frannie had it.

with a low shot past Stepney. Unfortunately Bobby Charlton then scored twice before half-time and City were still unable to clear perhaps the biggest obstacle of all. Towards the end of a game which had seen plenty of tough tackling, Bowles and United's Brian Kidd – ironically someone who was raised in the same Collyhurst streets as Bowles with just a few months age difference – tangled, with punches raining in from both sides. Only the quick thinking captaincy of Tony Book and Pat Crerand (claiming the 'exuberance of youth') saved the players from leaving the pitch early. The next day Bowles paid a visit to Kidd's house, posed for pictures and generally 'made up'. This idea came from Joe Mercer who couldn't stand violent behaviour of any kind on a football pitch.

Malcolm Allison remembers

My search for a goalkeeper ended when Ken Mulhearn arrived from Stockport County. Mulhearn had a reputation for being a good shot-stopper and he made his debut in the first 'derby' game of the season. Harry Dowd had dislocated a finger so giving Mulhearn his chance but I very nearly didn't play him. He was so nervous prior to kick-off that I locked him in the medical room away from the other players. He was as white as a sheet and looked capable of throwing up at any moment. I think it was simply the fact that his last game was in front of a few thousand whereas this one would be played in front of a sell-out 63,000.

Fortunately he got over his nerves and took his place between the posts and must have been even more reassured when Colin Bell gave us the lead early on. It was my turn to be sickened later when two Bobby Charlton goals gave our old enemies the points. Despite all our good work off the pitch and our recent successful run on it, we still couldn't manage to pass the ultimate test which would convince everybody that City had 'arrived'; that of beating Manchester United. The game finished with Stan Bowles again in the thick of it, although a punch-up with Brian Kidd was not exactly what was required at the time.

Tony Book remembers

Looking back we didn't start the season too well, but we then won five games on the run which gave us all a real boost. We signed Ken Mulhearn and then came up against United. We used to have a laugh with all our goalkeepers when we told them they'd only have to make an odd save because the ball wouldn't get through to them very often! Once I was living in Manchester I got to know all about the rivalry and the clamour for tickets and the build up to all the 'derby' games back then was tremendous. We knew that there wasn't that much of a difference between the two sides and we were always prepared to take them on. I can even remember on one occasion, Malcolm took us all out on to the pitch at Old Trafford and we applauded the Stretford End!

The disappointment of the 'derby' defeat travelled to the north-east seven days later as City went down 1-0 thanks to a goal by Neil Martin at Sunderland. In a game dominated by the Blues (even the great former Sunderland player Len Shackleton wrote that City were unlucky) they managed to hit the woodwork three times with no success. Martin's decisive strike went in off the post; such is football. Despite being on the losing side, goalkeeper Ken Mulhearn later described the game as his best of the season, commenting in particular on one double-save from former City player Ralph Brand. Two days after the defeat at Roker Park, City broke their transfer record when they spent £60,000 on Francis Lee.

Lee's arrival did indeed provide just the spark that up until then had been missing. His dynamic speed over the first five yards and directness towards goal caused huge problems for opposition defences and the goals began to flow. His debut came against Wolves on 14 October and although Lee himself failed to score, he must have been impressed by Doyle's effort from the edge of the box and Young's spectacular volley.

Malcolm Allison remembers

About ten days after that defeat by United, Francis Lee arrived at Maine Road. It was a terrific signing for Manchester City and Joe was absolutely right when he described Francis as "the final piece of the jigsaw".

Both Joe and myself had been impressed with Francis when he'd played for Bolton against City in the League Cup the previous season. I'd also crossed swords with him at Bath when we played them twice in the FA Cup, so I was already well aware of his qualities as a player. I loved the way Francis played and I was convinced his power and style was just what was required at Maine Road. I went to Liverpool with Joe one day to watch him and his performance convinced us both that we must have him.

On a personal note, Francis was building up a successful waste-paper business as well as some property interests but was dissatisfied with his future prospects at Burnden Park. So dissatisfied in fact that one day he actually went in to see manager Bill Ridding – himself once a player at Maine Road – and asked for his cards. Wolves and Stoke City were monitoring the situation but Joe Mercer was 100 per cent right when he said City were just one player short and Francis was that player.

Joe said to me: "Go and see Francis Lee. See if you can talk him into coming here." I was shocked by this request because it was the first time Joe had never mentioned money when we discussed a possible transfer. The top six in the division and an average home crowd in the region of 35,000 meant finally the club had some finances to speak of. It was a good job too. Francis would eventually cost City a then, club record fee of £60,000.

I arranged a meeting in a Bolton restaurant with Francis and his partner in the waste-paper business, Peter James. During the meal I turned to Francis and said: "Come to Manchester City and I'll make you a good player". I found out later as I was in a taxi going back to the ground, Francis said to his partner: "Make me a good player! He's a big-headed bastard isn't he"! Years later when Francis was a subject on the *This Is Your Life* television show I reminded him of that story and said: "I told you I'd make you a good player didn't I"?

Ironically Francis Lee's debut for City was against Wolves, a team he could quite easily have been playing for. We won 2-0 and remained unbeaten in the next ten League games.

Joe Corrigan made his City debut in the next game, a League Cup-tie against Blackpool at Maine Road. Unfortunately for Corrigan he had the misfortune to let a shot from John Craven squirm through his legs for the visitors' goal although Summerbee later saved his blushes as the game finished 1-1. The same two players were on target again in the replay but this time Craven could only manage to deflect a shot from Young into his own net. Summerbee's ability to be "deadly from three yards" showed itself again as he poked home the Blues' second goal whilst sat down inside the six-yard area!

Francis Lee's first goal for City came in driving rain at Craven Cottage as the Blues returned from the capital following a 4-2 win at Fulham on 21 October, a game that was goalless at half-time. Joe Mercer remembered Lee's 20-yarder as "a blur. The goalkeeper didn't see it at all. It hit him on the shoulder and shot into the top of the net." Two more from Summerbee (the most kicked player in the country according to Allison) and one from Young completed the scoring in the only First Division game of the day due to the Home Internationals. The win moved City up two places to sixth and left Fulham still second from bottom. At the end of the season City had progressed to first place; Fulham had gone even lower and were relegated.

Despite Fulham's low-standing, the Blues were unable to repeat their League success and lost 3-2 (Bell and Oakes) at Craven Cottage in the fourth round of the League Cup just ten days later. Back in the League, Colin Bell's header and a point blank save by Mulhearn were enough to earn the points against a powerful Leeds United side, and David Connor scored his only goal of the season in a 1-1 draw at Everton (despite a controversial 'offside' equaliser by Ernie Hunt) to keep the Blues just three points away from Bill Shankly's Liverpool at the top of the division.

Things couldn't have been better for the Blues when old cup adversaries Leicester (with Peter Shilton in goal) were beaten 6-0 and the Blues moved to third position, two points behind the new leaders Manchester United. Alan Oakes opened the scoring with a close-in shot and would later describe the game as his best of the season. He said: "I can't remember anything going wrong and we paralysed them." Doyle joined Oakes on the scoresheet, with Young and Lee scoring two each. Lee's excellent start to his Maine Road career continued into the next match as well, a 3-2 win against a West Ham side that contained all three of their World Cup stars. Tony Book's cross from the right-wing was caught perfectly first-time on the volley by Lee from fully 25 yards for the first of his two strikes. Lee's two and one from Summerbee overcame the goalscoring efforts of Geoff Hurst and Martin Peters.

Harry Potts brought his Burnley side to Maine Road the following week, fresh from an 8-1 annihilation at West Bromwich Albion and looking to restore some pride. Unfortunately for them City were in no mood for generosity as they battled it out at the top and ran out 4-2 winners. Lee missed out on this occasion, leaving the honours to Summerbee, Young and two from Coleman. That win moved City to just one point behind Manchester United and level with second place Liverpool. Any visit to Hillsborough in those days was always going to be difficult, more so on this occasion as Sheffield Wednesday had gone 18 games unbeaten at home. An Alan Oakes 'special' gave City the lead in the first minute of the second-half and it looked as though the Yorkshire defences had finally been breeched, only for fate to intervene in injury time when a lucky bounce (or sleight of hand depending on whether you come from Sheffield or Manchester) allowed John Fantham to avoid Oakes and slot home the equaliser. Despite the disappointment of losing a point at such a late stage, City fans behaved themselves impeccably, causing one Owls' fan to write to Joe at the club praising their behaviour and 'sporting manner'.

City had now gone eight games without defeat, scoring 22 against eight in that period and collecting 14 out of a possible 16 points. The programme notes for the game against Tottenham on 9 December asked was it too greedy to ask for more? Even if the answer was "yes" City continued their wonderful run and the game proved to be one of the most memorable in modern times. On an ice-bound pitch – indeed there was more than one occasion when the game was doubtful – City destroyed Spurs 4-1 and gave an exhibition of attacking football which made of a mockery of the conditions. Jimmy Greaves opened the scoring for the visitors after just seven minutes but, if anything, his goal seemed to inspire City more. Bell equalised before half-time following a goalmouth scramble in front of a snow-covered Open End, the outcome of a constant siege on Jennings' goal. There was more of the same in the second-half as wave after wave of attacks reigned down on the Londoners' defence. Having been denied by a fine save from Jennings in the first-half, Young then hit the bar with a ferocious shot in the second as the pressure mounted. Summerbee's header from Young's cross made it 2-1, Coleman 3-1 when he followed up Lee's shot against the post, and Young himself got the fourth from close range after Bell had collided with Jennings. City were robbed of a fifth when somehow they managed to hit both posts in a single attack.

Neil Young remembers

The game against Tottenham on the ice was absolutely tremendous to play in. We had nails coming out of our studs just so we could stand up! Back then you never got your boots checked by the referee. He'd just come into the dressing room before the game and say: "Have a good clean game lads", and that was it. Although I'm sure it was illegal, we put some little pins in the end of the studs, but even then we were slipping. Our control and passing that day was unbelievable. We really did murder them, and they had a class side, full of internationals.

Joe Mercer had earlier commented on BBC Television: "We do everything quick and simple and we're remarkably fit. We don't mind who comes and sees us training or who sees us playing. It's a simple game and we try to keep it simple." Manchester City's entire philosophy of the time captured in just three sentences. And yet absolutely true. The Spurs game was shown on BBC's Match of the Day (as well as going down in Maine Road legend) and City's performance brought letters of praise from as far a field as Glasgow and Dorset – and Tottenham! - although one man had other opinions. Liverpool's Bill Shankly (City's next opponents) warned Allison: "You're not going to tear our team apart like you have torn the others apart, you know." Was he confident or trying to hide any possible fear? The game at Anfield finished 1-1, a surprising scoreline when even the Liverpool Echo commented: "The frequency and power of City's shooting was amazing." Lee's sixth goal in ten games kept the Blues joint second with Liverpool, although Manchester United's 3-1 win against Everton at Old Trafford had now increased their lead to two points.

Malcolm Allison remembers

Following Francis Lee's debut for City was against Wolves -ironically a team he could quite easily have been playing for – we remained unbeaten in the next ten League games. Those 11 games contained eight wins and three draws and included the famous 4-1 victory over Spurs, affectionately nicknamed 'The Ballet on Ice'.

Dixie Dean, the great Everton and England centre forward and good friend of Joe's came to watch that game. By then of course, he'd lost both legs and after the game I met him in his wheelchair in Joe's office. This was a great thrill for me because Dean had always been one of my heroes. Joe made the introductions and I asked Dixie if he had enjoyed the game. He said: "That's a very good side you've got there. A very, very good side." I was delighted with his comments because I thought that's as big a praise as you can get from anyone. Dean went on to say: "What I liked about them was the fact they played on the surface as if everything was OK," and he was absolutely right. I'd drummed it into the players before kick-off: "Don't think about the ground. The ground is only there to be run over." As soon as the referee had said the game could be played, I took the players out on to the pitch for a 45-minute training session!

Mid-table Stoke failed to halt City's by now unbeaten run of ten League games when they lost 4-2 at Maine two days before Christmas. Lee two, Young and Coleman put paid to a Stoke side which had former City favourite Peter Dobing wearing number nine and getting his name on the scoresheet.

City entered the Christmas period just one point off the top spot with the prospect of back to back games against West Bromwich Albion, a side full of confidence after two successive away wins, at West Ham and Chelsea. For the away game on Boxing Day, City were without both Doyle and Bell and lost the game 3-2, despite Francis Lee (one of the scorers along with Summerbee) recollecting: "Even though we lost, we still murdered them!" City had clawed their way into the match despite being two goals down at one stage only to lose to a goal by Jeff Astle in the second minute of injury time. West Brom. had been fancied by some as an outsider at the start of the season and were in seventh position (five points behind City) when they arrived at Maine Road for the return game four days later. Still without Doyle and Bell, City gave a first start to youngster Johnny Clay and continued with their usual attacking style. City lost 2-0 with Allison claiming full responsibility for not changing the formation and trying to defend more. It had been a bad holiday season for Mercer and Allison's men. There was certainly nothing festive about it as Manchester United had done the double over Wolves and had increased their lead to five points over City who'd slipped to fourth place in the table.

The Blues first game of 1968 was a trip to tenth place Nottingham Forest. In the programme notes, Tony Book replied to a question about City's chances of winning the Championship: "I'll let you know if we really are good enough if we can beat Nottingham Forest", he said. Book had apparently been looking at Forest's recent home record, impressive as it was with only three losses in the previous 39 matches stretching back 16 months. Mercer and Allison's side made it four losses in 40 for Forest as they completely dominated the game and ran out convincing 3-0 winners. Summerbee, Young and Coleman all on target as the Blues put the misfortunes of Christmas – and West Bromwich Albion – well and truly behind them. Meantime Manchester United were putting three past West Ham thereby keeping their five point lead at the top.

A sudden cold spell forced City's next game – at home to Coventry – to be postponed but instead of a few days off, the players were taken to Southport on the Saturday night for three days of 'relaxing and toning'. When Derek Ibbotson had them running through the sand dunes in winds up to 70 mph, the players must surely have had other descriptions of their time at the seaside! The salt water and fresh air appeared to clear up Colin Bell's niggling ankle injury and he was back in a full-strength City side that travelled across the Pennines for the next game with Sheffield United. City had beaten the Blades 5-2 at Maine Road back in September and once again were victorious by a three goal margin. For the second successive away game, City won 3-0, with long-range efforts from Bell and Doyle, and Francis Lee's penalty separating the sides.

As usual January brings around the third round of the FA Cup and with the visit of Third Division Reading to Maine Road, it gave the Blues a respite from the chase for the title. It almost brought about the proverbial 'banana skin' as well as City (wearing all maroon) were held 0-0 in a game which also saw Tony Coleman blast a penalty way over the bar at the Platt Lane end. Not surprisingly Reading were mightily pleased with themselves as only Liverpool and West Brom had prevented City from scoring at Maine Road so far that season. Four days later in the replay, Reading were completely helpless in stopping a rampaging City side that won by an amazing 7-0 scoreline. Summerbee with three, Young, Coleman, Heslop and Bell scoring the goals that once again earned City praise from their beaten opponents.

Malcolm Allison remembers

In the FA Cup Third Division Reading held us to a goalless draw at Maine Road and quite frankly we were poor on the day. When the top sides draw teams from the lower divisions in cup competitions the attitude of the top players changes immediately. Before a ball is even kicked they think they have won the game. All they have to do is to turn up. A similar thing happened a few years later when we were drawn against Wigan Athletic.

I was livid when the final whistle blew on the Saturday. Firstly because of the way the team had played and secondly because my old friend Dave Bacuzzi had gone back down south with such a terrific result. In those days I used to carry an old baseball bat around in the boot of the car and the walls took some beating that night!

Former City favourite Peter Doherty – thought by many to be City's greatest player ever – and my racing pal and Joe's ex-team-mate former Arsenal player Arthur Shaw came to watch the replay four days later and the contrast couldn't have been greater. Determined not to slip up again we absolutely tore them apart, winning the game 7-0 with Mike Summerbee scoring a hat-trick. As the teams left the pitch the public address announcer claimed: "You have just seen the best side in England". Such was the style of our play that night we even got complimentary letters from some Reading fans in the weeks afterwards. Doherty described it as "a quite brilliant performance". Arthur's interest in football had waned since he retired from playing but he assured me after that game it was now as strong as ever, indeed he became a regular traveller to games at Maine Road, often bringing his little daughter with him. I still keep in touch with Arthur's daughter even today. She is now a successful producer with Paramount Pictures in Hollywood and I get regular little gifts from her. And, like many, many others, she still has soft spot for Manchester City.

The visit of Arsenal always guarantees a difficult game and the clash at Maine Road on 3 February proved no exception. Against a strong Arsenal side, the bulk of which would provide their double-winning team of three years later, City could only manage a 1-1 draw whilst Manchester United were extending their lead at the top with a 2-1 win at White Hart Lane. George Graham had given Arsenal the lead only for the Blues to equalise when Coleman's collision with goalkeeper Jim Furnell allowed Lee's lob to drop over both players and enter the net.

In the FA Cup fourth round, City were once again drawn at home, this time against a side they knew only too well from cup encounters in recent years, Leicester City. It was to be the fifth time in three seasons the clubs had met in cup competitions, and to date, City remained unbeaten. As with the Reading game, despite efforts from Bell and Summerbee in particular, and Coleman's terrific performance against Welsh international full-back Peter Rodriguez, City were unable to find the net and the game finished goalless. The replay at Filbert Street the following Monday saw seven goals shared but also City's apparent 'hold' over Leicester broken as the Blues lost 4-3. Joe Mercer gave Matt Gillies' side perhaps the ultimate compliment when he said: "They ran us off our feet", a statement which couldn't be said of most of City's opponents at the time. City's scorers on the night were Lee, Bell and Summerbee it was the first time the famous triumvirate had all scored for City in the same game.

As Gerry Harrison commented in the programme for the visit of Sunderland five days later, the defeat at Leicester had closed another doorway into Europe and now City must concentrate all their efforts in maintaining a top four position, one which would qualify them for the Inter-Cities Fair (now UEFA) Cup. Mike Summerbee missed Lee's goal and with it the 1-0 victory against Sunderland; he was busy making his England debut in a 1-1 draw against Scotland at Hampden Park in a European Championship qualifier. It was the first of his eight caps and was just reward for some sterling performances in City's colours over the previous three years. Prior to Summerbee, the last City player to be capped at full international level had been Don Revie over 11 years earlier.

City's next opponents, Burnley, had beaten leaders Manchester United at Turf Moor two weeks before City's visit on 2 March. The Blues were not to suffer the same fate as Francis Lee coolly sent Harry Thomson the wrong way from the penalty spot for the only goal of the game and to inflict on Burnley their first home defeat of the season. With Chelsea beating Manchester United 3-1 on the same day, the win at Burnley put the Blues within four points of their neighbours and with a game in hand.

March 9 was FA Cup fifth-round day but with City's interest in the competition over for this year at least, the postponed League fixture with Coventry was rearranged. The Midlanders were third from bottom but despite a recent run of good form they were not good enough to stop a City side who'd dropped just one point in the League since the turn of the year. More than 33,000 saw Bell, Summerbee and Young score for the Blues in a bad-tempered 3-0 win, as well as Coleman and Coventry's German-born defender Dietmar Bruck sent off. Coventry were still generous towards the City cause seven days later when they beat Manchester United 2-0. City meantime were thrashing Fulham 5-1 at Maine Road, a victory that took City to the top of the division – albeit on goal average – for the first time. Young took his total to 15 in the League with two goals in this game; Summerbee, Bell and Lee contributing one each, all this after Allan Clarke (later to become the 'sniffer' with Leeds United) had given the visitors the lead.

Neil Young remembers

I'd done well in the Fulham game against George Cohen, and managed to score a couple, and afterwards Malcolm said to me: "You've just murdered the right-back of England." He'd often come out with little things like that to the players and it would make them feel ten feet tall. Even if the team had lost or you'd not played so well, he knew exactly what to say and at what time to say it.

When we were top, Joe came into his own and was brilliant with us. He often said:

"It took you years to get into this position; don't let it slip. Don't get big-headed because there's always someone waiting around the corner waiting to take it away from you". Malcolm would always bull you up, bull you up, but Joe would also tell you the pitfalls as well. His honesty made us think that although we were good, we could also still be beaten.

In true Manchester City style, City then lost their next game, United won theirs and things were back to 'normal'. United's 3-0 win at home to Notts. Forest moved them above City, but not to number one; that place was now held by Don Revie's Leeds United following their 2-0 triumph over Mercer and Allison's men. Although the Blues had shown tremendous spirit at Elland Road with Oakes, Doyle and Book warranting special mentions, players, officials and fans knew that they'd have to overcome their disappointments quickly as the next game was so crucial it could decide the whole outcome of the Championship race.

Old Trafford, Wednesday night, 27 March 1968; Manchester United in second spot behind Leeds United on goal average only against Manchester City just two points behind them in third position. At the best of times a game in which no quarter is given or taken on either side. This was one of the biggest 'derby' clashes in the battle's 74-year history. Just 38 seconds into the game, George Best took advantage of an error by Tony Book to score past Mulhearn. Yet again it looked as though the biggest obstacle in City's way would not be overcome. After a nervous opening ten minutes City finally settled down and began to take control of the game, thanks largely due to the performance of Colin Bell in midfield. In the 15th minute it was Bell who started and finished a move that saw him blast the equaliser high into the helpless Stepney's net. City's pressure continued into the second-half and when Coleman's free-kick was met by George Heslop's head in the 57th minute, the lead was no more than they deserved. Heslop had played his 100th League goal for the club just a couple of weeks earlier against Coventry, but, until that header in front of a silenced Stretford End, had failed to score. What a sense of timing the man had!

Despite being in front City still pushed forward and when, in the dying minutes, the rampant Bell was unceremoniously hauled down by a trailing Francis Burns inside the penalty area, it gave Lee the chance to put the game – and the points – beyond doubt as he blasted home the ensuing spot-kick. Burns' attempt to stop Bell resulted in the only dark spot on an otherwise wonderful night for Manchester City as the Blues' midfielder was carried off on a stretcher and would miss the next four games. Not only was it a key result in the season it was also a key result in the history of Manchester 'derby' matches. City were at last top dogs in Manchester; United would win just one of the next 13 League matches against City.

Malcolm Allison remembers

As far as the League was concerned, we'd lost only once in eight games when the return 'derby' at Old Trafford came along. We 'scraped through' 3-1. We fucking murdered them! Without question it was one of the greatest nights of my life.

We'd just been knocked off the top spot after a 2-0 defeat at Leeds so it vital we got back to winning ways as soon as possible. Our players didn't let me down. To a man they were magnificent with Colin Bell in particular, turning in a quite staggering performance.

Things could have started worse for us however when George Best scored inside the first minute following a rare mistake by Tony Book. I said to Tony before the game: "I want you pick Bestie up, really mark him tight." After that early goal I quickly changed my mind: "Cancel that Tony, play your normal game, just let him come to you", I shouted at him. It worked immediately. Best hardly got a kick from then on but that is perhaps not too much of a surprise because I always rated Tony Book as the best full-back in the country. With the threat of Best extinguished it was no more than we deserved when Colin Bell started and finished a move that brought us level.

George Heslop scored his first City goal after about an hour and when Francis Lee converted a penalty the game was all but over. The only blemish was when Colin Bell was stretchered off causing him to miss the next four games. Matt Busby was a very subdued man that night. He wasn't used to being second best in the country let alone in Manchester. His side was beaten by one that was much better conditioned and more highly skilled.

The balance of power in Manchester football was beginning to swing strongly in our direction. Even if the years of disappointment and humiliation hadn't been wiped away completely, they had at least been erased. City supporters had every reason to be happy that night. By winning at Old Trafford so late in the season it put us in the position of knowing that if we could win all our remaining games there was absolutely nothing they could do about it.

As I was leaving the ground after the game I could hear all sorts of conversations but one in particular stuck in my mind. Two City fans were talking and one said, gleefully rubbing his hands: "Do you know George, tomorrow will be the first day in my whole life when I'll be pleased to go to work. I'm really gonna' give those Reds some stick!"

That night set up the championship for us; psychologically it was a massive game. One of the things that pleased me the most was the difference in attitude between the side of just 18 months earlier which didn't even want to go out on the pitch. That one game confirmed that we had finally closed the gap.

Four days before the triumph over United, Cliff Richard's latest song *Congratulations* entered the UK Top 40. Seven days later it was in the Top Ten and would eventually reach number one. It was a most appropriate song, released at a most appropriate time. Did City's successes over the next three months help to sell a few more copies for the Dorian Gray of the pop world?

Neil Young remembers

We knew, deep down, that we were better than United. The thing with us was we didn't know how to defend. It's no use going to places like Old Trafford and packing the defence with up to nine men. It's just asking for trouble. We always knew that if the opposition scored one, we could always score two; we had the players to do it. If say,

Mike and Colin were having an off day, then Frannie would score or Doyley would knock one in from a set-piece. We always had it in the back of our minds that we'd score in every game.

Tony Book remembers

We had a difficult time over Christmas and New Year when we lost twice to West Bromwich Albion and some people thought we might be losing our way. But by the time the return game with United came around we'd got back to winning ways and were right up with the leaders again. There was something like three points between us, Liverpool, Leeds and United at the top and it was all very tight. The game at Old Trafford couldn't have started worse for me when the ball bounced over my head and George Best scored in the first minute. But after that the team played really well and I thought it was our best game of the season, especially to come back after such a bad start. In the last five or ten minutes we were just passing the ball about for fun and were giving it the 'ole's' at one point. I remember even I kept it for something like eight passes in the corner. After such a great result, I really thought, and perhaps for the first time, that we had a real chance of winning the League.

Following their emphatic win at Old Trafford City were brought down to earth with a bump in their next game, away at Leicester and lost by the only goal of the game. As with the Leeds game two weeks earlier, it seemed that City were taking one step forward and two steps back in their attempts to win the Championship. Meanwhile Manchester United had returned to winning ways with a 4-2 win at Stoke. In order to keep pace with the leaders it was vital for City to win the Good Friday home clash with Chelsea. Heslop contained the obvious threat of Osgood up front, and Pardoe turned in an outstanding performance despite a temperature of 102 and a kick in the mouth. More than 47,000 saw Doyle clinch the points for the Blues and he was on the scoresheet again 24 hours later when another London side, West Ham United, were beaten 3-0. Neil Young scored the other two goals whilst down on the south coast, Southampton held Manchester United to a 2-2 draw. There was still a long way to go in the Championship race although City's route faltered again in the return game with Chelsea. Still with Doyle replacing Bell at number eight and Bobby Kennedy coming in for Doyle, City again lost by a solitary goal when Alan Birchenall scored for the home side.

Bell returned for a trip to Wolves on 20 April and although the team was back to full strength the game produced no goals but a point each. With Manchester United beating their Sheffield namesakes 1-0 at Old Trafford it looked as though single points would not be enough and City were slipping 'at the last' as they chased the title. With just four games left, the Blues were lying third, one point behind Leeds and four behind leaders Manchester United with a game in hand on both. The Blues then left for another short break at Southport where the players were given a lambasting by Mercer, who told them, in no uncertain terms, the Championship was theirs for the taking. Not unlike Allison, Mercer too knew the effects of psychology and would leave the run-in entirely in the hands of those who'd come so far, so quickly under his stewardship; namely the players themselves.

Alan Oakes played his 300th League game for the club in the 1-0 home win against Sheffield Wednesday, a game played unusually for those days on a Thursday night. Lady Luck was on City's side as Neil Young's deflected free-kick flew past Springett to give City the only goal of the game, and, more crucially, two valuable points. The Blues had now used their game in hand on Manchester United and were just two points behind their neighbours with Leeds separating the two Manchester sides in second place. For the last home game of the season, City played hosts to Everton. With Manchester United travelling to West Bromwich on the same evening, City knew a win was vital as the Blues two remaining games were away whilst the Reds two were at home. With a rare goal from skipper Tony Book and another from Tony Coleman (his ninth of the season) City won 2-0 against a full-strength Everton side which contained three players who would later have Maine Road connections. To round off a perfect night for City, news came through from the Midlands that West Brom had beaten Manchester United to allow the Blues to return to the top.

Tony Book remembers

I got my only League goal of the season in the 2-0 win against Everton. The ball just popped up on the edge of the box and, of all things, I hit it with my left foot and it's gone in. Although I was the occasional penalty taker, this one was a real collectors' item!

All City had to do now was to win their last two, very difficult games; whatever Manchester United did would make no difference. The penultimate game was at Tottenham, a team which City usually did well against at Maine Road, but were less than successful against on their travels to London. Once again Allison's tactics were to the fore as another superb Colin Bell-inspired City team overran Tottenham to win 3-1. Almost from the first whistle, Tottenham were pulled apart by a team full of running and commitment with no shortage of skill. Bell scored twice with Summerbee netting the other goal as City went the half-time break with a three-goal advantage. Perhaps not surprisingly after their first-half efforts, City began to tire in the second-half and when Heslop handled the ball inside City's area it gave Jimmy Greaves the opportunity to pull a goal back. Thinking they could still get something out of the game, Spurs put City under tremendous pressure for the final 20 minutes but an exhausted Blues managed to hold firm and earn two vital points. Some City fans in the crowd of 51,000 that day had paid 36 shillings to Fingland's Coaches for the trip down. A look at some of the star names in the Spurs team – Mullery, Mackay, Venables, Chivers and Greaves – meant the money was extremely well spent. Whilst City were winning at Tottenham, Manchester United were beating Newcastle United (ironically City's last opponents) at Old Trafford to ensure an already fantastic season would go 'down to the wire'.

The match at St.James' Park on 11 May 1968, was one of the most important in the club's history. If City could win, they'd be crowned First Division Champions and an estimated 17,000 made the long trip from Manchester up the A1 to witness the events. Closest rivals Manchester United had the easier (on paper at least) game at home to a Sunderland side languishing too near the bottom of the table for comfort. Liverpool too still had an outside chance of the title but City's biggest problem was to overcome a Newcastle side determined (and quite rightly) not to make life easy for the Blues.

As early as the third minute Newcastle nearly took the lead when Jim Scott's shot from the edge of the area beat Mulhearn only to rebound off the bar. A crowd of 46,300 – many sat around the edge of the pitch – watched a nervous start by the Blues, one that was completely foreign to their usual style of play. Far too often they gave the ball away and had to defend constantly against a Newcastle attack led by the imposing Wyn Davies. After 13 minutes Summerbee won a free-kick out on the right-wing. Doyle took the kick to Bell and received the ball back before having a shot across goal which was turned in by Summerbee. City led 1-0 but the goal had no time to settle any nervousness as within a minute of the restart Bryan 'Pop' Robson had equalised for the Geordies.

There was more concern for City shortly afterwards when Davies beat Mulhearn to a cross but fortunately for City, captain Tony Book was on hand to clear the goal bound header off the line. Undoubtedly a second goal was required and it came shortly after the half-hour mark. A shot from Oakes was charged down on the edge of the Newcastle box and Young swivelled to crash a volley past McFaul in the Newcastle goal. A thrilling, end-to-end match was far from over as Heslop's poor clearance was returned straight to Jackie Sinclair who smashed a second equaliser high into the net with Mulhearn completely stranded. Young scored again only to have his effort ruled out for offside against Lee and a pulsating first-half finished level at 2-2.

Within four minutes of the restart City had their noses in front again. McFaul parried Bell's shot into the path of the onrushing Young who made no mistake with his trusty left foot from six yards to notch up his 21st goal of the season in all competitions. That goal calmed the nerves and City's style of play resumed to its more reassured ways. Another goal was ruled out when Lee's effort was disallowed but in the 63rd minute the same player then beat the offside trap to latch on to Bell's through ball before delicately chipping over the advancing goalkeeper. Lee was swamped by excited fans as well as his team-mates, and Doyle grabbed hold of the nearest person in a celebratory bear-hug. Unfortunately for Doyle it was the referee who threatened to book him if he did it again! Surely now they'd now done enough to win? There was to be one last turn in this remarkable game when John McNamee powered a header past Mulhearn in the 86th minute. It made the dying moments enthralling and nerve-racking for both sets of supporters, in fact Mike Doyle was convinced that many Newcastle supporters were actually willing City to win, so impressed were they by the style of play of the men from Maine Road.

At 4.45 p.m. the referee blew his whistle for one last time, scores of delirious fans rushed on to the pitch and Manchester City – interestingly with 11 Englishmen in the side – were Champions of the English First Division. It was a fantastic achievement by a club that just over two years previously had been in the Second Division. Not surprisingly (and deservedly) Joe Mercer and Malcolm Allison received great praise for the club's success but apart from the obvious ability, fitness and stamina of the players, the one thing that was constant throughout was a tremendous team spirit.

Tony Book remembers

We went to Tottenham with two games left, knowing that we could beat them. We used to enjoy travelling to London and we had a lot of good results down there. Once again the team played really well and the win set us up for the last game at Newcastle, a game we had to win. The team had always had a belief that if we let one in we could score two at the other end and so it proved. We had a shaky start and the game was end to end all the time. I managed to clear one off the line and both Frannie and Neil Young had goals disallowed. It was a fabulous game to play in and of course the win meant we were First Division Champions. I think in all my years in football the victory at Newcastle has to be my finest moment. I always measure footballers – as individuals and as a team – against their ability to play well, consistently over a period of time. You have to do that to win the Championship. I remember being carried off the pitch shoulder high at the end of the game, but my biggest single memory has to be the sheer number of fans on the way back home. The number of cars and coaches following us from Newcastle was just amazing. I personally couldn't believe it as just two years ago I'd been playing part-time and laying a few bricks. I said when came to City I'd be happy with two seasons but when the bandwagon started rolling, no one wanted to get off; success breeds success.

For the record, Sunderland managed perhaps a surprising victory at Old Trafford, giving City a final winning margin of two clear points.

Neil Young remembers

Like the game against Spurs at Maine Road, the game at Tottenham was a marvellous match to play in. We played really well on the day and in all honesty that game won the Championship for us. We were at Spurs all through the game, we never let them settle, and I can't remember them having a shot in the first-half. After we'd scored the first goal we thought: "This is it. We can do this". It seemed to lift us another 10%. Even though we still had one game left, the victory at White Hart Lane really sealed it. Coming back on the train Joe and Malcolm both said: "That's it lads; there's no way we'll lose next week".

There were a lot of nerves in the build up to the game at Newcastle. People seemed to be on to us all the time looking for any bits of news and what the team was going to be. Malcolm knew we were going to win and simply told us to "Get used to it". We carried these nerves out on to the pitch as well and we didn't start the game too well. We always had the belief but needed something to bring it out, a sort of fuse paper to light if you like.

It was a hell of a game. We'd score then they'd equalise and then we'd score again and on it went. The nerves seemed to vanish after Mike had scored the first goal for us although we couldn't seem to hang on to the lead for very long. I got the second when I turned round on the edge of the box, caught it just right and it flew in. It was one of those goals that I just knew when I'd hit it, it had a good chance of going in. After the game I was interviewed by one of my all-time favourite players, former Newcastle hero Jackie Milburn, who was covering the game for a local newspaper. He said to me: "I'd have been proud of that first goal". I said: "Oh my God, I don't believe what you just said. You were my idol. It should be me interviewing you". Milburn just started laughing and said: "I'm a Geordie and appreciate good football whoever's playing".

When I got my second and City's third, the goal looked as though it was about a quarter of an inch in size. The ball came to me at such an acute angle and I thought all I've got to do is to hit it true. It could have hit someone and come back out again but it just flew in again. Sometimes you can hit them and they fly over the stands; the next time they go in. The last few minutes were really nail-biting but in the end we hung on and won. I even remember Malcolm shouting at us that United had lost and we had to keep what we had.

When I was just getting into the team as a teenager, I didn't think too far ahead. When you're that age all you want to do is play and when the game's finished you think about next week. Everybody wants to play at Wembley or to win the League and when you achieve that playing for the team that you've supported all you life – in my case I could only ever see blue – then it's absolutely brilliant.

Malcolm Allison remembers

Joe described the last two games as: "Like climbing Everest and K2 in a week." Not a bad description! The game at Tottenham was a brilliant tactical success. The plan was to isolate the ageing Dave Mackay in the centre of the Spurs defence. Francis Lee would pull Cyril Knowles out wide on the right whilst Mike Summerbee would do the same on the other wing with Mike England. This would leave a huge gap in the middle for the rampaging Colin Bell to run at Mackay. The plan worked beautifully. We won 3-1, with Bell scoring twice and Summerbee providing the other. I think Colin Bell now realised what everyone else had known for a long time; namely what an exceptional talent he was.

Dave Mackay left Tottenham for Derby County in the summer and years later I asked him why. "Malcolm," he said: "I've never been so insulted in my life as I was on that day. You absolutely slaughtered us in that match. That was the reason I left Tottenham!"

With Everest out of the way, all that was left was K2, or St.James' Park, Newcastle. We were now level on points with United at the top but they had a superior goal average. Just to make things even more interesting, United had, a supposingly easier game, at home to lowly Sunderland.

Although I knew it would be a tough game I had great faith in our players and was confident in not only winning the game, but the Championship as well. We'd had some problems with niggling injuries but such was the character and determination of the side that we were able to play our strongest 11 on the most important day of the season. It seemed like the best part of 20,000 City fans made the trip to Newcastle forcing Geordie boss Joe Harvey to say: "This is the first time I've been beaten at home before the game started". We knew a point was no good to us; we had to go for both.

Surprisingly our defence started badly and Newcastle hit the bar very early on. George Heslop in particular seemed overawed by the whole proceedings and 'froze' on more than one occasion. Mike Summerbee gave us the lead but the joy was short-lived when Bryan 'Pop' Robson equalised for the home side a minute later. Neil Young gave us the lead once more but further defensive frailties and poor clearances allowed them another equaliser, this time from Jackie Sinclair.

With score 2-2 at half-time and the way we'd defended, I had every intention of giving the team a real going over during the interval. When I got there though, I could clearly see how tense they were and realised a rollicking was not the answer. I simply told them they'd had 45 minutes to get used to it, and now they had to go out and play.

Minutes after the restart Neil Young scored again and when Francis Lee made it 4-2 I knew we were home and dry. Both those players also had goals disallowed but in the end it made no difference. A late goal from John McNamee made the last few minutes interesting but we hung on and eagerly awaited the result from Old Trafford. We didn't have to wait long to find out Sunderland had somewhat surprisingly won 2-1. The First Division Championship was coming to Maine Road, once the trophy had been 'found' at Old Trafford where it had apparently gone 'missing'.

It seemed everyone not connected with Manchester City was convinced the title would remain at Old Trafford. The FA had apparently issued instructions along the lines of "Leave the trophy where it is," and even the Match of the Day cameras covered United's game expecting some kind of celebration afterwards. How wrong can some people be!

I have to admit to feeling drained in the changing rooms after the game. I'm not sure if I had taken in what we'd actually achieved. Obviously the players were in terrific spirits – Lee and Summerbee were jumping in and out of the bath, although both Doyle and Pardoe, players who'd seen the bad times as well, did shed a few tears – and corks were popping and the champagne flowing. I think I was probably a bit stunned by the whole thing. The celebrations, which started in the changing rooms, continued on the coach home, a journey that took much longer because of the huge traffic jams. I got out of the coach at one point and began dancing in and out of the cars, joining in with the hundreds of delirious City fans. We had a celebratory party at The Cabaret Club back in Manchester and I think it was only then that things really began to sink in. Manchester City had carried off the greatest prize in English football in a style admired by all who saw it, even George Best who said he'd like to play a game in our side just to see what it was like.

Despite only managing about an hour's sleep, I was on a high when we held a press conference at Maine Road the following morning. The press had been very supportive of our style of open, attacking football, and whilst Joe was telling them calm, sensible tales about strengthening the squad for next season, I somewhat extravagantly claimed: "We'll be the first team to play on Mars!" It was at this press conference that I also made my now infamous: "We will terrify Europe!" remark. Well, we did, two years later when we beat Gornik to win the European Cup-winners' Cup. Now will people believe me when I say I was ahead of my time!

Within a month of that never to be forgotten day at Newcastle, Manchester United beat Benfica at Wembley to carry off the European Cup. It was the only thing that could have spoiled the season for me. But in all honesty, it didn't. We were quite happy; we knew what we'd done and we'd proved we were a better team than they were. I based my comments to the press on Manchester United's success in Europe because I knew if they could do it then we certainly could. When I first came to Maine Road a friend told me that as well as beating United I'd have to beat the press as well. They lost a game 4-2 once and I remember the newspaper headline said "Six-goal thriller!" Things like that used to really annoy Mike Doyle in particular as he hated them. That victory at Old Trafford meant so much to the City fans that whatever was written or said about United later would not change a thing. We had thrashed them and were now a power in the land again. No longer did the red shirts monopolise the parks. There were many, many sky blue ones on show now and it was a great feeling.

Once the trophy had been 'found', Joe arranged a friendly with Bury at Maine Road on the following Tuesday. Tony Book led the team on a lap of honour and City won 4-2. A young lad called Bobby Owen scored twice for Bury. I substituted George Heslop in the second half and brought on a very useful player. Me. Denied a goal by a fine save by the Bury goalkeeper I then managed to score a perfectly good goal only for it to be ruled out. The referee was rubbish! The cries of 'Allison for England' from the crowd was the icing on the cake.

The national newspapers were hugely complimentary over the next few days, with words such as 'magnificent, wonderful and buccaneers' being used to describe City's first Championship success in 31 seasons. The late Eric Todd, writing in The Guardian said: "If they play attacking football as they have done these past months whatever the state of the game, then they will be welcomed and acclaimed wherever they go."

The final words on this most memorable of seasons should be left to Joe Mercer who said at a press interview just minutes after the final whistle at St.James' Park: "We are Champions because we deserve to be. Because we are very, very fit. There is a lot of team spirit and we have allowed people to express themselves naturally. We work hard, we play positively. And the players we have – and we must never forget that these are the men who really did it – are better than even we realised."

1968-69
Europe Not Terrified... Yet!

THE close season of 1968 was a busy – if sometimes unfortunate – one for Manchester City. As Champions of England they embarked on a tour of the United States, Canada and Mexico, a tour lasting just over a month, and one that was both disappointing and, at times, controversial. In the commemorative magazine *"We Are the Champions!"*, City physiotherapist Peter Blakey chronicled the tour in detail and below is a short summary:

"It was an exhausted – and depleted – City party which arrived back via a Pan American jetliner on Monday, 17 June, from a 20,000 mile tour of three countries. The 32-day trip, with nine games squeezed into the schedule and a succession of plane-hops all over the place, swept players through Canada, America and Mexico. The tour raised only one victory and four drawn games. Not champion form ... unless you know the circumstances.

Internationals Colin Bell and Mike Summerbee were absent on England duty, Mike Doyle flew in from the England under-23 trip to catch only two games (sent off in the first and injured in the second), Alan Oakes was excused from the trip, promising youth players were committed to a tournament in Germany, and injuries piled up so high that coach Malcolm Allison and goalkeeper Harry Dowd turned out among the forwards.

Two players, Neil Young and Stan Horne, were sent home early suffering from serious injuries; while seven of the returning party were nursing painful knocks.

No wonder manager Joe Mercer said on his return: "Never again".

Blakey's report goes on to describe schoolboy-size pitches, small crowds, toilets for changing-rooms, bizarre refereeing decisions, stitches in wounds galore, sendings-off and spitting. Even Tony Book demanded a dope test on Malcolm Allison after a goalless draw against Scottish side Dunfermline in Los Angeles! The trip to Mexico proved worthless as both the arranged games were cancelled by the Mexican authorities because of City's inability to field the same side that had clinched the Championship at Newcastle.

Back home, the club was invited to a Civic Reception in Manchester's Town Hall at the end of July. Already back in training and under a drinking ban, the players became restless and after an hour or so, began to sneak out of the function. Later on they were discovered in a Manchester night-club, alongside Malcolm Allison who had apparently led the escape party. Joe Mercer was furious, saying this was no way for the Champions of England to behave. The newspapers picked up on the story and splashed it all over the back pages. It was a less than auspicious start to the new season.

Neil Young remembers

I remember going out to the pictures with George Heslop in New York. After the film we were walking along Broadway and we spotted this little pizza restaurant so we went in. We'd just finished eating and then all of a sudden, bang! This fella had shot this woman about four of five tables away from us. Well George and me just shit it! We were out of that restaurant so quickly nobody would have caught us running down Broadway. We just took the trip really for a bit of a holiday; we weren't interested in winning anything. I got injured about three weeks into the trip when we played Dunfermline. It was a bit of a rainy night and the pitch was a bit greasy on top. None of us wore shin-pads then, and, as I knocked the ball to the side of the full-back, he came sliding in and caught my left leg about halfway up. I tried to play on for a few seconds before looking down at it and the whole leg was covered in blood. It was a right mess. I signalled immediately for Johnny Hart. He came on and inside a few minutes he'd wrapped the leg in towels and ice and we were on the way to hospital. They got us inside a cubicle and before they even looked at the leg the nurse said: "We're not doing anything until you've paid the bill." Well of course neither of us had any money on us as we'd both rushed straight their from the ground. Johnny had to go back to the ground and get some money before they started on me. In the end I had 48 stitches in my leg and flew back to England with Stan Horne who'd damaged his Achilles tendon.

Another setback was the Achilles injury picked up in training by Tony Book. The seriousness of the injury was not known at the time, but it would prevent him from playing a game until January.

The versatile David Connor took Book's place for the Charity Shield clash with West Bromwich Albion at Maine Road on 3 August. Tony Coleman also missed the game with an ankle injury, causing Neil Young to wear number 11 and giving a debut to new boy Bobby Owen at number ten. Owen had impressed Mercer and Allison last year at Bury where he finished top scorer with 25, and had joined City a couple of weeks earlier for £35,000. His start could not have been better. In gloriously sunny conditions, City gained revenge for the two defeats suffered last Christmas and completely outplayed the visitors to win by a 6-1 margin. Owen scored twice on his debut – the first inside 60 seconds – to go alongside two from Lee, a strike from Young not too dissimilar to his second at Newcastle, and a tremendous headed own goal by West Brom's unfortunate Graham Lovett.

Malcolm Allison remembers

Before we began the 68-69 season we went to America for a pre-season tour. There was a funny incident when Neil Young – who was always a quite lad – was in a restaurant and witnessed a dispute on another table about who should pay a bill. All of a sudden this guy pulls out a gun and Youngie was mortified. He came back to the hotel mumbling: "What a place this is!" In another incident Tony Coleman was refused a drink in a bar because he looked under-age and the bartender asked him for some identification. T.C. started to get stroppy and they sent for the police to have him arrested! One of the best stories though concerns the shooting of Bobby Kennedy. Joe and the chairman, Albert Alexander, stayed in their rooms one night whilst I went with the players downstairs to the piano bar. Joe was watching Bobby Kennedy on television making a speech in Los Angeles when this guy comes right through the crowd and shoots him. I think it was about 12 o'clock at night. Joe then rings the chairman and says: "Mr. Alexander, Bobby Kennedy's been shot." The chairman said: "What's he doing out at this time of night?" Talk about one-track minds with football people.

Neil Young remembers

Before the new season started the players upset Joe and managed to get him annoyed, something that was very difficult to do. We'd gone to a reception at the Town Hall to celebrate the Championship success. This was a new thing for us at the time and we didn't really know what to expect. We had to sit through a lot of speeches and we couldn't move anywhere to get a drink in about an hour. Well, a room full of 20-odd-year-old footballers told to keep still for any length of time is bound to make them restless. Somebody suggested we should try and leave and go to The Cabaret Club. Before long we'd all managed to sneak out, including Malcolm! Joe was fuming with everyone the next day.

It was a dream start to what Colin Bell would later describe as "a very hard season for us. Because we were Champions everyone seemed to be that bit more keyed up when they played us". Francis Lee was also philosophical years later: "We started off so well by thrashing West Brom in the Charity Shield that everyone thought we could just go out and play and carry on from there. And then suddenly we started to struggle; we got a bit over confident. We thought we would win every game by loads of goals and we weren't really playing well when the European Cup came around. Everybody thought we'd easily beat Fenerbahce and again we were over confident. We ended up drawing at Maine Road and losing in Turkey".

Tony Book remembers

We came back from the trip to America and were back in pre-season training and the injury hit me. I think it was probably because we were training on the hard pitches but the Achilles just flared up and we couldn't get rid of it. They wouldn't operate on it because of my age and they just left it. In the end I don't know what it was that cured it because we'd tried everything on it. It was in plaster but the injury just seemed to go on and on and on. They tried me in a reserve game and it went again on me. I came off just after half-time and Sidney Rose stuck a cortisone injection into it. It was then that I wondered whether or not I'd ever get back. I went to Christie's Hospital and they gave me a shot of something or other and I don't know if it was that that cured it but I did then begin to feel better. I played a friendly up in the north-east at Crook Town and it held up and next thing is I was back in the reckoning. I think my wife Sylvia was as much relieved as I was when I started playing again. She'll tell you that I'm not a great spectator!

Manchester played Merseyside in the opening League games as City began the defence of their title. Colin Bell got over a bout of tonsillitis to take his place in an unchanged team from the Charity Shield game. In front of 51,000 at Anfield City lost a rousing game 2–1 despite going ahead in the seventh minute thanks to Neil Young's right-foot shot. Lee nearly made it two when his shot struck the bar, but Liverpool fought back and goals from Bobby Graham and Peter Thompson clinched the match for the home side. Controversy reigned after the game when several City players claimed another shot by Lee had actually struck the stanchion at the back of the net before bouncing back into play. Liverpool hardman Tommy Smith 'introduced' himself to Owen and received a booking whilst Malcolm Allison was 'sent off' for his outburst when the same Liverpool player hacked down Summerbee.

Malcolm Allison remembers

We bought Bobby Owen for the simple reason we didn't have a great deal of cover. If Francis Lee had been injured we didn't have another centre-forward. We could have played Mike Summerbee there, and although he was a great player his strengths were holding the ball up and letting other people in. Anyway we didn't have another right-winger. We never had a huge squad really, certainly not in comparison to today's teams.

Before the next game with Wolves four days later, transfers and contracts were the talk of Maine Road. Goalkeeper Harry Dowd, currently on the transfer list at his own request and disappointed at being number two to Ken Mulhearn, had settled his differences with the club and signed a new contract. Meanwhile top-scorer Neil Young was seeking more money but the club were standing firm and described the result as a 'stalemate'.

For the Wolves game Bobby Kennedy replaced Connor who hadn't fully recovered from a leg injury sustained at Anfield and after 51 minutes City led 3–0. For that period City dominated the game and ripped the bewildered Wolves' defence apart. Two goals from Summerbee and one from Lee separated the sides before Frank Wignall scored twice for Wolves to make the last quarter of an hour interesting. Kennedy – the replacement for Connor who was, in turn, the replacement for Book – damaged a knee and was for a while, doubtful for the next game, against Manchester United at Maine Road.

In the event, Kennedy recovered and played in the 79th Manchester 'derby'. So much was expected of the two best sides in the country but in the end it proved to be a disappointing goalless draw as both sides struggled to break down the others' defences. Young had a goal disallowed and both Bell and Best hit the woodwork, but, by and large, it was a game easy to forget.

Another less than memorable performance came at Leicester, a side well-known to City and one which contained, at the time, Britain's costliest footballer. Allan Clarke was a record £150,000 signing from Fulham in the summer and had secured the game with a hat-trick before half-time. Thanks largely to the efforts of Mulhearn, Leicester could manage no further goals, whilst at the other end, attempts by Bell, Lee and Young all failed to trouble Shilton. It was Leicester's first win of the season although it was their third successive victory over City.

Three drum-beating supporters on the side of the pitch awaited City as they travelled to Queen's Park Rangers for the fifth game of the season. They also found another high-profile striker lying in wait for them, this time in the shape of Barry Bridges, the former Birmingham, Chelsea and England star. As with Clarke at Leicester, Bridges too found the net, volleying in from a corner on his debut. City's performance improved in the second half and their efforts were rewarded when Doyle headed in the equaliser just after the hour. Once again City had Mulhearn to thank for some fine saves but it was still proving a struggle to find that elusive second win of the season.

Malcolm Allison remembers

I thought Tony Book could have gone on forever. Every season, from 29 onwards, he just seemed to get better and better. He was a super athlete, almost freak-like. We tried to replace him during his injury but we really missed him.

Perhaps Highbury was not the place to go looking for it but as it was their next destination, City had no choice. The Blues' defence was described in the *Daily Telegraph* as 'pathetic' and Arsenal moved to the top of the First Division with a very one-sided 4–1 win. Bell's header from Coleman's corner was the only consolation on a night when Arsenal scored twice in each half. Despite the defensive frailties shown at Highbury, Joe Mercer later named an unchanged side for the visit of First Division newcomers Ipswich Town the following Saturday, saying: "It's not really a vote of confidence in the side, but at present this is our strongest available line-up. It is no use singling out individuals; we will only solve this problem collectively. The loss, through injury, of skipper Tony Book's leadership and the fact that several players have failed to hit form this season has seen us only playing in flashes."

The performance against Ipswich showed some improvement, at least until the last minute. Ken Hancock in the Ipswich goal kept the visitors in the game with a series of 'quite fantastic' saves with both arms and legs until Colin Bell's left-foot shot finally beat him in the 41st minute. With the exceptions of Connor, Bell and Coleman, City overall were below standard and their failure to capitalise on many chances, particularly in the first-half, backfired on them when Ray Crawford pushed the ball into an unguarded City net for an 89th minute equaliser. City had now let in 13 goals in seven games, with only four clubs in the division fairing worse. Interestingly enough one of those was Manchester United who'd conceded one more.

This alarming drop in form forced Mercer to ring the changes for the League Cup second round tie at Huddersfield. Heslop, who'd been under pressure for the last few games, saw his place taken by 18-year-old reserve centre-half Tommy Booth for his debut, whilst Owen returned to the first team line-up at the expense of Young who found himself on the substitute's bench. It was the first time the reigning Champions had entered the League Cup but City's stars lost both heart and their tempers in the game and looked far from Championship material.

Despite being in the bottom half of the Second Division, Huddersfield had reached the semi-final of the League Cup the previous season, eventually losing 6-3 to Arsenal over two legs. They carried on their good form and had it not been for Mulhearn again, City's interest in the competition could have been all over inside the first ten minutes. The Blues' all-star forward line barely had a look-in all night and City were more than pleased when the home side finally ran out of steam late on and the game finished goalless. After a somewhat shaky start, Booth "settled down well" according to Joe Mercer, and was rewarded with a suspected broken nose and concussion for his efforts.

Both Heslop and Young returned to the side for the visit to Stoke, a side without six of their usual first team players, including the legendary Gordon Banks. Stoke need not have worried as the Blues continued their poor run of form and lost by a solitary Terry Conroy goal with just three minutes of the game left. Once again City's marking left a lot to be desired as Conroy was one of two unmarked Stoke attackers converging on Mulhearn when he scored. Ironically City had their performance at Stoke covered by F.I.F.A. as part of a two-week programme which would feature in an official coaching film. Future students of the game would have seen very little to impress them on City's recent showings.

It was a concern to supporters that seemingly the majority of players had all happened on a poor run of form at exactly the same time. The Board announced that money was available and newspapers immediately linked the names of Barnsley's Pat Howard, Bob Curtis from Charlton and Bolton's Dave Hatton as all possible candidates for a move to Maine Road. In the end none of the stories proved true, but the more optimistic fans felt that one good win would put a stop to the bad run and all would be well again.

Neil Young remembers

We absolutely pulverised West Brom. in the Charity Shield game and then for about the next ten games, I think we only won once. I can't really put my finger on the reason why, possibly because we were a bit too confident after last season. After the West Brom. game we all thought "this is going to be a great season" and it was really difficult. I'm sure other teams raise their game against the Champions but it took us until September-time before we got going again.

That win finally came in the League Cup replay against Huddersfield, and it provided a welcome tonic for all concerned. Although most people knew they could still play better, City found the net again, winning easily 4-0 and secured a trip to Blackpool in the next round. Before being substituted because of a calf injury, Young was back to his best, and it was his (albeit miscued) shot which was deflected into his own goal by Huddersfield's centre-half Roy Ellam for City's second. Summerbee scored twice with Bell getting the other on a night in which City scored more than they had done in the previous seven matches. Any prospects of continuing this sort of form in the League was halted abruptly by a cynical Southampton side when they travelled north three days later. In one of the roughest and crudest performances ever seen at Maine Road, Terry Paine's men took away a point in a 1-1 draw, but certainly no friends. Mike Summerbee was unceremoniously hacked down by centre-half John McGrath who then went on to punch Francis Lee full in the face. By all accounts the officials completely lost control of the game, City were denied two clear-cut penalties and Tony Coleman was picked out constantly for the day's heaviest treatment. On one occasion he was removed from the field of play by the raised knee of full-back Denis Hollywood, a disgusting incident which caused an incensed crowd to rise to its' feet in united protest.

Perhaps not surprisingly, because of the opposition's spoiling tactics, (Southampton made six changes to the side printed in the programme and included a young Mike Channon at outside-left) City were unable to find any sort of rhythm and went behind early on when Ron Davies scored after ten minutes. Despite being the victim of regular premeditated attacks, Coleman kept bouncing back for more and was rewarded for his aches and pains when he equalised with a real 'corker' of a volley (and with his right foot) in the second half.

It was hardly the ideal preparation for City's first ever game in Europe when physio Peter Blakey 'welcomed' Summerbee, Lee and Coleman to his treatment room, where they joined the already injured Pardoe and Young prior to the visit of Turkish Champions Fenerbahce. Their coach, Hungarian-born Ignace Molnar watched the game against Southampton and felt heartened by what he'd seen, saying, in optimistic tones: "I wish my club had been playing City today."

Fenerbahce had played previously at Maine Road, back in 1953, in a friendly under City's new floodlights. Then City won 5-1, but on 18 September 1968, things couldn't have been much different. Even though they'd lost their last nine European ties away from home, the Turks had conceded just 12 goals in their last 34 games and were the best defensive team in Europe last season. And, just for good measure, they won five competitions as well. Thanks largely to an outstanding performance by 21-year-old Simsek Yavuz in goal, they maintained their impressive statistics and left England with a valuable goalless draw. With all the injury worries behind them, a full-strength City side produced some of their most cohesive football of the season and constantly laid siege to the Fenerbahce goal. However it was simply one of those nights in football when fans know, no matter how long the game goes on for, their side just will not score. Lee, Bell and Coleman all went close to breaking the deadlock but the two easiest chances of the night fell to Summerbee who was going through a terrible patch and had probably his worst game in City's colours. At one point he was even booed by a small section of the crowd. Perhaps in an attempt to boost morale, Mercer later told the press: " Fenerbahce are a good team but I don't know if they can play any differently on their own ground than they did here. I don't plan to watch them in the meantime. I've seen all I want to see of them and I shall be very surprised if we don't beat them in Istanbul."

Neil Young remembers

To this day I still don't know how we didn't manage to beat Fenerbahce 10-1. In the first-leg we did everything apart from score. I think this was one of Malcolm's biggest mistakes during his time at Maine Road. He never had them watched and I know he'll admit this as well. We went into the game blind. We didn't know what we were up against. Even so, we still should have beaten them. In Turkey we took the lead and then threw two stupid goals away. The fans went berserk at the end. It was a real hostile environment to play in. Their fans would start getting to the ground in the morning for a 7 o'clock evening kick-off and they'd let them in. They got into our hotel as well and I can remember them knocking on our doors at two and three o'clock in the morning trying to disrupt us. We were on such a high and to lose the tie like that was a real kick in the teeth.

Any disappointments from Wednesday night were quickly forgotten by weekend. City went to Sunderland, played out a goalless first-half, and then, in the second-half, at last found the Championship form that had been missing so far this season. Unfortunately for the Roker Park side, it was they (and fans knew it had to be someone eventually) who caught the backlash of this season's disappointments and were ripped apart by a City side back in top gear. So good was City's performance that even the most ardent Wearsider applauded City's play. The players who had struggled for form for so long – namely Oakes, Heslop, Bell, Doyle and, especially, Summerbee – all turned in fine performances, indeed Summerbee scored his first goal in eight League outings when he opened the scoring with a header midway through the second half. It was the first of three City goals in a seven-minute spell – Bell and Lee scoring the others – that tore the heart out of the home side. Lee also had an effort ruled out for offside but in the last minute he scored City's fourth from the penalty spot after Bell had been brought down by Sunderland's Irish international full-back Martin Harvey.

Joe Corrigan joined Shrewsbury Town on loan as City prepared for the third round League Cup-tie at Blackpool. On the same night as Manchester United were losing 1-0 in Buenos Aries to Estudiantes in the World Club Championship, City lost by the same scoreline at Bloomfield Road. Bobby Kennedy passed a late fitness test on an injured groin only to injure his ankle during the warm-up and missed the game. Perhaps then the writing was on the wall for the kind of night it was going to be. Lee hit a post and a Bell header bounced off the top of the bar but the game was just another example of City's inability to score this season as chance after chance went begging. In the end a free header from Blackpool's Tom White after 15 minutes was enough to separate the sides as The Seasiders gained some revenge for last year's FA Cup defeat.

In typical City style, they found form again in the next game, against, of all teams, Leeds United, pretenders to City's League crown. Leeds were unbeaten until their trip to Maine Road and had conceded no more than two in a single game so far this season. On the day a rampant City side could easily have doubled their total. Bell scored twice (his first after just four minutes), hit the bar again and forced the save of the match from Gary Sprake. Leeds were on the back foot all day and Young made it 3-0 with a superb swerving 30-yarder before a late consolation from Mike O'Grady gave the scoreline some semblance of respectability for the Yorkshire side who hadn't won a League game at Maine Road since 1936.

City left a rainy Ringway Airport on the morning of Tuesday, 1 October, bound for Istanbul and the return European Cup game against Fenerbahce. Knowing full well that they must score at least once (a goalless draw would have meant the tossing of a coin in those days – at least at that stage of the competition – to decide the winner), Mercer was 'fairly certain' Francis Lee would make the staring line-up after twisting an ankle in the victory over Leeds at the weekend. City's travelling party of 17 was made up of the side from that Leeds game, along with reserves Dowd, Booth, Bowles and Owen, and the injured skipper Tony Book who went along 'just for the ride'.

Against an official, extremely partisan crowd of 40,000 with approximately 15,000 gatecrashers, City silenced the countless claxon horns with some calm, controlled football in the first-half and led 1-0 at the break thanks to Coleman's goal after ten minutes. Within a minute of the restart, substitute Abdullah (he'd only come on at half-time) had equalised to give the Turks new heart. With just 13 minutes left, Mulhearn stood rooted to his line as a cross from Can was eventually scrambled into the net by Ogun for what turned out to be the winner. At the end of the game the crowd went wild with rockets lighting up the night sky, fires lit on the terraces and riot police called upon just to let the players off the pitch. It was a bitterly disappointed City side that left Istanbul the next day, although when Joe Mercer spoke to the press he was honest with his opinions: "The score was about right. We made mistakes and we paid for them. I thought both their goals should never have happened. They were both from scrimmages but we have no excuses. There is a very hard lesson to be learned. You simply can't make silly defensive mistakes in this type of competition and expect to get away with it. We lost the tie by failing to seal it up in the first leg at Maine Road".

Malcolm Allison remembers

Fenerbahce! The funny thing when I went over there later with Galatasary there were three teams in Istanbul; us, Fenerbahce and Beshiktas. I was there about two years and in all those 'derby' matches I lost one game. We slipped up badly against Fenerbahce because we simply underestimated them. That's one of the most important things in football – never underestimate your opposition. Teams play differently against different standards of opposition. Sometimes teams think so-called 'easier' games are a walkover and the performance suffers. The other side of the coin from that is when we drew Liverpool in the FA Cup. I thought it was a great draw for us but some of the others thought I'd gone mad but just look at the result. I think it's fair to say now that we were just too cocky and paid the price. Everybody mentioned my "we'll terrify Europe" comments. What they didn't know though was I meant the year after!"

City's first taste of Europe had ended in bitter failure at the first hurdle; had they beaten Fenerbahce they would have faced Ajax in the next round. Heslop and Mulhearn in particular were singled out for criticism for their poor performances, and Mulhearn was immediately dropped for the League visit to Goodison Park. Harry Dowd came back into the side as Mulhearn's replacement (Mulhearn had been a League ever-present since making his debut some 15 months earlier) although many thought that the former Stockport 'keeper was somewhat unfortunate, taking into account his hitherto fine performances and without the influence of Tony Book in front of him. Dowd and a brand-new, never-seen-before (at least on City) black and red striped kit failed to prevent Everton winning 2-0, with Alan Ball and Joe Royle scoring the goals inside a 12-minute spell midway through the first-half. Colin Bell played his 100th League game for the club and Mike Summerbee was carried off on a stretcher after an aerial collision with Brian Labone, returning to the action nine minutes later. It was the end of a busy week for Summerbee, what with travelling to Turkey and finding the time to get married as well!

Tony Book remembers

Colin Bell is right when he says the start of the 1968-69 season was a really difficult one for us and we weren't playing well when the European Cup came round against Fenerbahce in September. Although playing in Europe was 'foreign' to us we could have won the tie in the first leg at Maine Road. We had so much of the play at home that we really should have taken a big advantage with us to Turkey for the return leg. Even though I didn't play in either game because of the Achilles injury, I did travel with the party to Turkey. Believe me it was a real eye-opener. I remember getting up in the morning and looking out of the hotel bedroom window. It was about ten o'clock and even then people were making their way towards the ground. We were staying at The Hilton, perched high on a hill and in the distance we could see the ground. Even at such an early hour it looked very nearly full. Once we got there, we saw armed troops round the pitch and the whole experience was completely new to us all. None of us – including Joe and Malcolm – had ever seen anything like this before. All in all, it was pretty frightening and I think the whole atmosphere got to us in the end. Even though we started well when Tony Coleman scored it was hugely disappointing night and I can remember just sitting on the bench slowly watching the game slipping away from us.

Bert Trautmann brings off a diving save at Blackburn in April 1959. Bill Leivers, another survivor of the 1956 FA Cup Final victory over Birmingham City, is in the centre of the picture. City lost this match at Ewood Park 2-1 and finished the season in 20th position, avoiding relegation by just one point.

'Burnden Ballet' – Bert Trautmann foils Nat Lofthouse (on ground) in November 1960. City lost 3-1 and Lofthouse scored his last-ever League goal at Burnden. On the same day 16-year-old Francis Lee made his debut for the Trotters and scored against the club he would serve with such distinction in future years.

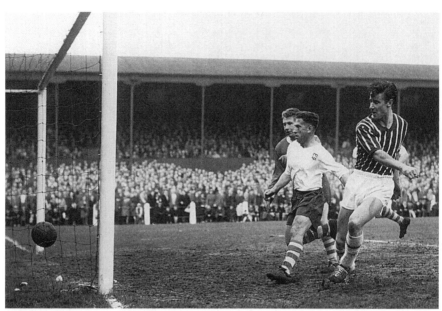

City's Gerry Baker nips in front of Preston's Fred Else to score in the 1-1 draw at Deepdale in April 1961. At the end of the season City were in 13th place in the old First Division.

The City team which lost 4-1 at Blackburn in December 1961. Back row (left to right): Bobby Kennedy, Jackie Plenderleith, Harry Dowd (making his debut), Cliff Sear, Joe Hayes, Alan Oakes. Front row: Dave Wagstaffe, Peter Dobing, Barrie Betts, Neil Young, Paul Aimson. City finished the season in 12th position.

Liverpool goalkeeper Jim Furnell blocks a shot from City's Peter Dobing at Maine Road in August 1962. Ron Yeats and Gerry Byrne are in attendance. Neil Young scored both City's goals in the 2-2 draw. It was the start of a dreadful season for City who were relegated in 21st place at the end of it.

Manchester City pictured at the start of the 1964-65 season. Back row (left to right): Vic Gomersall, Derek Kevan, Roy Cheetham, Harry Dowd, Alf Wood, David Shawcross, Jimmy Murray. Front: Bobby Kennedy, Dave Bacuzzi, Cliff Sear, Alan Oakes, Dave Wagstaffe, Glyn Pardoe, Matt Gray.

"It's somewhere in there, lads." A scramble in the 5-2 win at Deepdale in November 1964. Derek Kevan scored a hat-trick and Neil Young netted the other two. Bobby Kennedy is on the ground supported by Vic Gomersall (centre) and Matt Gray (right). City ended this season 11th in the Second Division.

Manchester City chairman Albert Alexander, whose family had been involved with the club for over 70 years, and who made one of the most important signings in City's history when he brought Joe Mercer to manage the club.

In March 1966, on the eve of the transfer deadline, City signed 20-year-old Colin Bell from Bury. Bell immediately impressed, scoring on his City debut, at Derby. His Maine Road career saw him score over 150 goals in almost 500 games and win 48 England caps.

Joe Mercer, brought back into football after leaving the game when he became unwell while managing Aston Villa. It was a masterstroke to bring him to Maine Road.

Malcolm Allison had also been forced out of the game through ill-health. He returned as a coach but was out of work when Joe Mercer, realising he needed a younger presence on the training ground, telephoned with a job offer.

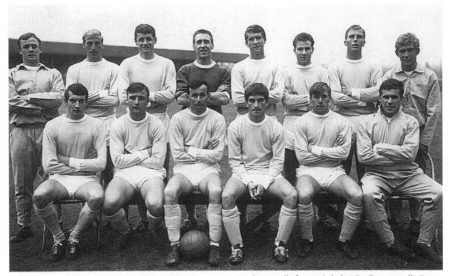

Manchester City pictured in the 1965-66 season. Back row (left to right): Vic Gomersall, Dave Bacuzzi, Roy Cheetham, Harry Dowd, Mike Doyle, Bobby Kennedy, Alan Oakes, John Clay. Front row: Neil Young, Glyn Pardoe, Jimmy Murray, Johnny Crossan, Dave Connor, Alan Ogley.

Fallowfield-born Neil Young had been switched around in the City forward line before Mercer and Allison settled him in the number-10 shirt, after which his career blossomed. Young made 413 senior appearances for City, scoring 108 goals, one of them the fine left-footed shot that won the 1969 FA Cup Final. He enjoyed all City's triumphs in the Mercer-Allison years.

Johnny Crossan, an inspirational midfielder who skippered Manchester City to promotion in 1965-66. Crossan missed only two League games that season and was second-highest scorer (behind Neil Young) with 13 goals.

73

A smiling Joe Mercer with his happy City squad.

Menu cover from the celebration dinner held at Manchester Town Hall in July 1966, to celebrate City's return to the top flight as Second Division champions.

CITY OF MANCHESTER

Alderman Mrs. Nellie Beer, O.B.E., J.P.
Lord Mayor

DINNER

IN THE TOWN HALL

TO CELEBRATE MANCHESTER CITY FOOTBALL CLUB'S CHAMPIONSHIP OF THE SECOND DIVISION OF THE FOOTBALL LEAGUE

THURSDAY, 21st JULY, 1966

Tony Book joined City from from Plymouth Argyle in July 1966, for £17,500 and two months short of his 32nd birthday.

Colin Bell hammers over a fierce cross against Sheffield United at Maine Road in May 1967. The result was a 1-1 draw and City were on their way to finishing 15th in their first season back in the old First Division.

Colin Bell chips Burnley goalkeeper Adam Blacklaw to score in City's 3-2 win at Turf Moor in October 1966.

Glyn Pardoe, a cousin of Alan Oakes, made 378 appearances for City between 1961-62 and 1974-75. He played in every position except goalkeeper and centre-half and was the regular left-back in the First Division championship-winning season. His career was effectively ended after he suffered a broken leg in the December 1970 Manchester derby game.

Tony Coleman joined City from Doncaster Rovers in March 1967, although Joe Mercer had reservations about his reputation. Happily, Coleman scored 16 goals in 102 games for City and helped them to a League Championship title and an FA Cup victory.

Alan Oakes was a remarkable player who made a club record 676 senior appearances for Manchester City. His Maine Road career began in April 1958, when he signed as an amateur, and continued until he joined Chester for £15,000 in July 1976. In between he had helped City to every senior domestic honour and to European glory, yet remarkably his only major representative honour was an appearance for the Football League. In 1967-68, he missed only one League match as City lifted the First Division title.

City at the start of the 1967-68 season. Back row (left to right): Tony Book, Stan Horne, George Heslop, Alan Ogley, Harry Dowd, Alan Oakes, Glyn Pardoe, Mike Doyle. Front row: Mike Summerbee, Dave Connor, Colin Bell, Johnny Crossan, Chris Jones, Neil Young, Tony Coleman.

"What's up ref?" Coleman, Young and Summerbee want to know from Clive 'The Book' Thomas during a League game at Burnley in March 1968. George Heslop is about to join in. City won 1-0 with a goal from Francis Lee.

Although he made only 13 appearances when City won the Championship in 1967-68, Wythenshawe-born Dave Connor enjoyed his best days with City in the late 1960s. Altogether he made 154 appearances in two spells with the club.

Chairman Albert Alexander, manager Joe Mercer and coach Malcolm Allison pose proudly with City's League Championship and FA Charity Shield winning squad in the summer of 1968. Back row (left to right): Albert Alexander, Johnny Hart (trainer), Glyn Pardoe, Alan Oakes, Ken Mulhearn, Mike Doyle, George Heslop. Front row: Francis Lee, Mike Summerbee, Colin Bell, Tony Book, Tony Coleman, Neil Young, Dave Connor.

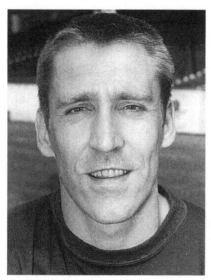

After struggling at both Newcastle and Everton, centre-half George Heslop never looked back after Joe Mercer and Malcolm Allison took him to Maine Road and he missed only one League game in the 1967-68 League title-winning season.

Goalkeeper Harry Dowd, above, was a solid performer but at the start of 1967-68, Malcolm Allison was on the lookout for another 'keeper. He found one in Ken Mulhearn, below, who made his debut against Manchester United and retained his place for the rest of the season as City won the title.

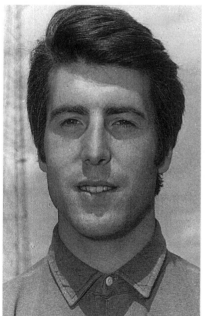

In 1967-68 Mike Summerbee, with 20 goals, was City's second leading scorer in all competitons behind Young. Summerbee was Mercer's second signing in 1965 and went on to share in City's triumphs under the manager who had played alongside his father during the war. He made 449 senior appearances for City, scoring 68 goals and winning eight England caps before being transferred to Burnley for £25,000 in June 1975.

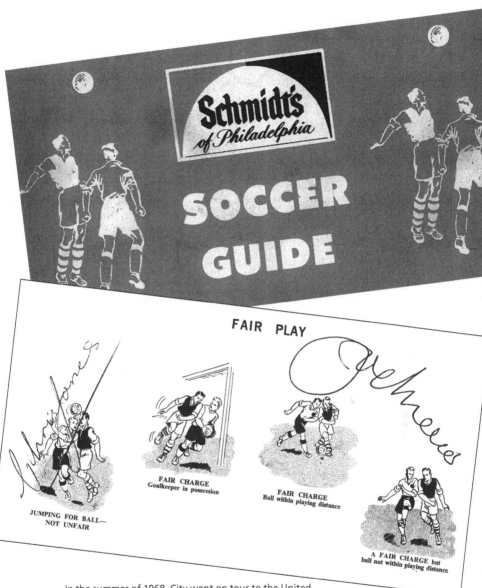

In the summer of 1968, City went on tour to the United States. Uninitiated local spectators were given this guide to the strange game of soccer.

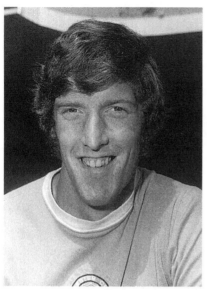

Joe Mercer (left) and Blackburn Rovers manager Johnny Carey, the former Manchester United star, meet before the FA Cup fifth-round tie at Ewood Park in February 1969. City won 4-1 with two goals each from Francis Lee and Tony Coleman.

Local boy Tommy Booth made his debut for City in September 1968, at the start of a career that would bring him 487 senior appearances, 36 goals and a host of medals.

FA Cup winners. Manchester City in 1968-69. Back row (left to right): George Heslop, Mike Doyle, Alan Oakes, Harry Dowd, Arthur Mann, Glyn Pardoe, Tommy Booth, Tony Coleman. Front row: Dave Connor, Bobby Owen, Colin Bell, Tony Book, Francis Lee, Mike Summerbee, Neil Young.

George Heslop made Mercer's selection problems easier for him by picking up a virus two days before the midweek clash with Arsenal. Heslop was still struggling with his form in the defeat at Everton and it gave an opportunity for Tommy Booth to make his League debut. Interestingly enough, contemporary newspaper reports this same week suggested City were currently keeping an eye on an up-and-coming young centre-half by the name of Dave Watson, at the time establishing himself in the first team at Tommy Docherty's Rotherham. Arsenal left Maine Road with exactly what they came for; namely a point. City were unable to break down a strong London rearguard expertly marshalled by Frank McLintock and it was the Scot's long pass to centre-forward Radford that gave the visitors the lead on the stroke of half-time. Bell equalised three minutes into the second-half but a largely stale game petered out into the inevitable draw with many fans not realising the referee had blown the final whistle, such was it's demise.

Joe Mercer now made a slight change to the managerial structure when he 'banned' Malcolm Allison from watching games from the touchline, telling him: "You must sit with me in the Directors' Box." The decision came following Allison's latest brush with a referee who reported him to the FA after the recent ill-tempered game against Southampton. The new seating arrangements – which were also confirmed to have been in force for the last two games –would now feature a 'phone link-up between Allison and Johnny Hart in the trainers' dug-out.

From his new vantage position in the stands, Allison (and guest of the club, Hollywood star Jane Russell) sat back and watched a true vintage performance as City beat Tottenham 4-0. Two goals in the first ten minutes – firstly by Lee and then by Coleman – set the Blues on course for the win in front of a windswept 38,000 crowd. In the second-half Lee scored City's third when he sent Pat Jennings the wrong way from the penalty spot before Connor rounded off a fine performance both personally and by the team when he started and finished a 70-yard move for the fourth.

Around the time of the Spurs' game, City were attempting to arrange a series of friendly matches against top overseas sides as they tried to learn from their Fenerbahce experience in anticipation of further European campaigns. It was also announced that the new red and black kit as worn recently at Everton, was to be the club's official change kit. The board had asked director John Humphreys (the owner of Umbro) to design the kit, as certain sections were unhappy with the all-maroon strip.

The new kit got its second outing in City's next fixture, a 1-1 draw at Coventry. The Blues took the lead in the first-half when Coventry full-back Dietmar Bruck deflected a cross from Lee past his own goalkeeper after 29 minutes. Coventry equalised in the second-half, Pardoe's error allowing Coventry's new £80,000 acquisition from Liverpool Tony Hateley, to squeeze a low shot past Dowd.

Off the pitch, Joe Mercer accompanied Malcolm Allison to an FA Committee meeting in Leicester. After a 40-minute hearing, Allison was fined £100 and banned from the touchline for life following 'abusive remarks' made to a linesman during the recent Southampton game. It was the seventh time the flamboyant coach had appeared before an FA Disciplinary Committee and their decision only rubber-stamped the moves already made by Mercer and the Board at Maine Road.

The continually impressive Booth kept his place in the side as bottom club Notts. Forest visited Maine Road at the end of October. In a pathetic second-half performance, City squandered a 3-0 half-time lead to give Forest a share of the points. Bell scored in the 11th minute and then two shots from Young were deflected in by the unfortunate Nottingham full-back paring of John Winfield and Peter Hindley. Thanks largely to the performance of Ian Storey-Moore, a revitalised Forest scored three times in 18 minutes in the second-half and in the end could easily have gone away with both points.

Chelsea had failed to score in any of their previous four games as City travelled to Stamford Bridge without the injured David Connor who'd damaged an ankle in the recent friendly against Ajax. They remedied the situation after just seven minutes when Tommy Baldwin beat off tackles from both Booth and Doyle before firing a shot past Dowd which went in off the post. Two minutes before the interval, Chelsea's John Boyle was sent off after a clash with Coleman, in the referee's eyes the final act of a private feud that had been going on all afternoon. Despite being down to ten men, it took the home side just five minutes of the second-half to score their second goal and effectively finish the contest. Played on-side by Booth, Peter Osgood collected Baldwin's through ball before side-stepping Dowd for the simplest of goals.

Twenty-four hours after the Chelsea game, there was a full turnout of players and staff for Mike Doyle's wedding in Reddish. Glyn Pardoe was best man and later made a speech, as did manager Joe Mercer although both Alan Oakes and Colin Bell declined the speech-making on grounds of 'lack of training and preparation'. Bell went straight from the wedding to the ground to collect his kit, then to make for London en route for Bucharest to join up with the England party for a friendly with Rumania. He then realised he had left his ticket at home and had to dash back for it. By all accounts he made it to Rumania on time although in the end he took no part in the game that finished goalless.

The game with Sheffield Wednesday was in doubt up until 30 minutes before kick-off owing to thick fog swirling around Maine Road. In the end it was perhaps a pity the game took place as City lost at home for the first time in nearly a year. Despite the fog and the Arctic conditions, both sides played out a fast-paced game, with Wednesday's Young England 'keeper Peter Springett denying City on at least six occasions with some superb saves. Heslop replaced the injured Coleman on the hour and it was his misdirected clearance that gave Peter Eustace the chance to score the only goal of the game from close in. As at Chelsea the previous Saturday, once again the ball struck the post before nestling in the back of the net.

Coleman's pulled leg muscle prevented him from travelling to Newcastle, the scene of City's Championship celebrations six months earlier. His absence gave a debut to the 17-year-old Ian Bowyer. In a drab and dreary match – one that contrasted hugely from that last 4-3 thriller – City looked set for a share of the points until the head of Wyn Davies settled things with just 30 seconds left. That goal left City without a League win in over a month. It was also the third consecutive game in which they'd failed to score. Angered by what he thought was an infringement prior to the goal, Mike Doyle was escorted off the pitch by police after allegedly swearing to some local supporters in the crowd. Mercer headed north after the game at Newcastle to check glowing reports on the Hearts full-back Arthur Mann, a player rated in the £50,000 class. It was believed Mercer focussed his attention towards Mann after being turned down flat by Arsenal in an attempt to buy Ian Ure. Whilst Mercer was looking to strengthen the squad, Birmingham and Newcastle were making moves towards the out of favour Heslop and Mulhearn respectively.

On the same day as City eventually announced they'd agreed terms with Hearts for the services of Arthur Mann (a new record signing of £65,000) Tony Coleman was disciplined by the club and dropped for the game against West Bromwich Albion. Coleman apparently broke club curfew rules when he was found drinking by Allison at 1 a.m. in The Cabaret Club, Manchester. With both men being of a somewhat fiery temperament, the meeting soon evolved into a row and brawl and Coleman was immediately reported.

With the memory of the Charity Shield still reasonably fresh in their minds, West Brom. did one better this time; they only lost 5-1. In easily the most entertaining game of the season so far at Maine Road, City were two goals up in the first 16 minutes thanks to Bell and Young. It remained that way until ten minutes after the interval when Doyle's shot from the edge of the penalty area increased City's lead. Tony Brown – a player who was always likely to score – pulled a goal back for West Brom. before Bell and Young doubled their personal tallies to complete a five-star performance by the Blues on a mud-laden Maine Road pitch. Young was later denied a hat-trick when a volleyed goal was ruled out for offside against Bell. Malcolm Allison missed this more than welcome return to form by the Blues; he was laid up in bed with 'flu.

New record signing Arthur Mann made his debut in the 2-1 defeat at West Ham. There was still no place for Coleman following the nightclub incident although he had by now publicly apologised to the club who, in turn, had accepted and offered him another chance. Two headed goals by Geoff Hurst and Martin Peters inside the first quarter of an hour made things even more difficult for City and it was the sharpness in front of goal exemplified by these two that was the difference on the day. Despite creating several good chances, City only had Lee's second-half penalty to show for their efforts and once again returned home empty-handed. Whilst City were losing at West Ham, on Merseyside, future City boss Joe Royle was scoring a hat-trick in Everton's 7-1 demolition job on Leicester. It took the impressive Royle to 17 for the season, or, put another way, more than half of City's total.

Three weeks earlier, Burnley's impressive run of eight successive League victories had come to an end when Wolves held them to a 1-1 draw at Turf Moor. Since then they'd suffered three successive defeats and Mercer and Allison's men were keen to increase that run. Watched by

Conservative leader Edward Heath and England manager Sir Alf Ramsey, City battered the much-lauded young Burnley side 7-0, although with two disallowed goals, a missed penalty by Lee and two efforts cleared off the line, a larger winning margin would not have been too unjust. Young with two, and Bell led the way before the interval with Coleman, Doyle, Lee and Bell again completing the job in the second-half. So impressed was Ramsey with the performances of Bell and Lee that he named them both in his line-up for England's game against Bulgaria at Wembley the following week. It was Lee's first full international cap and Bell's third; his first had come back in May against Sweden.

As Mike Summerbee was battling against an ankle injury in an attempt to play at Tottenham, 17-year-old Glaswegian Willie Donachie was putting pen to paper after being on trial for four weeks. Another 'one for the future' was Youth Team captain Tony Towers who travelled with the first team to London 'for the experience'. On a bone-hard, frost-covered pitch, City were unlucky to fall behind to Mike England's header after 15 minutes. Just a few weeks earlier and such an early goal would have put paid to the Blues but their newly restored resilience and confidence once again came to the fore enabling Lee to volley home a spectacular equaliser ten minutes before the break. Despite dominating the game for large periods – and Lee having a goal disallowed – City reluctantly had to settle for a point; Tottenham were more than grateful for a share of the spoils. Once again it appeared the Blues saved their best performances for Tottenham.

Neil Young remembers

The whole season was a real topsy-turvy one. We all knew we could still play but we seemed to have lost a bit of consistency. Scattered amongst the games like Fenerbahce were great wins against West Brom. (again) and Burnley when we scored seven. We used to have these six-week training sessions at Wythenshawe Park, six weeks on, six weeks off, with people like Joe Lancaster, on Mondays. When we'd just finished a six-week stint and we had a couple of games in quick succession it was great and we inevitably played well. However if we had a couple of tough games during a six-week stint then we invariably struggled. I don't know if that was the reason but these sessions were really intense – killers – and maybe it was little bit too much for the games we were playing. We still trained during the six-weeks 'off' but nowhere near the same intensity. I've seen many a player physically sick in Wythenshawe Park. However these sessions paid off in games when we'd come on strongly against teams in the last 20 minutes.

There was great news for City on 16 December when Tony Book came through his first full match of the season with no ill effects from his Achilles injury. Book played on the left-wing in an almost full-strength City team sent to amateur side Crook Town to inaugurate their new floodlights. The north-easterners proved no match for Francis Lee in particular as he scored a hat-trick in the 6-1 win on a snow-covered pitch. The following day Malcolm Allison was approached by managerless Queen's Park Rangers to take over the reigns after their previous manager, Tommy Docherty, had resigned after just 28 days. Allison later told the press: "I had a telephone message asking for a meeting to discuss the position. But I haven't followed it up because I don't fancy the job!" In the same week, Mike Doyle was fined £50 by the FA for 'making an ungentlemanly gesture' at a linesman at the end of the game at Newcastle the previous month. Things certainly happened all day, every day, during those halcyon days at Maine Road!

Tommy Booth received an early Christmas present when he scored his first-ever League goal for the Blues in a 4-2 win against second to bottom side Coventry. It wasn't a classic strike be any means as Booth, after a solo run into the penalty area, seemed to 'stumble' the ball slowly past Glazier in the Coventry goal and into the net. Nevertheless it cancelled out a surprise fifth minute opener by the unmarked Trevor Shepherd for the visitors. Five minutes before half-time Young gave City the lead with a trademark 30-yarder and the same player made it 3-1 two minutes after the break despite desperate pleas for offside from the Coventry defence. Centre-half George Curtis deflected Bell's shot into the net for City's fourth before Hateley completed the day's scoring when he beat Dowd with just over ten minutes left. It wasn't quite a textbook performance by the Blues; in fact one newspaper at the time said: "They (City) played only as well as they had to."

A pity then that they didn't carry on in the same vein for the Boxing Day clash with Everton, at the time one of the top three sides in the country and strong contenders to take over City's mantle as League Champions. Joe Royle gave Everton the lead in the first minute when he raced past a standing Doyle to head Morrissey's cross past Dowd. Eight minutes later City were in more trouble when full-back Tommy Wright beat off challenges from Pardoe and Mann before scoring Everton's second. Bell pulled a goal back for City but Everton could have scored at least three more before Jimmy Husband secured the points for the visitors with just seven minutes left. The game was won and lost in midfield where Mike Doyle's poor performance caused him to be dropped for the next game, away at Notts. Forest. However the hitherto ever-present Doyle earned a reprieve when the game at Forest was abandoned owing to a frozen pitch with only two First Division games – at Burnley and Sheffield Wednesday (neither place renowned for its tropical climate!) – beating the big freeze as 1968 turned into 1969.

City's first game of the New Year was a third-round FA Cup clash with Third Division Luton Town, a game that brought back memories of the famous Denis Law 'six-goal' game eight years earlier. On the day City struggled to an unconvincing 1-0 win with Lee providing the only goal of the game from the penalty spot. Once again the Blues failed to convert a good number of clear-cut chances and but for a superb one-handed save by Dowd from Bruce Rioch's header in the closing minutes, the game could have gone to a replay. City's reward for a hard-fought win was a trip to Newcastle in round four.

Tony Book was finally restored to his rightful position when he returned to the side (although not as captain; that job was still left in the hands of his deputy Alan Oakes) for the visit of Chelsea on January 11th. Book had played just one friendly, one reserve and one 'A' team game since injuring his Achilles in pre-season training. Somewhat surprisingly it was club record signing Arthur Mann who made way for Book with the amicable Scot admitting: "Although I'm disappointed, I accept that I haven't been playing that well lately. But don't worry, I'll be back."

Standing in for the injured Mike Summerbee, Bobby Owen took advantage of a rare opportunity by scoring twice in a 4-1 win. Book eased his way back into first-team action (and a new shirt after his original one had been ripped off by Houseman) with a solid performance but the star rating went once again to Tommy Booth in defence. Peter Houseman had given Chelsea an early lead only for Young to equalise with a fine shot into the top corner ten minutes before half-time. Before Owen got into the action with his first League goals for the club, Lee scored City's second after good work by substitute Bowles, the replacement for Bell who'd left the action with a knee injury.

With Bell out for the next game at Sheffield Wednesday, City welcomed Summerbee back into the fray after a niggling ankle injury. A thrilling, end-to-end game with chances for both teams ended 1-1 and was a fair reflection of the day's proceedings. After a goalless first 45 minutes, the home side took the lead when full-back Wilf Smith crashed a long-range shot past Dowd in the 55th minute. It was Smith's first goal for the club in 152 League appearances. Young's reply five minutes later after Lee's shot had been parried by the goalkeeper, levelled the scores and both sides – with their minds on difficult FA Cup-ties next weekend – went away happy with a point each.

Mann, Bowles and Connor were added to the team that drew at Sheffield as the Blues travelled to Newcastle for the fourth-round FA Cup-tie. A sternly fought game finished goalless with the home side having more of the game territorially and City having more of the clear-cut chances. With only the goalkeeper to beat Lee saw his shot hit the bar but the main talking point of the afternoon was the alarming miss (from barely a yard out and in front of an empty net) by Owen when McFaul had parried Young's shot against a post. If the former Bury striker was the villain on Saturday, he was the hero on the following Wednesday. In front of a crowd touching 61,000 (some 5,000 more than had seen the first game at St. James's Park) Owen made the first for Young and then scored the second himself in a 2-0 win. It was a game City won in some comfort and could easily have scored considerably more on the night. Even so there were a couple of scares on Dowd's goal, firstly when 'Pop' Robson hit the bar and secondly when the normally calm Book (aiming to concede a corner) nearly put through his own goal with a spectacular banana shot. City fans left Maine Road still smiling about the result and the effort by Book, and could look forward to a trip to Second Division Blackburn Rovers in round five. The draw caused some believers in fate to note the following pointer; the last time City met Blackburn in the FA cup was in 1934. The Blues won 3-1 and went on to win the Cup by beating Portsmouth in the Final.

Newcastle were once again visitors to Maine Road just three days after the FA Cup replay. The Geordies had stayed in Blackpool all week and for the League game they included their recently signed striker from Middlesbrough, Arthur Horsefield, for his debut. Horsefield immediately made an impact. By the third minute he'd given the visitors the lead and broken Dowd's nose into the bargain when he scrambled the ball home. Despite the continuous fierce, driving rain, both sides produced some good football before Owen splashed through the mud and equalised for the Blues in the 32nd minute after good work on the left by Young and Coleman. However nine minutes later, with the pitch resembling a lake and after yet another torrential downpour, the referee had no option but to call the game off. Joe Mercer fully supported Mr Corbett's decision: "It was right. Conditions were becoming absolutely farcical."

Neil Young remembers

T.C. always fancied himself as a penalty taker but knew Frannie was our regular. In the Cup-tie with Luton, we were awarded a penalty and Frannie put the ball down on the spot and turned round back to his mark. T.C. comes rushing past him, out of nowhere, and before you knew what was happening, he's ballooned the ball high up into the Platt Lane stand. Frannie couldn't believe it. Fortunately it didn't cost us anything and we got through to play Newcastle in the next round. It was very tight up there and finished goalless before we beat them 2-0 at Maine Road. I managed to score at Maine Road and the next morning there was great photograph of me in the papers flying through the air.

Malcolm Allison missed the events at Maine Road as he was accompanying chief scout Harry Godwin on a spying mission to Ewood Park. City's Cup opponents Blackburn Rovers played hosts to Crystal Palace but what information was collected must surely have been slight as that game too went the way of the one at Maine Road, this time after just 18 minutes.

On Monday, 3 February 1969, everybody connected with Manchester City was delighted when the board announced that Malcolm Allison was staying with the club. For the previous few days, Allison's old West Ham colleague Noel Cantwell had been desperately trying to lure him away from Maine Road and join forces with him at Coventry. Allison had been offered considerably more money than he was earning at Maine Road (despite two Championship successes) and was also very close to Cantwell. Allison himself admitted at the time that he thought long and hard and had been undecided, but Mike Summerbee knew exactly where he stood: "If Malcolm leaves, there's a transfer request coming from me and probably from Colin Bell and Tony Book. I've crossed Malcolm often enough, but he's made us into good players and made us into a good team. I wouldn't want to work for anyone else." In the end the players' minds were eased when Allison signed a new four-year contract saying: "I never really wanted to leave. This is the greatest club in England."

Once the off the field events had finally been laid to rest, thoughts turned back to football and the FA Cup. However once again the weather intervened, this time though rain was not the culprit. The heaviest snow falls in years blanketed Blackburn's Ewood Park ground with up to six inches falling inside a few hours. Despite valiant attempts by the groundstaff, the game was called off 24 hours before the scheduled kick-off. On a positive note, the delay gave Colin Bell an extra four days to complete his rehabilitation from a knee injury sustained at Chelsea a month earlier. In the end, Bell had even longer to recover. Although the weather changed sufficiently for playing conditions to be described as perfect, an outbreak of 'flu took a hold on the players, with Blackburn having six of their starting line-up unable to play. City were hit on a smaller scale with Young definitely out of action and Lee and Bowles 'on the mend'. Blackburn boss Eddie Quigley made a 'phone call to the FA headquarters in London and was granted a postponement until the following Monday.

A case of "here we go again" struck Maine Road, just 48 hours after the game with Blackburn was abandoned. Heavy snow returned to the north-west and the six-inch covering of the pitch made it impossible to stage the League game with West Ham. It meant that City had not played a competitive game for 17 days, and that was only 41 minutes of the rain-affected game with Newcastle. Not surprisingly, Joe Mercer worried about his players being rusty when the apparently jinxed clash with Blackburn should eventually take place.

The snow that hit Manchester also travelled to East Lancashire, stopping off on its way at Ewood Park, and caused the fifth-round FA Cup-tie to be postponed for an amazing third time. It appeared that City would never have the opportunity to stop a sequence of results that had seen them fail to win at Blackburn in nearly 40 years. Three postponements became four when the snow turned to ice and the game rescheduled for Thursday, 20 February was also called off, stretching the Blues' period of inactivity to 20 days.

Blackburn and Burnley are two Lancashire towns in such close proximity that if the weather affects one, the chances are it will affect the other. Back in February 1969 this proved to be exactly the case. City's League game at Turf Moor was cancelled when, despite a slight thaw, the pitch was covered with two inches of snow at one end and, thanks to drifts, several feet at the other. At Maine Road things had improved considerably and City's reserves beat Coventry 2-0 with Coleman converting a penalty and Bowyer providing the goals.

Coleman had been given a run out in the reserves following a stomach upset and was back in the first team when Blackburn and City finally met on Monday, 24 February, 16 days after the game was initially scheduled to have been played. Rain finally washed away the remains of the snow and City – with Bell in particular outstanding – found their Championship form of old to win 4-1. The Blues took full advantage of some poor defending by the home side and with Lee and Coleman both scoring twice, they eased their way through to the quarter-final and Tottenham.

Neil Young remembers

It took ages for us to get the cup-tie with Blackburn played. Because of all the snow and ice I don't think we played a game for about three weeks and Malcolm wanted to take us all away for a break. Then someone said what if there's a sudden thaw and the team's not in the country. In the end we all stayed and had to contend with five-a side and head tennis in the gym. We daren't go out on to the pitch because it was far too dangerous. After the Blackburn game we began to seriously think about Wembley and my mind went back to the Everton-Sheffield Wednesday Final the previous year. All the team was at the game and I remember Malcolm saying to us: "You'll be here next year."

Because of the Blackburn postponements, City's next game was that FA Cup clash with Tottenham, a club (like Everton) that had been negotiating with City for the past few weeks over the future of Blues' utility player David Connor. Any contest between City and Spurs is usually one guaranteed to produce a flowing, attacking game. However on this instance, only one of the two sides was interested in playing this way. Spurs decided the only way to stop City was to man-mark Bell, showed scant regard for anything resembling a fair tackle and generally replaced fair play with strong-arm tactics from the outset. It took City until half-time to counter the visitors' style of play. After the break Doyle (who's form had improved considerably since the return of Book behind him), Summerbee (who seemed to be regaining his) and Lee really got involved in the game and began to create chances. In the 65th minute, Summerbee headed down Coleman's overhead kick and Lee hooked an awkward volley past Pat Jennings for what turned out to be the only goal of the game. Young later had a shot headed off the line by Cyril Knowles, but Lee's goal proved enough to send City to an FA Cup semi-final for the first time in 13 years. Their opponents would be Everton, a side that had already done the double over City and had just won 1-0 at Old Trafford thanks to a goal from Joe Royle. Matchwinner Francis Lee commented after the game: "It was a half-chance; it could have gone anywhere. In fact I'd had two chances. The first I took a smack at and it soared into the terraces. The second time I tried to keep it down and it went in. I was delighted." So too was Joe Mercer: "I got knocked out of the semi-finals twice when at Aston Villa, once against Wolves and once against Notts. Forest. It must be my turn to be lucky! I never expected Spurs to play like that. They were hard – uncharacteristically hard – but we have no complaints."

Tony Book remembers

The club had had some bad luck at right-back that season. Apart from myself, there were three or four other injuries and I was delighted to get back into action in a friendly at Crook Town. Fortunately the injury held up and I was back in the first-team at Chelsea in January, just in time for the FA Cup, although I'd already missed the third-round tie with Luton. We had a couple of great games with Newcastle before beating Blackburn in a game we thought might never get played what with all the postponements. It was after the 4-1 win at Blackburn that thoughts began to turn to Wembley. We had enough belief in ourselves and I always thought we were more of a Cup side than a Championship side. Even though we'd won the Championship, I never felt we had consistency over a few seasons. We certainly had it in one, but couldn't seem to find it again and played all our best football in cup games.

Francis Lee suffered a thigh injury against Spurs and it forced him to miss the rearranged clash with Burnley at Turf Moor. Burnley's 2-1 victory on the night moved them up to sixth place in Division One, and their victory was in no small way owed to the terrific performance of winger Dave Thomas. Coming on as a first-half substitute, Thomas terrorised the Blues' defence all night, scoring the first goal himself and later setting up the winner for centre-half Dave Merrington. Bell had opened the scoring on the half-hour for City but in the end it was a fair result. With Doyle also suffering from a gash to his calf, it perhaps wasn't the greatest preparation for a trip to Old Trafford, although when City's reserves triumphed 2-0 (Bowles and Mundy) over their illustrious neighbours on the Friday night, it must have caused a few smiles at Maine Road.

Their were even more smiles on the Saturday; Mike Summerbee scored his first goal for nearly six months as City came away with both points. Alex Stepney made a fine back-breaking save to keep out 'Buzzer's' chip only for the ball to run loose back to Summerbee for him to crash home the game's only goal in the 38th minute. Both sides had further opportunities to find the back of the net – Best, Charlton and Young all hit the woodwork – but with Dowd and Book outstanding at the back, City withstood some second-half pressure from United and held on for their second successive win at Old Trafford. Once again coach Malcolm Allison was on a high: "On chances we should have walloped them 9-2. Blimey, things were getting so one-sided I even had to call Francis Lee off to give 'em a chance! We've given United 19 years start and passed them in three. We've beaten them twice here in two years – and we'll go one doing it." Although less exuberant than Allison, Mike Summerbee too was delighted with his afternoon's work: "It's given me a lot of confidence back. I began to feel my feet again immediately. Two weeks ago I would not have got a second chance, let alone scored from one."

With Lee, Bell and, for the first time Oakes, called into the England squad for the game with France at Wembley, City also gave a well-earned rest to Harry Dowd for the trip to Ipswich. Dowd's absence provided the opportunity for the 19-year-old, 6ft 4ins tall Joe Corrigan to make his League debut. Having gone in front after just nine minutes through Doyle, City left East Anglia empty-handed as Ronnie Wigg and John O'Rourke replied for the home side. Things could and should have been different when Peter Morris hauled down substitute Bowyer from behind inside the penalty area for arguably the most blatant 'non-penalty' of the season; only the referee didn't see it. *The Daily Telegraph* reported: "Bowyer fell like a tree. In the directors' box Malcolm Allison was up on his feet with the expression of a man who had just been given out caught off his pads one run short of a triple century, while Joe Mercer, that most undemonstrative of men, shook his head."

City left Ipswich for London on the way back to the north-west in readiness for the game against Queen's Park Rangers four days later. The squad took in England's 5-0 drubbing of France as Francis Lee and Leeds' Mike O'Grady supplemented Geoff Hurst's hat-trick in England's biggest win since before the 1966 World Cup. Winger Tony Coleman also stopped off at Highbury to make use of their medical facilities – especially the x-ray machine – to check on the ankle injury he sustained at Ipswich. Unfortunately for Coleman and City, the ligament damage proved to be serious and the ensuing plaster cast made him miss City's 3-1 victory. Against QPR Harry Dowd was back in the side at the expense of Corrigan although when he collided with Mike Summerbee in training on the Friday before the game, he must have thought otherwise. A gash to Dowd's eyebrow required stitching before the 'plumber' was passed fit. Dowd's apparent liking for collisions with his own players continued into the game itself when, in an attempt to punch the ball clear, he only managed to poleaxe Doyle with a right cross. It was a leisurely win for a City side playing well within itself as the vital semi-final tie with Everton (who had Alan Ball watching from the stands) was by now only seven days away. The Blues played the first-half so leisurely that they went in at the interval a goal down; Mick Leach beating Dowd with a low shot after seven minutes. Ten minutes into the second-half City pulled level when Lee converted a penalty kick after a despairing Alan Spratley in the Rangers' goal had brought down Young. In the 65th minute, and with Lee receiving treatment on the touchline, Pardoe forced a fine diving save from Spratley who was unfortunate when he saw the ball roll towards Bowyer who smashed it home from an angle. It was Bowyer's first goal in League football. The victory was complete a few minutes from the end when a stunning 35-yarder from Young sealed the points. Queen's Park Rangers returned to Manchester five days after being beaten at Maine Road. At Old Trafford, they went in at half-time 1-0 down but the wheels really came off in the second-half as United eventually won 8-1. Rodney Marsh scored the consolation goal in a game watched by United's lowest crowd of the season. City were now 13th in Division One, a massive 25 points behind leaders Leeds United. The only way back into Europe, at least for this season, was by winning the FA Cup. The small matter of third placed Everton and the semi-final at Villa Park – and injuries to Coleman, Lee, Bowyer and Doyle, and Bell with 'flu – stood between City and a Wembley appearance.

In the end Lee was the last of the injured party to be passed fit but unfortunately Coleman's ankle refused to respond to treatment and he missed out; his place being taken by Connor. Everton meantime were able to play their full-strength side for the first time since the third round back in January. The inclusion of Connor proved decisive in City's 1-0 win. His outstanding performance in completely stifling the efforts of Alan Ball prevented Everton from gaining any sort of superiority in the crucial midfield area. It was a typical semi-final, dour, hard and uncompromising with thrills at a minimum but tension uncontrollable. There was no doubting City's superiority, especially in the first-half when they should have been two up only for Gordon West to make two great, point-blank saves to deny firstly Young, and then Lee. The nervous tension that is often so evident in these matches left its mark and perhaps surprisingly it was Everton who suffered more in this respect. They rarely found their rhythm and blend in midfield or up front.

Colin Harvey tried as hard as anyone to get the Merseymen ticking, but his link-up play with Ball never materialised because of the superb marking job done by Connor. In the end

Ball's frustration at living with Connor for so long in such close proximity earned him a booking as he finally lost his patience and fouled City's utility man. Lee was also booked shortly afterwards after a flare-up with the same disgruntled Everton player. Just a few weeks earlier, Harry Catterick had tried to persuade Connor into joining him at Goodison Park. Now he must surely had wished he'd have tried somewhat harder.

Mike Doyle turned in a sterling performance despite leaving the field for a while in the first-half after a collision with Joe Royle. He returned to the action with a heavily strapped ankle and, along with skipper Tony Book and young centre-half Tommy Booth, was one of City's best players on the day. Booth completely dominated the threat of Royle and it was fitting in the end that it was he who got the vital, last-gasp goal. In the final moments of the game Young was through on goal with only the goalkeeper to beat. On the run, he hit a swerving, dipping left-foot shot that struck West high on the shoulder and flew away for a corner. Many thought it was City's last chance for glory, but from the ensuing corner, the brave Doyle climbed high to head the ball down, Summerbee flicked it on and Booth crowned a brilliant performance when he volleyed home the winner.

Neil Young remembers

When I was through on goal with only Gordon West to beat, in all honesty, I probably should have scored. I think what happened was I struck the ball too cleanly and it hit him somewhere up on the arm or shoulder before going for a corner. Gordon said to me later: "Neil, I didn't know where that ball was going. It just hit me." Tony Book in particular used to say I could never pass a ball straight. It would always go up and down, left and right and he'd say: "Never mind all these foreigners. Youngie does all that stuff every day in training." Anyway I took the corner and Tommy Booth scored the goal that took us to Wembley. It must be terrible to lose in a semi-final. That Everton side was a very good one and would be Champions in a couple of years. It was the first time I'd seen players leaving the field in tears at the end of a game. If you get through to the Final then that's great. At least if you get beat, you've been there and had your day out. But if you lose in the semi-final, you might never get there.

The goal was a memorable moment for the young Langley-born player: "I could hardly believe it when the ball bounced at my foot. I shoved Colin Bell out of the way and rushed past Frannie Lee to belt it in. The awful thing is, it could have gone anywhere. My left foot's not my best. It might have gone out of the ground instead of into the net." Joe Mercer was also delighted, as well as relieved: "What a display from Tommy Booth. He's going to be better than Stan Cullis, and that's saying something. We will play football at Wembley – win or lose. We don't mind who we meet. The tension is now off."

Just two days after the tremendous semi-final success, City were once again back on League duty. With five players missing from the win at Villa Park, the Blues lost 1-0 to a Nottingham Forest side languishing too near the foot of the table. Harry Dowd was rested for the game and

Malcolm Allison remembers

Tommy Booth won the game for us in the last minute against Everton. He was a brilliant reader of the game and was underestimated as a centre-back. I went to watch him as a youngster with Harry Godwin at a local park where he was playing inside-left and I could see then he was a good footballer with two good feet. He wasn't the fastest player but could hold his own and I told Harry I liked him. Anyway he came down for trials and we signed him on. He wasn't a traditional 'stopper'; he was a good passer, had good control and was good in the air, very similar to the great Stan Cullis. I always had confidence in him. After the game Alan Ball went on to describe David Connor as the best man-to-man marker in English football. Connor was a terrific athlete and tremendous competitor and the thing he loved, his forte, was not giving his opponent a kick in the 90 minutes. I remember walking to our dressing room at the end of the game and saw Everton's goalkeeper Gordon West standing outside their dressing room on his own. I asked him what he was doing there and he said: "I can't go in there, the boss (Harry Catterick) is going berserk." I said: "Oh we can't have that – come in ours!" And he did!

it gave Joe Corrigan a rare opportunity for first-team action. The young' giant goalkeeper had an outstanding night and earned rave reviews, the *Daily Telegraph* in particular describing his performance as "brilliant". After just 30 seconds Corrigan performed a "cat-like" leap to prevent a goal from winger Barry Lyons. It was the first of many superb saves on the night, however he was finally beaten just a quarter of an hour from the end when Henry Newton scored with a low shot to secure two valuable points for the home side.

On Saturday, 29 March 1969, City found out who their FA Cup Final opponents would be when Leicester City beat West Bromwich Albion 1-0 at Hillsborough thanks to a 20-yard left-foot volley from Allan Clarke. Joe Mercer and Francis Lee watched the game from the stands. Mercer: "I am expecting a very hard match at Wembley. I've seen Leicester twice recently and they have really impressed me – especially their defence, at Liverpool and again today. We will certainly not be underestimating them. Whether the Final will be a classic, no one can say. Still, we might get a better idea after we've met Leicester in the League next Friday." Francis Lee spoke the same way as he played – straight to the point: "I think we'll be able to beat Leicester. If our forward-line can strike true form, I just can't see us losing at Wembley."

Tony Book remembers

We played really well in the semi-final against a very good Everton side. We had to be at our best to beat them, especially in defence, and Dave Connor did a super job on Alan Ball. Even though we were always in the game and made a few chances, we couldn't make the breakthrough until the last minute when Tommy Booth scored from a corner after Youngie's shot had been saved. It was a nice time for it to come. There was no way they could come back from it.

Whilst Mercer and Lee were at Hillsborough, Allison was taking charge of City's 3-1 win against Stoke at Maine Road. Despite City's victory, the game showed all the hallmarks of one typically played towards the end of the season when both sides show no more than an academic interest in the points. City – missing the directness of both the injured Lee and Coleman – started the game well when Bell followed in Bowyer's shot in the ninth minute. Apart from a couple of half-chances, Bell's goal was the only talking point of a disappointing first 45 minutes. Stoke equalised just before the hour when a mishit cross from full-back John Marsh floated over Dowd before dropping into the net. The goal seemed to kick-start a hitherto lacklustre game with both sides playing some good football and creating chances. In the 70th minute Doyle restored City's lead from the penalty spot after Stoke's Northern Ireland full-back Alex Elder had hauled down Summerbee. Dowd and Doyle then combined to clear a point-blank effort from former City favourite Peter Dobing before Owen sealed victory in the dying minutes with a header past Banks. The brightest aspect of the game as far as City were concerned was the great display of youngster Ian Bowyer on the left-wing. He was consistently City's most dangerous forward and was desperately unfortunate not to find his name on the scoresheet despite a succession of fine shots at the Stoke goal.

Despite Bowyer's efforts against Stoke, he lost his place to the returning Coleman for the FA Cup Final rehearsal against Leicester on Good Friday. Also back from injury was Francis Lee who'd scored five times in the week in a testimonial game for Bolton's Roy Hartle. Playing at centre-half behind Lee in that game was none other than Malcolm Allison. With Bowyer on the bench, City's team had an all too familiar ring about it, and, barring injuries, was the full-strength side that would play at Wembley. Leicester on the other hand were without their star striker Clarke, and his absence was all too apparent up front for the visitors as City won 2-0. Mike Summerbee found the net for the first time for the Blues since his winner at Old Trafford five games earlier. Still with the ability to be 'deadly from three yards', Summerbee scored with his foot at the Scoreboard End and his head at the Platt Lane end to secure City's mid-table position and to deepen Leicester's relegation worries. Leicester supporters in the sun-drenched crowd of more than 42,000 returned home disappointed and knowing their team would have to show a marked improvement if they were to have any chance at Wembley.

Twenty-fours later, City travelled across the Pennines for a visit to Leeds against a side that currently led the First Division by five points from second placed Liverpool. Desperate to maintain their position at the top, Leeds laid siege to City's goal for long periods, but their over anxiousness in front of goal resulted in some poor finishing. Joe Corrigan was given another chance and once again turned in a superb performance with saves from Peter Lorimer, Mike O'Grady and Terry Cooper in particular warranting special mention. In the 62nd minute City suffered a double blow. In an attempt to stop a shot from Cooper, Book was injured and was replaced a few minutes later when Jimmy Mundy was given his first taste of senior football. Book's attempt to stop Cooper failed as the Leeds player blasted a hard shot on target that Corrigan failed to hold on to. The ball broke lose and Johnny Giles gleefully accepted the opportunity to smash the ball high into the net for what turned out to be the only goal of the game. Unfortunately for Corrigan it was a single mistake in an otherwise faultless performance. After the game many people – including followers of Leeds – tipped him to go on to great things. One of those was City boss Joe Mercer: "Young Joe Corrigan had a great game, a magnificent game today – but he will not, definitely NOT be playing at Wembley. Harry will be in goal at Wembley, unless of course he is injured before the Final, in which case Joe would come in over Ken Mulhearn who is not yet fully recovered from a cartilage operation. Joe is already a great asset to us this season and will be even more so next. We brought him in to combat Jack Charlton's goalmouth moves and it paid off. Malcolm Allison must take all the credit for young Joe making the grade. I must admit even I had my doubts about him and I once told Malcolm he might be wasting his time by persevering with the boy, but he was stubborn. He took three stone off the lad and now you can see the result."

The Blues had a break on Easter Monday but were back in action on the Tuesday. Having already beaten Wolves at Maine Road back in August, City faced a side that were without their captain, contained three reserves and had not won for six League games. It was the ideal opportunity for City's first 'double' of the season. Everything seemed to be in City's favour, particularly when they took the lead after just 15 seconds. Lee seized on to a quick throw-in from Young on the left before cutting infield and squeezing the ball between Phil Parkes and the near post. Booth (who later suffered concussion and double vision) then survived an anxious moment when his own-goal was ruled out for offside and City went into the break still one goal to the good. Two minutes into the second-half Wolves were back in the game as Peter Knowles headed in Derek Dougan's cross. Dougan himself gave Wolves the lead 12 minutes later and when Frank Munro scored a third in the 86th minute the match was over. Only Bell, Pardoe and Dowd (who was largely responsible for keeping the scoreline down) showed anything like their true form as City struggled against an 'old-fashioned' Wolves side content on the long ball and full-cry attack.

Forty-eight hours after the defeat at Wolves, City had reason to celebrate when skipper Tony Book was named as joint Footballer of the Year alongside Dave Mackay of Derby County. It was the first time in the 21-year history of the award that it had been shared. Book's return to the City side after a long absence at the start of the season had seen the Blues' return to something like their normal form and he would be leading the team out in the FA Cup Final in two weeks' time. Mackay, discarded by Spurs after twice breaking a leg, joined Derby for a bargain fee and had already led them to promotion to the First Division. It was a warranted award for the two 'old men' of English football.

Although successful in the next home game – a 1-0 win against Sunderland – City's performance did little to encourage the supporters with Wembley literally just around the corner. The Blues' inability to break down a poor Sunderland side intent solely on defence earned them the slow handclap from the terraces on more than one occasion. Interestingly enough the game was watched by a crowd of 22,842, Maine Road's lowest of the season so far.

With the exception of Summerbee, City's strike force was below its' best with plenty of chances going begging as the game dragged on in blustery conditions. With Coleman leaving the field with an injured foot, the game appeared to be dragging itself towards the inevitable goalless draw until, in the very last minute, Young atoned for his earlier misses when he fired a low shot past an off-balance Jim Montgomery after good build-up work by Doyle and Lee.

Tony Book remembers

It was fantastic for me to pick up the Footballer of the Year Award with Dave Mackay but in all honesty I felt if I was ever going to win it, I should have won it the year before. I never missed a League game in that Championship season but lost out to George Best because of United's European success. I thought my chance had gone but when I came back after such a long injury and then to carry on again, well maybe they made the decision on my performances over both seasons. Nevertheless it was a proud moment for me and a great honour to share the award with Dave Mackay.

Pardoe, Doyle and Booth were all in the England Under-23 team to face Portugal Under-23s at Coventry on the same night as City played their re-arranged League game at The Hawthorns. With Bell unusually wearing the number seven shirt, City continued their apparent fear of scoring and lost the game 2-0, although with Osborne in fine form in goal for West Bromwich, Bell hitting a post and Owen seeing his header cleared off the line, at least they now seemed to be on the road to recovery. Two goals in the first-half by Dick Krzywicki and a deflection by Tony Book proved enough to win the game. City had been back to the Midlands three times since the FA Cup semi-final triumph over Everton. On each occasion (at Notts. Forest, Wolves and now West Bromwich) they had returned home empty-handed. For the record, England Under-23's beat their Portuguese rivals 4-0.

Another League game, another poor performance, another blank scoresheet and another defeat. Such was City's game at Southampton just seven days before the Cup Final. The home team – desperate for the points to secure a Fairs' Cup spot for next season – were by far the most interested of the sides on show. Two goals in four minutes just after half-time proved far too much for a lacklustre Blues' side (containing 16-year-old Tony Towers for his League debut) to recover from and they eventually lost 3-0. Bobby Stokes, Terry Paine and Michael Judd did the damage to a City side that waited until the 35th for its first attempt on goal; even then Coleman's shot presented more danger to the back of the stand than to Gerry Gurr in the Saints' goal. Not surprisingly Leicester sent their chief scout, Ray Shaw, to watch the game although it is not known exactly what opinions he formed after a spiritless City showing. On the Blues' part, they'd sent both Malcolm Allison and Tony Book off to Leeds to watch Leicester, who faired slightly better than City; they only lost 2-0. Obviously both sides had their minds on other things.

The other things of course were the events at Wembley Stadium on Saturday, 26 April 1969, the date of the FA Cup Final. For City it was their first appearance at the Twin Towers since 1956. For Leicester it was their fourth visit since the war; it turned out to be the fourth time they'd leave the famous stadium as losers.

Whatever fears and trepidations had worked their way into City's play over the recent few weeks were quickly forgotten in front of the capacity 100,000 crowd who'd paid a record £128,000 in gate receipts. As Frank McGhee reported the morning after: "City won the Cup elegantly, brilliantly and with a display of nerveless, almost effortless, superiority." It was just the kind of performance Joe and Malcolm had been looking for.

City went into the Final free of any injuries and having conceded just one goal in six FA Cup-ties so far. Leicester were also adept in keeping the opposition out and had let in just two goals in their seven outings. With both these defensive records it appears that the 1-0 scoreline was no more than could have been expected. However, although there was possibly a shortage of goals, there certainly wasn't a shortage of good football. City produced their best football – some even described it as 'Champion football' – in weeks and Leicester belittled their position at the bottom of the table by keeping Dowd busy in the City goal on more than one occasion.

Neil Young remembers

We didn't play well for a few games prior to the Final and in truth I think we were a bit nervous. Naturally we all wanted to play at Wembley – none of us wanted to get injured – and our form suffered. I must admit we did take our foot off the pedal a bit and we didn't give it our all in those last few games. On the morning of the Final itself Joe and Malcolm were absolutely brilliant. They weren't anxious at all, they were laughing and joking all the time and it rubbed off on the players. I suppose some managers might get worked up and tight and players can sense it. The press and television were with us in the morning and they all saw us very happy, just relaxing and enjoying ourselves. We weren't bothered by them being there as we were all nice and calm and relaxed.

Neil Young remembers

Once at Wembley we all walked out on to the pitch, had a good look around, and then went back into the changing rooms. Everybody has their own little ritual before a game, little things they do, and then as we were getting changed Malcolm came around and whispered a few things in everyone's ears, just last minute reminders and a bit of advice. I remember us walking out of the tunnel when the noise hit us, shaking hands with Princess Anne and then the game itself which really did just fly by. Afterwards I remember walking up the steps to get the Cup and the medal. It was fantastic day but it went by so quickly. People ask me all the time "What's it like to score the winning goal at Wembley?" Let me try and put it into perspective. When I was a little lad of about five or six, I used to dream of playing for City. I achieved that and then wanted to play for City in the Cup Final. To play for City and score in the Cup Final is even better. It was undoubtedly my day; a dream come true. If you can't play in front of 100,000 people on a Saturday afternoon in a Cup Final then you'll never be able to play. About five minutes before I scored I'd mishit a chance and thought to myself: "I'm 25 years-old, if I get another chance that one's going in." Mike rolled a great ball back to me, right into my path and I was running on to it. I knew as soon as I hit it, it was going in. I could tell by the sound. I caught it perfectly. The ball was in the back of the net almost before Peter Shilton took off.

Summerbee had an outstanding game, giving David Nish the Leicester captain and left-back a torrid time all afternoon, and it was his strength and skill that laid on the winning goal. In the 24th minute he collected a throw from Lee and fought his way past Alan Woollett on the by-line before rolling the ball perfectly back to Young on the edge of the penalty-area. City's prolific (and vital) goalscorer found himself with both time and space as he crashed a swerving left-foot shot high into the net past a diving Peter Shilton. It was a goal worthy of winning a Cup Final. And so it proved.

Coleman and Young again had chances to clinch the game for City whilst at the other end Dowd made a brilliant save to deny Man of the Match Allan Clarke and Andy Lochhead blazed a great chance over the bar. Miss of the match went to Leicester full-back Peter Rodrigues who got himself in a terrible tangle inside City's six-yard area and forced the ball wide when it seemed easier to grab the equaliser.

At the final whistle Malcolm Allison left his enforced seat in the stands and made his way on to the pitch to greet Joe Mercer and his delighted players. Joe sportingly congratulated the Leicester players for their part in a splendid game before joining in the celebrations with his own team. Neil Young's goal had secured a win that meant Joe Mercer was the first person to win the FA Cup as both a player and as a manager. The disappointment of losing a Cup Final was just the first piece of bad luck Leicester would suffer that season. Just over a fortnight later they would be relegated from the First Division as well. The last time a team had been FA Cup runners-up and relegated in the same season was back in 1926; the team then was Manchester City. As for Manchester City in 1969, they were once again bound for Europe, determined to take the lessons learnt from Fenerbahce with them.

Malcolm Allison remembers

I loved the red and black striped kit. I loved the sort of AC Milan-like invincibility it gave off. I remember Frank O'Farrell, manager of Leicester and an old friend from my West Ham days, came up to see me one day in Manchester shortly before the Final. He said: "Malcolm what are we going to do about the kits at Wembley? We're in blue, you're in blue." I said: "Frank, don't worry. I've already had a word with the chairman and we'll change." I'd never said a word to Albert Alexander. I just wanted so much to play in that kit. John Humphries from Umbro told me that it was their best-selling kit although I never saw a penny from it! They'd banned me from the touchline for the Final so I got a seat on the front row and I ended up nearer the action than those on the bench. I remember Leicester's outside-left Len Glover knocked the ball past Tony Book and I shouted out: "50 to 1 Bookie!". Tony said later he'd heard me, and he still got a tackle in. When he won the Footballer of the Year award it was a fantastic achievement. There was nothing between Tony and Dave Mackay and in the end I think it was impossible to split them. Just before kick-off at Wembley I was reported to have slammed the dressing-room door in a steward's face. He'd come in and told us we should all go and stand in the tunnel and get ready to walk out. I told him in no uncertain terms we'd go when I said we were ready; I wasn't going to have the players just standing around. I knew what time it was. There was another incident prior to kick-off that was a lot funnier and has been told many times. It concerns Tony Coleman but it had actually started a few weeks before, shortly after we'd beaten Everton in the semi-final. One Monday morning after training he came to see me and he was really worried. He said: "Mal, I can't shake hands with Royalty. I've got these tattoos on my hands." I couldn't believe it at first. I thought he was joking but it really got to him. Despite his tough-guy image it affected him badly. In the end I rang Christie's Hospital and finally got put through to the surgeon. The first thing I said to him was: "Who do you support?" I think he thought I was having him on but a bit later he said: "City." I said: "Right I've got two tickets for the Final for you if you can take a couple of tattoos off Tony Coleman's hands. He's embarrassed about shaking hands with Royalty with these tattoos." He simply said: "Send him round." They kept Tony in overnight and he turned up for training the next morning with his hands all bandaged up. I asked him if everything went alright and he said it had but his hands were still a bit sore. I told him not to worry about it; when the game comes along in three weeks time you won't notice a thing. After the operation, psychologically he was like a new man, as if a great weight had been lifted from him. On the day of the match, Tony Book went along the line introducing the players to Princess Anne. All along the line it was "Pleased to meet you ma'am." Until they got to the end and Tony Coleman. He'd been thinking: "I can't just say that I've got to think of something else." In the end he said: "Pleased to meet you ma'am. Give my regards to your mum and dad." I also remember Mike Summerbee tried to arrange a date with the Princess but I don't think anything came of it.

I said to Joe straight after game: "Joe, I'm a bit worried." Joe was shocked: "Why? We've just won the FA Cup. What's wrong?" I said: "What happened in '67? We didn't win anything!"

Tony Book remembers

We'd lost a few games just prior to the FA Cup Final. Joe and Malcolm made a few changes to the side and rested one or two players, myself included. I remember missing one game in order to spy on our opponents Leicester City. We travelled down to London on the Wednesday before the game, staying at the Selsdon Park Hotel. It was a very relaxed atmosphere. We went to the Football Writers' Dinner on the Thursday and then we all went for a meal to a restaurant on the Friday. We did hardly any training – the bulk of that had been done in Manchester before we left – and the whole camp was in good spirits. As for the game itself, despite Leicester struggling at the bottom of the League, it was very even-stevens. I felt that whoever took their chance on the day would win it. Leicester had a couple of opportunities through Andy Lochhead and Allan Clarke but Harry Dowd was on top form for us in goal. It took a great pull-back from Mike and a super strike from Youngie to decide the match in our favour. People say that the whole occasion is over in an instant and that's very true. The game starts, then its gone. The next minute it's the evening celebrations and before you know it you're waking up in bed the next morning. It's as quick as that; it flies by. We had a great 'do' at The Royal Garden when BBC's Match of the Day cameras turned up. The FA Cup spent the night in my room and I happily posed for photos with it the next morning. What had happened to me in the two or three seasons since non-League was incredible. I just couldn't believe it. It was just like a dream and I didn't want to wake up. I just wanted it to go on. Success was the great thing about it and it kept me going. There were some terrific sights the next day when we arrived back in Manchester on an open-top bus. To see all the people who turned out will stay with me forever.

In a true example of the kind of friendly team Joe Mercer, Malcolm Allison and the rest of the City management had built up, the Blues took their full Wembley side to Gigg Lane just two days after their FA Cup success. The occasion was a testimonial game for Bury's longest-serving professional Brian Turner. With the exception of Colin Bell who played the whole game for his old club, City's Wembley winners played the first-half before leaving for another engagement, their places taken for the second-half by a reserve side that contained Corrigan, Bowles, Donachie and record signing Mann. A crowd of 10,555 swelled Turner's bank balance to the tune of £2,294 as the home side won an entertaining game 6-5, the recipient himself netting a hat-trick.

Home supporters saw the FA Cup paraded on a lap of honour before the game against West Ham on 30 April, the first of three home games that would finish another successful season. Apart from Glyn Pardoe's first goal of the season, the sight of the old silver trophy was the only memorable event of an otherwise less than memorable match. City gave a disappointing performance after the highs of the weekend, going behind to a Geoff Hurst and Martin Peters combination eight minutes after half-time. Dowd was the busier of the two goalkeepers on the night; his opposite number – the unfortunately named D'eath – generally having the quieter time on his first and last League game for West Ham. One same night as City and West Ham shared the points at Maine Road, a Johnny Giles goal for Leeds United with just six minutes left in the home game with Notts. Forest clinched the Championship for the Yorkshire side.

Colin Bell and Francis Lee's absence with the England side in the Home International Championships gave Wythenshawe-born Jimmy Mundy an opportunity to start a League match as Newcastle United arrived at Maine Road for the penultimate game. Bobby Owen was also recalled to the side and was only one of four players in a Blue shirt (the others being Book, Summerbee and Young) who looked as though his heart was in it. The same could also be said about the visitors as they avoided injury at all cost in preparation for a Fairs' Cup semi-final against Rangers in a few weeks' time. The crowd had also decided in advance as to what kind of a game it was going to be; just 20,108, the smallest of the season at Maine Road, turned up to watch it. In the end, Young's 75th-minute shot after controlling Summerbee's pass was enough to decide, at least for posterity's sake if nothing else, where the points should go.

And so to the last game of the 1968-69 season, the visit of Liverpool – runners-up to Champions Leeds United – the return game of the season's opener. Francis Lee continued his terrific England form (having recently scored against both Northern Ireland and Wales) by scoring the only goal of the game three minutes after the half-time break. Joe Corrigan replaced Dowd for only his fourth League game of the season and it was his quick throw out from a Liverpool corner that set Summerbee on his way to create the chance for Lee. The majority of the 28,309 crowd went home happy; their side had not lost in the three games since Wembley.

The final League table shows City in 13th place in Division One, a small matter of 27 points behind Champions Leeds United, but well clear of relegated Leicester City and Queen's Park Rangers. A mixed season of 15 wins and 17 losses was over at least on the pitch; but not off it. The day after City's last game against Liverpool saw a disgruntled Tony Coleman hand in a transfer request (later to be withdrawn) and Italian giants Juventus then began a two-week "will he-won't he?" saga as they attempted to lure Malcolm Allison away from Moss Side and transport him to the bright lights of Turin. Backed by the financial clout of the Fiat Motor Company, Juventus offered Allison a reported £25,000-a-year salary, a car of his own choice, a villa in the sun, bonuses and a liberal expense account. Understandably Allison was tempted and, on more than one occasion, nearly put pen to paper. However, the one thing the Italians hadn't taken into consideration was Allison's heart; it belonged exclusively to Manchester City.

Manager Joe Mercer was delighted by Allison's decision not to go to Italy: "Just look what he has turned down. There aren't many men walking the streets who would have refused such a fantastic offer. It's obvious the money doesn't motivate him. And let's face it, if he'd gone, it would have been very dull without him."

Malcolm Allison remembers

We finished the season in 13th position and some said it was a disappointing year but the hardest thing when you've achieved something once, something big, is to go on and do the same again next year. I don't know why that is but it's certainly more difficult. Very rarely do teams do well season after season. Some will come back time and time again admittedly but maybe we simply didn't have the resources to maintain the run over a long period. I remember when I was in Portugal we had something like 27 or 28 first-team players; no reserves, just first teamers. At City we had about 15 or 16, give or take, to win those trophies.

Tony Book remembers

Malcolm went to Italy at the end of the season to have a look at a job offer from Juventus. Fortunately for City nothing ever came of it. Malcolm was great with the players. If you were on a downer, he was the one who'd get hold of you, he'd take you out, kick the ball around with you and all of a sudden you'd feel ten feet tall. If you were having a few doubts about your game he could talk you out of it. He was such a positive person. If he had gone it would have been a huge loss to the club. We'd have had to replace him quickly but in all honesty I don't know who could have done the same job.

1969-70
Goodnight Vienna

A CLUB the size and stature of Manchester City, especially when it's successful, never really closes down even when the teams aren't playing. Take for instance, the summer of 1969. In July, the draw was made for the first round of the forthcoming European Cup-winners' Cup. The Blues were drawn away first to the Spanish Cup holders Atletico Bilbao, with the game due to take place on 17 September. Bilbao were managed by the former West Bromwich Albion player and Wolves' manager Ronnie Allen, who, in his first season in charge in Spain, had guided Bilbao to success in the Spanish Cup Final against F.C.Elche. Bilbao were no strangers to English football having beaten Liverpool in the previous season's Fairs Cup and had also played at Maine Road before. In 1956 they beat Manchester United 5-3 in a blizzard in Spain, only to lose 3-0 in the return leg played at Maine Road because United at the time had no floodlights. Joe Mercer was in Geneva when the draw was made: "It's a tough one for us all right. But playing away first will help a bit. And, after all, you might as well have a tough one to start off with. However, it will be just like playing an English club for they have an attacking style of play familiar to ours."

Six players – Colin Bell, Francis Lee, Mike Summerbee, Tommy Booth, Mike Doyle and Glyn Pardoe – were all on Alf Ramsey's stand-by list for the 1970 World Cup in Mexico, although Joe Mercer did admit to be slightly disappointed at their being no place for either Alan Oakes or captain Tony Book. David Connor and Arthur Mann both got married in the close season, whilst Mike Summerbee's wife Tina presented him with their first child, a baby daughter, Rachel.

Even the ground itself witnessed some changes. A Players' Lounge was created, new licensed bars installed, a team of architects had been brought in to look at the possible covering of the Scoreboard End, a lick of paint applied to the main stand structure and the offices were completely renovated and modernised. Malcolm Allison was even given his own desk, although nobody ever saw him sitting at it! Groundsman Stan Gibson spent many hours producing a 'bowling green of a pitch' and even replaced last years' blue nets with brand-new white ones. He said: "I'm keeping the lucky Blues for the European games."

Prior to the first competitive game of the season, City played two friendlies, a 1-1 draw against a Caernarfon Select X1, and a 3-3 draw with Ajax in Amsterdam, a game much remembered for Stan Bowles missing the flight.

Malcolm Allison remembers

Before the season started, we went to Holland for a friendly against Ajax in Amsterdam. This was of course the game that produced Stan Bowles' vanishing act. I'd warned the lads before the game that it wouldn't be easy as the Dutch could play a bit. Mike Doyle seemed less concerned: "Don't worry about it," he told me. After the game (it finished

3-3) he came off the pitch and said: "Jesus, that Cruyff's some player." I said: "I told you he was." They genuinely thought the Dutch couldn't play. I'd had dealings with Ajax before, back in the 1950s. They asked me if I wanted the coaching job so I went over to meet them. I watched the training and the set-up looked really good. They offered me £34 a week and a house on the grounds. In the end I didn't think the offer was good enough as it would have meant me leaving my family and, for £34 a week, I wasn't prepared to do it so I turned them down. Much later I was offered a similar position with Juventus and again I turned that down. These were two massive clubs and I was delighted to have been offered both positions but I turned them down for different reasons. Ajax because I thought the money was too little and it would have been a big job and Juventus because they simply didn't want to play the way I wanted too. I suppose if I have any regrets in life then it's the fact that I didn't take either of these jobs. Of course if I'd taken either job I'd have never got to Manchester, or I'd have left earlier than I did.

As in the previous year City took part in the curtain-raiser to the season proper, the Charity Shield. On 2 August, as FA Cup holders, they travelled to Elland Road for the game against First Division Champions Leeds United. Like all of these games, it proved no more than a useful warm-up for the more serious months to come, although Leeds appeared the keener of the two sides to win. Both sides played their first elevens, Eddie Gray and Jack Charlton giving the Champions a two-goal lead in a three-minute spell in the second-half before Colin Bell's overhead kick pulled one back in the last minute for the FA Cup winners. The 2-1 scoreline went the way of the team who approached the game in a more serious vein.

Malcolm Allison remembers

We gave Joe Corrigan a chance right at the start of the season. He'd done well when he'd come in and he thoroughly deserved it. He'd worked really hard since he came to City and I was delighted for him. I knew goalkeepers were different animals than the outplayers – a race apart if you like – and I'd always spent a lot of time working with them, away from the rest of the side. Because he's an individual – the rest are a unit – he's the most important.

Sheffield Wednesday, a team that had finished two places below the Blues last season, provided the first opposition of the 1969-70 League campaign. Never one of the biggest spending clubs in the land, Wednesday had the country's youngest £100,000 player (Tommy Craig from Aberdeen) in their ranks and on paper at least, had a reasonable side. On grass however it was a different matter as City won easily 4-1. Joe Corrigan kept goal for the Blues, the first of 34 League appearances of a season that would see him finally take over the number one spot from both Dowd and Mulhearn. Francis Lee continued where he'd left off the previous campaign (an 82nd minute penalty), and Colin Bell and Neil Young with two (one with each foot) gave City a perfect start to the season. Sheffield's' token reply came when Peter Eustace converted a 62nd minute penalty. Had it not been for the efforts of Ron Springett in the Sheffield goal, the defeat would have been heavier. Joe Mercer was in good spirits as he celebrated his 55th birthday. Young, a prolific goalscorer in previous years for the Blues, suffered an ankle injury against Wednesday that caused him to miss the next eight games. By the time he returned (against Tottenham) City had scored 11 times, although seven of those were in two games. As for Sheffield Wednesday it was the first of their 25 defeats for the season. Perhaps not surprisingly when the end of April came around nearly nine months later, they found themselves rock bottom of the division and relegated.

Neil Young remembers

We started the new season with a great 4-1 win against Sheffield Wednesday. I managed to score twice and despite what some people said, the one with my right foot was not a mistake! Unfortunately though I got injured in that game and would miss the next eight matches. I turned my ankle over in a divot on the pitch and at first they all thought I'd damaged my Achilles. In the end it turned out to be some ligament damage but it took ages to get it right. I had some rest for a while but as soon as I tried walking and then some light jogging it just went on me again. Finally I was told to rest it completely for three weeks and stay away from the ground. Like Tony Book, I'm not a great spectator and never saw a game during the time I was out injured.

Youngster Ian Bowyer replaced Young for the second game, a Tuesday night trip to Anfield. In a stirring match (Alan Oakes' 400th first team game for the club) City led 2-1 thanks to Bowyer's terrific header from Summerbee's cross and a Tommy Smith own goal going into the dying moments. Unfortunately for the Blues they were unable to keep their concentration until the final whistle and allowed Roger Hunt and Ian St.John to add to his earlier, third-minute strike and lost 3-2. It was a bitter pill to swallow especially as the Blues had played so well with Joe Mercer calling it "a tough lesson in concentration" and Malcolm Allison admitting he'd never been so upset after a game in his whole career. A delighted Bill Shankly praised both teams' performances when he said: "If there were another war I'd put all you 22 players in the front-line – and we'd win it no time."

Four days later City suffered another disappointment when they made the long trip north to Newcastle only to lose 1-0. Bryan 'Pop' Robson scored the game's only goal early in the first-half from the penalty spot after Pardoe had felled Jim Scott. On the day, City turned in a poor performance, one that lacked ideas, drive and determination. In fact the reason for some improvement in the last 20 minutes appeared to be due entirely to a sudden downpour that roused the players from their collective slumbers.

The Blues didn't have to wait long for revenge against Liverpool, the opportunity given in just the next game, the fourth of the season. However once again, Shankly's side got the better of Mercer's by winning 2-0 in front of nearly 48,000 at Maine Road. City, now missing Oakes as well as Young, were no match for a very competent Liverpool side. To balance out Lee hitting the bar, Roger Hunt then hit a post before Bobby Graham headed the visitors in front right on the half-time whistle. Nine minutes from the end the same player scored again to seal a very professional victory.

Next up were League leaders Everton (a position they'd still be in at the end of the season) and City finally lost their losing habit, although when Johnny Morrissey converted a free header to give the visitors an early lead it looked as the Blues were still keen to hang on to it. The game developed into a real 'ding-dong' battle as could easily be expected from two of the top (and most attacking) sides in the country. In the second-half Bowyer equalised for City with yet another superb header and later very nearly won the game when he forced goalkeeper Gordon West to save bravely at his feet.

The Blues were not the only team to start the season with such mixed form. At the end of the opening month City were in 12th position with six points, nine places above bottom-placed Ipswich Town who had managed just one draw so far. Eight clubs had accumulated either five or six points. City's cause was helped considerably in the game immediately after the draw with Everton. Sunderland were brushed aside 4-0 at Roker Park with the ever-improving and free-scoring Bowyer adding two more to his season's tally, and Oakes and Bell finishing the job off. Newspapers described City (who were two up after just eight minutes) as 'ruthless' and overran a Sunderland side still awaiting its first win of the season. For the home side, their best chance fell to a 19-year-old Dennis Tueart, who, on this occasion at least, was wide of the target.

Malcolm Allison remembers

Ian Bowyer came into the side and did really well for us, continuing his scoring from last year. We'd had him from school as a 17-year-old and perhaps his only slight downfall was he lacked a little bit of initial pace. When Cloughie took him to Notts. Forest it was a great move him. Cloughie dropped him back into midfield and Bowyer did brilliantly from then on, still capable of nicking the odd goal.

Bowyer completed a hugely successful month for himself when he scored in the 1-1 draw at Burnley on 30 August. Amazingly his goal in the third minute (his fifth in seven outings and yet another header) was City's equaliser! Burnley had scored after just 25 seconds, Martin Dobson finishing off a slick Burnley move before any City player had touched the ball. Despite both sides having a goal disallowed, the ball shied away from the nettings for the remaining 87 minutes. After Bowyer's equaliser, the defences took control of the game and mid-way through the second-half both teams seemed equally happy with a share of the spoils.

With a seven-day gap until the next League game (against Chelsea), Joe Mercer and Malcolm Allison took the opportunity to fly from Manchester Airport to San Sebastian to check up on City's opponents in the forthcoming European Cup-winners' Cup-tie, Atletico Bilbao. The couple watched the Basque side take part in a pre-season game, inspected the impressive 45,000-seater San Mames stadium, and even checked on the team's accommodation on the outskirts of the thriving industrial city. Joe Mercer was adamant with his comments: "This time we shall miss nothing in our preparation."

Malcolm Allison remembers

We'd gone out to Bilbao before we played them just to have a look. The seats they gave Joe and me were awful, right behind a huge pillar in the stand so we moved somewhere else immediately. During the game I thought to myself if we put these under pressure we can beat them. I didn't realise just how good a couple of their forward players were but defensively was different, I knew we could cause them problems. The game over there, the 3-3, was a hell of a game, and of course when we got them back over here we murdered them.

Before the Chelsea game City faced a potentially embarrassing trip to Third Division Southport for a second round League Cup-tie. In a crowd of 11,215, City's allocation of just 425 seat tickets (at 9 shillings each) had been snapped up within a matter of hours. Many more stood (5 shillings for adults, 2 shillings for juniors) on the terraces of the compact Haig Avenue ground and saw City win comfortably in the end by a 3-0 margin. Not surprisingly, Southport came at City, occasionally with too much enthusiasm, with Doyle on more than one occasion finding himself in the thick of things. In a heated first-half of 27 fouls, Doyle managed to avoid the referee's notebook, something that could not be said about Lee. The first step of a journey that, at the time, no one could have realised would end in Wembley glory, was decided by Lee's 15th minute penalty, Oakes' conversion of Book's pass and Bell's 87th minute strike.

Somewhat surprisingly for Chelsea at the time, they came to Maine Road in a defensive frame of mind and returned to London with a share of the points and a goalless draw. Singer Matt Munro and comedy actor Lance Percival (City fans in their "few spare moments") saw Lee go closest for City when he curled a free-kick around the Chelsea wall only to see Peter Bonetti make a fine save at the foot of the post.

On the day City missed the goalscoring talents of Neil Young and they were delighted to have him back in the reckoning for the trip to Tottenham. He'd tried to make a comeback in a reserve game two weeks earlier, only to limp off midway through the game. Stan Bowles was the unfortunate player relegated to the substitute's bench at White Hart Lane, Bowyer's prowess in front of goal making the decision easier for Mercer and Allison. Mike Summerbee rejoined his team-mates fresh from scoring for The Football League in their 3-0 win over The League of Ireland at Barnsley as the Blues' travelled to London on the Friday, where, as guests of ITV, they watched the whole Spanish Cup Final from last year.

Neil Young remembers

I got back in the side for the game against Spurs. Four days later I was lining up against a very good Atletico Bilbao side for the first leg in Spain. The first 15 or 20 minutes were very, very tough. They just went through us like a dose of salts and were two up in no time. I learned in that game that the Europeans were much better – twice as quick really – at controlling the ball than we were. They were tremendously skilful players. Malcolm got some instructions out to the side along the lines of get tight on them, don't give them any time, don't let them turn with the ball. And that's what we did. We got right up on them and didn't give them any space and it stopped them playing. At the end of the game we knew we could take them at Maine Road. We knew how to play against them and were confident of getting through.

Despite goalkeeper Pat Jennings earning the plaudits as Spurs' best player on the day, they still lost 3-0 to a City side inspired by Oakes in midfield. Shortly before the interval Bowyer gave City the lead when he headed home Bell's cross although the game was far from over until Bell's header at the near post and Oakes' low shot – both in the 90th minute – confirmed the win. Bowyer was now the division's top scorer; Young had returned from injury with a brilliant display that rubbed off on Lee and City had turned in their best performance of the season. City left for Spain in the perfect frame of mind.

Tommy Booth was taken ill at Manchester Airport shortly before the flight with a temperature and all the symptoms of tonsillitis. In the end it turned out to be nothing serious and Booth took his place in an unchanged line-up from the Tottenham game. Joe Mercer announced City intended to play exactly the same way in Bilbao as they'd successfully played in London, namely defensive football in their opponents' half. He went on to say: "I believe this can be the start of an exciting new era for us – an era when Maine Road is going to reverberate to the pulsating thrills of top European football." Hours before kick-off, Malcolm Allison broke his own enforced European silence. This time though it was a more reassured man from the "We will terrify Europe" one of last year: "We are going to win 3-2," he said confidently. "Last season we failed abysmally in Istanbul. And I am the first one to hold up my hand and say we made a drastic mistake by not making more preparations. Those same mistakes have not been made this time. The players are in the peak of condition and we know all there is to know about Bilbao. I'll tell you this – you'll be proud to be British after you see the way we play tonight."

Tony Book remembers

The game with Bilbao was really difficult; they looked a very good side. Off the pitch there were no signs at all of the hostility we'd seen in Turkey last year. Ronnie Allen was in charge at the time and they made us all very welcome. Like I say the tie was difficult and they gave us a bit of a chasing, especially in the first-leg. I remember them going two up and in all honesty the tie could have been over. But we fought back well and to get three goals over there was a terrific performance. The papers said I personally had done well which was pleasing but all this European stuff was still new to me and I was enjoying it. I'd never played in Europe before so it was a fresh challenge for me. I'd had a little experience of the Italians when I played with Toronto City in Canada and I'd learn a bit about the way they played. Little things like never jump in; try and jockey the players for position.

Malcolm Allison wasn't too far off with his prediction as City came from behind to draw a thrilling game 3-3 despite going 2-0 down after just 11 minutes. The Blues defence started badly and appeared both confused and out-manoeuvred as Argoitia and Clemente gave the home side a dream start. It took City a long time to get going and it wasn't until Young converted Bowyer's pass via the goalkeeper's shoulder in the 42nd minute that the Blues were back in the game. City's defence was considerably tighter in the second-half (no doubt helped by Allison's instructions from the touchline which could still be heard above the 45,000 crowd) although there was another shock in store in the 57th minute. Argoitia's cross was met by centre-forward Uriarte's head leaving Corrigan with no chance to restore a two-goal advantage for the Basque side. City's goalkeeper was then called upon to make two further saves, from Argoitia and Rojo, and his efforts seemed to inspire his team-mates on to greater things. In the 68th minute, Summerbee's corner was cleared only to the edge of the penalty-area where Tommy Booth hit a low right-foot shot through a crowd of players and inside Iribar's far post to make it 3-2. With the Blues continuing to press for a deserved equaliser, the Bilbao defence wilted and, with four minutes left, they levelled a game that looked all over early in the first-half. Book, by far City's defender on the night, continued to urge his troops forward and sent Bell away on a run with a ball that split the defence. The England midfielder crossed the ball into the penalty-area only for full-back Echeberria to deflect it past his own goalkeeper. City had come back from a two-goal deficit as well as scoring three valuable away goals.

Not surprisingly the management team was delighted. Joe Mercer: "Strangely enough, I did not feel too badly when Bilbao's second goal went in. Once Young scored I knew we would do well. However, the game's not over by a long way. We will start the next leg as favourites, but it's still going to be very difficult for us to beat this side. Bilbao surprised me; they played far better than I thought they could". Malcolm Allison: "A wonderful result for us. We only started to play our normal game late in the first-half. I knew we would come through once we could get our game going. The lads were not satisfied. They are a bit niggled because they thought we could have won but just wait for the second-leg!"

Neil Young remembers

Malcolm had learnt his lessons after the defeat by Fenerbahce last year. For the European Cup-winners' Cup games he made sure all the opposition were watched before we played them. He knew exactly what sort of style and system they'd play. In training he used to play first team versus reserve team games and the reserves would play the same way the Europeans would. This was a big help to us. One of the big things was man to man marking. We didn't really play that way over here but we practised it in the reserve games so we knew what to expect on the night.

Tommy Booth picked up a bruised ankle in Spain causing him to miss City's next League game, against Coventry at Maine Road. It gave George Heslop a chance to impress yet again in the first team, and to interest any potential buyers. As usual Heslop did not let the side down, turning in a fine display alongside both Book and Oakes, as City played only as well as they had too against a Coventry side who started brightly and then faded. Some of the credit for the final scoreline of 3-1 was down to some poor defensive play by the visitors. With just 60 seconds gone, Bell found himself completely unmarked from Summerbee's free-kick and had the easiest of chances to score past Bill Glazier from five yards. In the 32nd minute, Coventry's Jeff Blockley missed his clearance completely and could only kick Neil Young full in the face. Francis Lee converted the penalty with his usual aplomb. City eased off in the second-half and allowed Ernie Hunt to pull a goal back for the visitors with ten minutes left. Determined not to make the same mistakes as Atletico Bilbao had against them, City piled on the pressure in an attempt to regain their two-goal advantage. Bell celebrated his best performance for weeks when he first forced Glazier to make a fine save at the second attempt and then, with two minutes left, slid the ball under the onrushing goalkeeper to seal the victory. The win moved City up to ninth position, eight points behind leaders Everton but with a game in hand.

Neil Young remembers

I'd been suffering from a heavy cold just before we played Coventry and was doubtful for the game. In the end I was passed fit but for a while wished I hadn't been. I remember bending down to head a bouncing ball and Jeff Blockley, their centre-half, kicked me in the face as he tried to clear it. Well I went down, and out! I was well out of it for a few minutes. Fortunately Frannie scored from the penalty spot and we won 3-1 but I can still remember that incident. And Blockley wasn't a small lad. He was built like a house door!

The League was forgotten about (albeit temporarily) as City prepared for their third clash in six weeks against Liverpool. The occasion was a third round League Cup-tie, and for the first time this season, City managed to overcome Bill Shankly's men. Once again the outstanding Book led by his example, inspiring his team to a 3-2 win in a real 'cracker' of a cup-tie. Doyle opened the scoring with a searing 35-yarder in the 12th minute only for Alun Evans to score a fortunate equaliser ten minutes later when Heslop's clearance struck him in the face and rebounded past a helpless Corrigan and Book on the City goal-line. Tommy Lawrence was much the busier of the two goalkeepers on the night and could do nothing to prevent first Young, and then Bowyer, from increasing City's lead. Bobby Graham scored Liverpool's second to make the last few minutes a tense affair, but in the end City deservedly hung on and were rewarded with another home game against the winners of the as yet undecided Arsenal-Everton tie.

Back to the League, unfortunately any further progress up the division was halted by a trip to The Victoria Ground, Stoke on 27 September. Stoke had recently entertained Brazilian side Santos in a friendly (Stoke losing 3-2, Pele two) and had obviously picked up a few pointers from the great South American. Helped by City's lethargy on the day, Stoke performed much better than the Blues and won 2-0, although the result did somewhat flatter the visitors who's only threat on Gordon Banks' goal came from Young's long-range efforts. A goal in each half – from Jimmy Greenhoff and John Ritchie –proved more than enough to beat City who also lost the fit again Booth in the last minute when he left the field with a head wound that required stitching.

One person who would not be available for selection for the return clash with Atletico Bilbao would be Championship and FA Cup winner Tony Coleman. He'd agreed a move to Sheffield Wednesday where he was guaranteed first-team football, something not possible at Maine Road owing to the arrival on the scene of Ian Bowyer.

Nearly 50,000 people crammed into Maine Road on 1 October for what would be the first of many tremendous Wednesday European nights. In a plan designed not to concede any further goals and hit City on the break, Ronnie Allen's side defended resolutely in the first-half, Iribar in goal saving splendidly from Lee and Young, although the latter did get the better of him at one point only to see his shot rebound off a post. In the 58th minute City finally broke through. Oakes intercepted a pass from substitute Ortuondo, raced through from the halfway line and, as Bilbao expected a pass, hit a left-foot shot high into a bulging net past a flying Iribar. Young then got into the action when his shot from out on the left beat the goalkeeper and was kicked off the line. The ball looped up invitingly for Colin Bell to nod home the simplest of headers from a yard out. The 3-0 scoreline was completed with five minutes to go. Once again Young was influential in the goal; this time the goalkeeper could only parry his shot and Bowyer volleyed home the rebound. With a 6-3 aggregate scoreline, City marched majestically into the second round. There was some controversy after the game when it was revealed that an incident had taken place in the tunnel as the players left the field at half-time. Eyewitnesses reported an alleged scuffle between Mike Doyle (City's star man on the night) and Bilbao's inside-right Betzuen. Betzuen did not come out for the second-half; his place was taken by 17-year-old Ortuondo. Bilbao's players visited the dressing-room of Hungarian referee Istvan Zsolt, who, after speaking to both managers, said he would not be making an official report. "I had to take him off – he could hardly breathe," said Bilbao boss Ronnie Allen, "after that, we were finished." Doyle gave a less-flustered response: "I don't know what all the fuss is about. There was a bit of bother just before half-time, but nothing serious." The draw for the second round paired City against Belgium side S.K.Lierse, a team like City, experiencing European competition for only the second year in their history.

When West Bromwich Albion visited Maine Road, they met a City side struggling to find the form that had devastated Bilbao. Although the Blues played well enough to win 2-1, it was a bizarre game that could easily have finished 6-6. With scrambles and incredible misses at both ends, particularly in the second-half, both defences looked suspect in a thrilling end-to-end game. Two minutes before the break Young finally got the better of John Osborne who, up to that point, had made a string of fine saves. In the second-half West Bromwich lost (somewhat unfortunately) the services of Dick Krzywicki when he was sent off for a foul on Lee. Glyn Pardoe levelled for the ten-men visitors, when, in an attempt to block Tony Brown's shot, he only succeeded in deflecting the ball past Corrigan; a goal typifying the entire afternoon. After 80 minutes Bell restored City's lead with a great header from Young's free-kick for his eighth goal of the season. Four minutes from the end, City brought on Derek Jeffries as a replacement for Lee, giving the Longsight-born youngster his first taste of senior football.

The same 2-1 scoreline was enough to beat Newcastle four days later, although the Blues left it very late, and won the game in controversial circumstances. Young had given City the lead with the by now, almost expected 25-yarder, only to see Bryan 'Pop' Robson capitalise on an error by Corrigan to level the game in the 70th minute. Both sides seemed reasonably happy with a share of the points until the events of the 90th minute gave City an opportunity to snatch both. Mike Doyle found himself inside the Newcastle penalty-area and went down heavily under a challenge from the visitors' Danish midfielder Preben Arentoft. At first the crowd of 32,172 thought a corner had been given but Wolverhampton-based referee Dennis Corbett thought otherwise and pointed to the penalty-spot. Despite both long and loud protests from the Geordies, Mr Corbett stuck by his decision, and Lee stepped up to smash home the ensuing kick and give City a somewhat fortunate victory.

Francis Lee was on target with his first away League goals of the season as City fought back bravely to earn a share of the points at Nottingham Forest. Unlucky to have gone two goals down (to Ian Moore and Barry Lyons) after an hour's play, City never gave up and after Bowyer had hit the bar, Lee produced a shot that proved too hot to handle for Alan Hill in the Forest goal. Switching Summerbee and Lee's positions in the second-half un-nerved Forest and Lee grabbed his, and City's, second with a rare headed goal from Book's cross eight minutes from time.

Neil Young remembers

Ian Bowyer came into the side to replace Tony Coleman and did really well for us. Unfortunately though the crowd didn't like him and it got to the point where he simply couldn't play at home. It was a great shame and in the end Joe and Malcolm just had to sell him. I was lucky in that respect, being born almost at the back of the Kippax stand gave me a great affinity with the fans and I never had any trouble. But for some reason or other they never took to Ian. He was a good steady player, with no shortage of skill and more than capable of scoring a few goals.

Thoughts then turned towards the League Cup and the visit of Everton, a side currently five points clear at the top of the First Division but without five regulars including Alan Ball, Colin Harvey and John Hurst, a man who would later become City's chief scout. With so many experienced first-teamers missing, Everton proved no match for a full-strength City side and had it not been for the heroics of Gordon West in goal, the result would have been more than the 2-0 final score. With the Blues dominating in midfield, City put persistent pressure on the Merseysiders and led 2-0 at the interval with a 25-yarder from Bell and Lee's penalty separating the sides. In the second-half City, aware of their heavy fixture commitments, eased off, although Bell, Bowyer and Young all missed chances to inflict a heavier defeat on a team that, up to then, had only lost one game all season. A second successive trip to Wembley looked even more possible when it was announced City had been drawn at home to Second Division side Queen's Park Rangers in round five.

City's unbeaten run of four games continued with a 1-0 win at Derby, a team that had surprised many after winning promotion from the Second Division last season. Brian Clough's team were lying in second place behind Everton but came up against a City side that attacked from the outset. Bowyer missed an early opportunity to give City the lead when he sliced the ball wide after Les Green in the Derby goal had dropped a shot from Young. It took City until the 67th minute to break down the Derby defence, organised by the hugely experienced Dave Mackay, and it was somewhat ironic that it was Mackay who gave the ball away in City's half, starting a move that led to the decisive goal. Summerbee ran 60 yards and outstripped four defenders before crossing for Lee to hammer the ball into the roof of the net. It was Lee's fifth goal in four games; it was Derby's second successive home defeat. The players went directly from Derby for a few days break in Blackpool, staying at a hotel on the North Promenade. Joe Mercer took advantage of a rare opportunity when there was no midweek game to reward the players "for the way they have played so far this season". They also took advantage of the crisp Irish Sea water to clear up Tommy Booth's niggling ankle injury.

Three days before City's next League game against Wolves, Joe Corrigan picked up his first international honour. Standing in for Peter Shilton who missed the game with a septic toe, Corrigan kept a clean sheet as England Under-23s beat Russia 2-0 at Old Trafford; the Everton duo of Jimmy Husband and Joe Royle getting the goals.

City were without Francis Lee for the visit of Wolves. He'd suffered a painful eye injury when a stone chipping flew off a piece of rock he was setting in the garden of his Bolton home. Another player with an injury was Stan Bowles who'd fractured a leg during training. Jimmy Mundy, City's 19-year-old reserve striker replaced Lee in a game City won 1-0 to make it seven successive home wins in all competitions. After having two confident penalty appeals turned down in the first-half, it was a case of third time lucky for City when full-back Derek Parkin unceremoniously pushed Mundy in the back three minutes after the break. Without Lee in the side it was left to Doyle to side-foot the ball past Phil Parkes in the Wolves goal for what turned out to be the winner.

Lee's eye injury cleared up sufficiently for him to be back in the side for the League Cup quarter-final against Queen's Park Rangers. In fact it hardly seemed as though Lee had been away as he had a hand in all of City's goals in a 3-0 win. Rangers – wearing the same red and black striped kit favoured by City – were out of the game by the ninth minute. The score then was 2-0, Bell following up his opening headed goal in the seventh minute with a fierce near-post strike two minutes later. In the 24th minute Lee brushed past two defenders on the right to roll the ball across to Summerbee for the easiest of tap-ins. Summerbee wasn't in the least bit bothered as to the simplicity of it all; he'd at last scored his first goal of the season. Eager for the semi-final, the crowd burst into a rousing chorus of "Bring on United".

The visit of City to Portman Road prompted the biggest gate of the season for Ipswich Town, 24,124 witnessing a 1-1 draw. The home side, struggling for points at the bottom end of the table, failed to match City for skill but were worthy of a point purely for their hard-running teamwork. Joe Corrigan was at fault for the Ipswich opener when he could only drop a hopeful 30-yard lob from Mick McNeil behind him and into the net. Fortunately for City (and Corrigan) Lee continued his rich scoring vein and was on hand to head home Summerbee's cross in the 67th minute. Derek Jeffries looked impressive as a replacement for the injured Summerbee as the Blues played six minutes with ten men with Doyle receiving treatment after being knocked out in a goalmouth scramble.

On 3 November, Frank Carrodus signed for City from non-League Altrincham for a fee of £3,000. Carrodus had impressed City's management recently with some fine performances and he was definitely 'one for the future' as far as Messrs. Mercer and Allison were concerned. On the same day as Carrodus put pen to paper, Stan Bowles was suspended for four weeks and fined £25 by an FA Disciplinary Committee in Manchester. Accompanied by Joe Mercer, Bowles' crime was swearing at the referee in a Central League game against Bury. The ban could have been worse for Bowles and City, coming as it did at exactly the same time as his right ankle was covered in plaster.

Colin Bell scored the only goal of the game in England's 1-0 triumph over Holland in Amsterdam on 5 November. Twenty-four hours later he was part of a City side on its way to winning the Daily Express National 5-a-side Championships at Wembley's Empire Pool. The Blues beat Coventry 3-0, Crystal Palace 3-1, Chelsea 4-2 and then Swindon 2-1 in the Final. The six-man squad was Corrigan, Book, Pardoe, Oakes, Bell and Young, with the goals coming from Young with six, Bell with five and one from Oakes. The selection of the squad had caused a little controversy in the dressing room with certain players less than happy with their being left out. One notice was pinned up on the wall: "To whom it may concern. Francis Henry Lee and Michael George Summerbee and three others, hereby challenge the so-called 5-a-side Champions of Great Britain to a match, with the same rules as at Wembley. Venue yet to be decided. The prize for the winners to be 14 days holiday in (1) Paris, (2) Blackpool, (3) Saigon". Competition and rivalry obviously fierce (if light-hearted), but, at the end of the day Manchester City had won yet another trophy.

City's impressive run of form in September and October with just one defeat from ten League games had seen them move up to sixth place when Southampton arrived at Maine Road. The Blues were without Neil Young who'd turned an ankle in the 5-a-side tournament as well as having a sore throat, his place in the starting line-up being taken by Tony Towers for his first full senior game of the season. A tough game in heavy rain and muddy conditions was decided in the 13th minute when Colin Bell scored the only goal with a spectacular strike from fully 30 yards. Although City dominated territorially they were unable to put the game further beyond the Saints' grasp, a fact noted by the treasurer of European Cup-winners' Cup opponents S.K.Lierse. Mr. Virbirts, leading a 20-strong party of Belgians on a spying mission to Maine Road said: "I think City will have to play better than this when they come to Belgium next week. We were not particularly impressed with their performance today."

Tony Book remembers

I remember the Five-a-side tournament vividly. It was the first time the club had entered and we took seven players down to London. Dave Ewing took the team, as Malcolm wasn't really that interested. I remember we played the first game and then someone said there was a bonus to be had. None of us knew anything about this so we all said to Dave: "Nip out and find out what this is all about." He came back and said there was something like a £500 win bonus each. That was a lot of money in those days and the lads started rubbing their hands. We'd only gone down in the first place for a bit of fun! Anyway we played some great stuff and ended up winning the tournament. Mike Summerbee and Francis Lee weren't in the party and when we came back we started taunting them a bit saying: "We don't need you. We won it without you." We wound them up so much they issued a challenge against us but nothing ever came of it. They weren't too clever those two indoors with head tennis and five-a-side and the like. Neil Young, Alan Oakes, Glyn Pardoe and Colin Bell had too much for Frannie and Mike indoors!

If they weren't impressed on the Saturday, they must surely have been on the following Wednesday. City welcomed Young back into the side and won the game at a canter 3-0 despite a plucky performance from the Belgian part-timers. With City three goals to the good, the game was wrapped up by half-time, many reporters commenting that the return leg at Maine Road two weeks later would be "just a formality". Some City supporters had travelled to Brussels via a special flight arranged by Roy Clarke in the Social Club. The cost of the one-hour flight (on a Comet jet) including meals out and back, hotel with bed and breakfast, travel to and from the game and a match ticket, was just £23. Lee opened the scoring after seven minutes when he hooked a shot through the hands of Engelen in the Lierse goal. In the 35th minute, the England man doubled the Blues' advantage, collecting a pass from Young before scoring with a left-foot shot that went in off a post. Doyle then aggravated a thigh injury picked up in training the night before, his place taken by Heslop, and with a minute to go to the interval, Bell completed the scoring after good work by Lee on the right. City dominated the game from the start and came through with an emphatic victory in front of a crowd of 19,000 in a neat, compact ground, located in the market town of Lier, ten miles from Antwerp. Joe Mercer said after the game: "This was a very pleasing result for us and one that I thought was right in every way. Lierse gave us a good fight and they played better than I had thought possible." Malcolm Allison was also pleased with the outcome: "We played extremely well in our third European test, and we were altogether too strong and professional for the Belgians. I thought Tommy Booth had a splendid match and was also pleased to see

Joe Corrigan make a couple of saves near the end." Despite Doyle's injury – on more than one occasion making him doubtful for the game with Manchester United in three days time – he was still delighted, saying: "Now that one's over, let's get at those Reds." Victory in Belgium was the perfect preparation for the 81st Manchester League 'derby'.

If the preparation was perfect, then so too was the outcome of the game. In a game described as 'the most one-sided 'derby' of all-time' City destroyed United, winning 4-0, although the dominance was so extreme that the scoreline could easily have been doubled. Doyle revelled in the slaughter and gave a superb performance in the middle of the field, although to isolate the well-known 'United hater' for special praise would be unjust on the others. To a man, City were outstanding, constantly harassing the United defence whilst easily handling the forward-line which contained no less a threat that the Best, Law and Charlton triumvirate. Despite their obvious superiority, it took City 38 minutes to make the breakthrough when Neil Young, wide out on the left-wing near to the Kippax Stand, beat Alex Stepney on his near post with a vicious swerving left-foot shot. Lee had the ball in the net a second time right on the half-time whistle only for the 'goal' to be disallowed by referee Gordon Hill who'd already called 'time'. The decision only delayed the inevitable. After the break City continued their dominance and in the 55th minute, Bell scored City's second after a 50-yard run by Oakes had split United's defence. Two minutes later, David Sadler, harassed by the persistent Bowyer put through his own goal and it was all over – not that United ever had much chance. A minute from time Bell completed the rout when he poked home City's fourth from close in. The Blues left the field to a standing ovation. It was the first time City had won a Maine Road 'derby' since September 1959. There was now no doubt who was the best team in Manchester. Joe Corrigan, in the first of his record-breaking 26 derbies, watched most of the proceedings as a lone spectator, probably wondering what all the fuss was about Manchester United.

Neil Young remembers

We beat United (murdered them actually) 4-0 at Maine Road in the League and I scored from right out on the touchline – not far from the corner flag – near the Kippax. I used to have this thing where if I could get a cross in, I'd hit it as hard as I could, but try and keep the ball low. That way it could hit a knee or an ankle and go anywhere. This particular time I struck it well and it swerved and beat Alex Stepney at the near post. He had no chance with it really as I'm sure he was expecting a high cross to the far post.

City were now fourth and with injury doubts to Corrigan, Lee and Young, travelled to Highbury to face a side they hadn't beaten in six years. Arsenal, unusually for them, were experiencing a difficult time, and had won only five of their 19 matches to date. In the end, Joe Mercer was able to announce a full-strength City 11 and came away from one of his old 'stomping grounds' with a well-earned point from a 1-1 draw against a strongly-built side. The home team had taken the lead in the 22nd minute, when Corrigan, slow to leave his line, hauled down George Graham, resulting in a penalty-kick converted by the Arsenal skipper Terry Neill. Two minutes before the break, City levelled through Bowyer, a hotly disputed goal in the eyes of the Arsenal defenders who were convinced Bowyer had handled before shooting past goalkeeper Geoff Barnett. The goal ended a lean spell for Bowyer – it was his first in 11 outings – and extended City's unbeaten run to 13 matches.

Tony Book remembers

I was having quite a good run in the side round about September-October time. We'd beaten United again in the League and began to do well in the League Cup. I felt really good after the long lay-off through injury and was in good nick. It was a fresh start and things started to happen. I was having a good time and hoping it would continue. I was fortunate that I never had any reoccurrence of the Achilles trouble because there was more than occasion when, during the lay-off, I thought my career was finished.

With the Cup-winners' Cup-tie against Lierse apparently already a foregone conclusion, Joe Mercer took the opportunity to rest Neil Young and Joe Corrigan, both of whom had picked up niggling toe and groin injuries respectively at Highbury. Young's replacement was the 18-year-old self-styled 'joker' of Maine Road Derek Jeffries (his first senior start) whilst Ken Mulhearn deputised for Corrigan, ironically for his first game since the defeat in Fenerbahce 13 months earlier. The pundits were right with their pre-match predictions; apart from a couple of early chances, Lierse were ripped apart by a decisive City performance. The first of five on the night came from Summerbee when he scored with a low, left-foot drive from the 18-yard line after 21 minutes. There were no more goals in the first-half, but after a change of footwear at the break to combat a frosty pitch, City scored four in the second 45 minutes. Lee scored in the 48th minute following up Bowyer's header and then again seven minutes later with a neat back-header after good work from cousins Oakes and Pardoe. Tony Towers replaced Oakes shortly before Bell got into the scoring action. His first effort was a header from Summerbee's cross, followed in the 72nd minute by his 17th of the season, a side-footer past an advancing Engelen. A crowd of just 26,486 had seen City win 5-0 and stroll into the last eight of a major European competition. Everyone knew things would be harder next time, although they'd have to wait nearly four months, until March, to find out.

Neil Young remembers

Malcolm really conned us before we played Lierse. I remember he came back after watching them and said: "It's going to be very difficult against them. I've just seen them and they are a very good side. It won't be easy." In the end we beat them 8-0 on aggregate and, as the scoreline suggests, they were never in it. Malcolm knew we'd beat them easily but was trying to keep our feet on the ground and focussed for the tie.

Again he'd learnt from Fenerbahce. I missed the game at Maine Road through injury, which was disappointing for me, but it was a convincing win and once again proved just how good Malcolm was with psychology.

Although conditions were icy for the game with Lierse, the cold spell worsened as the weekend neared and four of the 11 First Division games were postponed owing to heavy snow. The pitch at Maine Road was bone-hard, but according to referee Burtenshaw of Great Yarmouth, playable, and the game with Leeds took place; the majority of players turning out in training shoes. At five o'clock City fans wished it hadn't. Leeds won at Maine Road for the first time in 33 years with a goal in the 88th minute. They'd gone ahead in the 19th minute when Eddie Gray's cross struck an unknown City body and looped agonisingly over Mulhearn and into the net. Despite the conditions City played some fast, attacking football and always looked as though they may equalise with Lee in particular (not to mention the Leeds' goalkeeper Gary Sprake) looking the most likely. In the 57th minute they finally managed it. Summerbee's cross-cum-shot struck Terry Cooper's hand at point-blank range and the referee pointed to the spot. Francis Lee did the honours by sending Sprake the wrong way with the ensuing kick. Mick Jones, the Leeds centre-forward (never one to shirk a tackle – like the rest of his team-mates) was then booked for a vicious-looking foul on Tommy Booth right in front of the tunnel. The tackle angered many supporters in the main stand (some of whom were led away by the police) with the unfortunate Leeds' chairman Percy Woodward bearing the bulk of their wrath in the absence of Jones. Two minutes from time Jack Charlton knocked the ball from Mulhearn's hands as the City 'keeper tried to hang on to a corner. In the ensuing scramble, Charlton poked the ball over the dead-ball line. The referee gave Leeds another corner which the unmarked Jones converted with his head to give Leeds a fortunate 2-1 victory. Three 'lucky' goals but the outcome did not please Malcolm Allison, already angered by Jones' tackle on Booth: "Charlton admitted to me that he was the man who nudged the ball over the by-line. It was a diabolical decision by the ref." He went on to say: "The tackle by Jones was the worst I've seen in 25 years of football."

The Sunday papers were full of the controversial Leeds winner the following morning. One of them, *The People*, also had an exclusive story about Harry Godwin and Johnny Hart checking on the current form of Queen's Park Rangers' star striker Rodney Marsh. The difference between watching Rodney Marsh and signing him would be two-and-a-quarter years.

The Blues had just four days to put the memories of the Leeds game behind them. Many said the events of that game would only increase the players' determination as they prepared for the League Cup semi-final, first leg against Manchester United at Maine Road.

If City had lost the game with a controversial goal on Saturday, then some (especially those from the other side of town) said they won by one on the Wednesday. The Blues beat their old enemy 2-1 and were halfway to Wembley for the second successive season. Still smarting from their 4-0 drubbing at Maine Road less than three weeks earlier, United were desperate to avoid

119

a repetition and very nearly managed it. The game turned in the last minute when Ian Ure's clumsy challenge on the rampaging Lee sent the City player sprawling inside the penalty-area. Despite long and heated protests form those in red, referee Jack Taylor stuck to his guns and awarded the penalty. The protests didn't bother Lee; he simply put the ball down and crashed it inside Alex Stepney's right-hand post. No prizes for guessing who the coolest person in a crowd of nearly 56,000 was! City had taken the lead in the 13th minute when Bell scored with a low drive, and but for Stepney, Bowyer and Lee would have clinched the tie by half-time. Twenty minutes after the interval, Bobby Charlton, United's best player on the night, equalised when he gave Corrigan no chance from close range. Over the 90 minutes, United's defence was the busier of the two and it appeared they'd done enough until Ure's tackle on Lee. A highly-charged night finished with a still-angry George Best knocking the ball out of the referee's hands in the tunnel at the end of the game. City weren't bothered; they looked forward to the second-leg in a fortnight's time with a vital one goal advantage.

Another Best – Clyde – faced City for West Ham in the next League game. Like his more illustrious namesake, he too finished on the losing side as City ran amok with a superb performance and came away with a 4-0 win. Lee gave a brilliant display on a heavy pitch and continued his recent scoring form when he beat Bobby Ferguson with a skimming 30-yarder to give City a first-half lead. In the second-half Bowyer scored two fine headers before Doyle rounded off a great all-round performance with City's fourth in the 88th minute. The win moved City to fourth position in the table, behind Liverpool, Leeds and leaders Everton.

It was a busy few days off the field before the next League game. On Monday the FA Cup third round draw paired City with Second Division Hull; on Tuesday, Queens' Park Rangers were reported as having turned down a new British transfer record fee of £170,000 from City for Rodney Marsh whilst on Wednesday the draw was made for the quarter-finals of the European Cup-winners' Cup. On the same day as the Blues were drawn against the Portuguese students from Academica de Coimbra, their centre-forward, Antonio, was playing for his national side against England at Wembley. Colin Bell and Francis Lee played in England's 1-0 win with Lee, extremely unusually for him, blasting his penalty kick yards wide of the target. Thursday saw Bell with his arm x-rayed and in a sling following a heavy fall at Wembley and on Friday the week finished with Corrigan's troublesome groin strain flaring up again causing him to miss the match with Spurs.

Once again the more than capable Mulhearn replaced Corrigan and had a very quiet afternoon against a Spurs side content with a point from the outset and with an eight-man defence. Especially without the drive of Bell in midfield, City struggled to break down the visitors' heavy fortifications, his replacement Connor being given such a heavy burden to carry. Against almost one-way continuous pressure, Spurs surprisingly opened the scoring in the 77th minute when Neil Johnson finished off a move started by Jimmy Greaves. Their joy was short-lived when, a minute later, Oakes finally got the better of Pat Jennings with a stunning 30-yard shot. The goal set the scene for a grandstand finish with the Spurs' goal bearing a charmed life. Twice Jennings made incredible point-blank saves (one from Book's header) then, in the game's last attack, they had fantastic luck when Mullery, under pressure, headed Summerbee's cross against his own post.

Neil Young remembers

We always looked forward to playing United back then. We knew we had the upper hand and couldn't wait to get at them. Frannie never dived for that penalty! It was almost expected really but it was simply the way he played. He'd run so quickly at defenders that it took just the slightest of touches and he'd be over. There was even more controversy at Old Trafford – again involving Frannie – in the return leg. He said he never saw the ref's arm indicating an indirect free-kick and he just blasted the ball through the wall. In Alex Stepney's defence though, what do you do when you're a goalkeeper and you see the ball coming straight at you? It must be very difficult not to try and stop it. Unfortunately for him he couldn't hang on to it and Mike's followed up and knocked it in. Bobby Charlton went absolutely berserk at Stepney but by then of course it was too late.

And so to Old Trafford, 90 minutes away from Wembley and a League Cup Final date with West Bromwich Albion. Like the first-leg, this game too was a fiercely contested affair. After 17 minutes Young's shot was blocked on the line by Ure; Stepney failed to hold a second shot from Lee and Bowyer was on hand to give City a 1-0 lead on the night and 3-1 on aggregate. Six minutes later United were level when Paul Edwards gave Corrigan no chance with a searing right-footer in front of a delighted Stretford End. It really was now "game on". Lee then had a couple of half-chances but the teams went in for the half-time break level with everything to play for. Disaster struck for the Blues on the hour mark. Best beat two tackles on the right before firing in a fierce shot which Corrigan could only parry. Unfortunately the ball fell to the feet of one of Britain's greatest ever goalscorers, one Denis Law. The tie level on aggregate and United now with the upper hand, if only for a while. Despite the home side's efforts, City withstood everything they could throw at them and nearly regained the lead when firstly Edwards almost turned Young's corner past his own goalkeeper and then Summerbee missed a glorious chance in front of goal when he was unable to convert Lee's cross. In the 81st minute he more than made up for his miss. Willie Morgan fouled Bowyer two yards outside the penalty area. Referee Jim Finney immediately signalled an indirect free-kick as United's defenders assembled their wall. In his typical forthright manner, Lee blasted the ball towards the goal, presumably in the hope of a deflection causing some damage. The ball flew straight through to Alex Stepney in the United goal who instinctively attempted to save it but could only manage to knock it down directly into the path of the onrushing Summerbee. Deadly from three yards, Summerbee dutifully finished the job off and City were back at Wembley thanks to one of the most talked about 'derby' goals of all times. If Stepney had the let the ball through, the 'goal' would not have stood. Not content with a draw, City could have scored again when both Lee and Young had chances. In the end though a draw was more than enough; the Blues could look forward to another appearance at the famous Twin Towers. Joe Mercer was full of praise for his players afterwards: "I thought we had the better chances and just had the edge in a fine match. We knew it would be tight and close and it was. The last thing Malcolm and I told the players was to concentrate on football no matter what happened. They did this splendidly and deserve to be at Wembley again. This was another example of our growing maturity. United are used to semi-final situations and we have beaten them."

Tony Book remembers

We got through to Wembley after beating United in the semi-finals. Alex Stepney saved Frannie's free-kick and Mike's finished it off. We always seemed to well against them during that time and we were never afraid of going to Old Trafford. I remember Mike Summerbee would always get their supporters going and Malcolm would go the Stretford End before the game and show them the score with his fingers! None of us were frightened of playing there.

Unfortunately the highs of Old Trafford didn't travel to Stamford Bridge three days later. Without four members of the side who played against United, a somewhat makeshift City side crashed 3-1 with two of Chelsea's goals coming inside three minutes and from the unusual source of defender David Webb. The craggy centre-half scored 21 League goals in 231 appearances for Chelsea, or, looked at another way, 10 per cent of his goals in three minutes. Another bizarre fact that could only happen to Manchester City. Things got even worse in the 43rd minute when the Blues failed to clear the ball and Ian Hutchinson (he of the enormous windmill-like throw) made it 3-0. The home side seemed keen to increase their already sufficient lead even more in the second half. Corrigan made fine saves from both Eddie McCreadie and Charlie Cooke and when Peter Osgood's header did get past him, Tony Book was on hand to clear off the line. Scant consolation on an otherwise disappointing day came when Summerbee headed in Young's cross in the 88th minute.

Francis Lee recovered from a calf injury sustained at Old Trafford and returned to the side as City continued their League travels to top of the table Everton. The Blues turned in a much better all-round performance although still returned home empty-handed following a 1-0 defeat. With several of the side suffering from 'flu, City managed to hold out until the 78th minute when Joe Royle nodded down a cross into the path of Alan Whittle who beat Corrigan from six yards. Earlier Royle had struck a post with his penalty-kick after George Heslop had fouled the same player. It was Royle's second penalty miss inside three days. On the Saturday he'd had his spot-kick saved by Derby's Les Green. The defeat at Goodison Park, and new injuries to Bowyer and Summerbee took the edge of the players' Christmas party.

The last game of 1969 (and the 1960s for that matter) was the home clash with Burnley on 27 December. Or rather it wasn't. A thick blanket of fog attached itself to the Black

Country and the north-west causing the games at Maine Road, Anfield, Burnden Park and Molineux to be postponed. Ironically groundsman Stan Gibson had given up most of his Christmas break to lay the club's new £3,000 plastic and foam rubber pitch covers to ward off the snow and frost that was threatening. Stan's hard work had produced, in the words of secretary Walter Griffiths, a "pitch in perfect condition", however not even one of Maine Road's greatest characters could get the better of the fog. On a positive note though it did give City an extra week to get their casualties fit in readiness for the FA Cup-tie with Hull.

As is the way of most Cup-ties when a major club visits a so-called 'minnow', the Blues trip to Humberside was far from easy. For the first 20 minutes the home side threw everything at an uncertain-looking City and were unlucky not to take the lead when a shot from Chris Simpkin flew past Corrigan only to hit a post. Bowyer replied for the Blues by hitting an upright at the other end and then Ken Houghton fired a shot into Corrigan's side netting. With Bell back in the side City were at full strength and needed to be against some tremendous Hull pressure. Young then left the field with a leg injury leaving the Blues with just ten men for an even more nervous few minutes. Despite all the home side's pressure, City's defence, with Book and Doyle in particular outstanding, managed to go into the break level at 0-0. In the second-half, the Blues looked a little like their old selves and the game was more evenly balanced. Only Lee of the forwards posed any real regular threat until the 70th minute when Book launched a 40-yard pass through the Hull defence and into the path of Young. The ball bounced head-high but fortunately for City, Young's long right leg got there before Ian McKechnie's arms and the Blues' Cup-winner from last year had continued where he'd left off. It couldn't have come at a better time for Young. He'd not scored since the 4-0 League victory over Manchester United back in November and it was only his second strike in 17 games.

City's reward for the win at Hull was a fourth-round clash with Manchester United at Old Trafford – tickets 5 shillings for adults at The Scoreboard End. Malcolm Allison said in his usual confident style: "They aren't half giving them a few chances to get their own back!"

Neil Young remembers

At Hull, Tony Book pushed forward with the ball and I called for it. His pass must have been 40 yards or so. Despite what people said, it was a pass from Tony Book, and not just a big 'hoof'. Admittedly it was unusual for him to launch a pass that far – he was normally a ten to 15-yarder to either Mike Summerbee or 'Tommy' Doyle – but in this case it was a genuine pass. I was moving in from the left for it, with the goalkeeper and a defender coming in for it at the same time. I just got my foot to it – my right foot – to flick it over the goalkeeper's head. Once I saw it clear him I thought it was pretty certain to go in the net. I suppose it was about head high when I got to it. I'd been in some pain most of the game after that knock but I can't remember feeling it during that incident. I had a couple of stitches in the leg but when you score you never feel any pain.

Young's injury failed to clear up in time for the rearranged League fixture against Burnley. Stan Bowles was his replacement and although he was City's star-man it was Lee who scored City's goal in the 1-1 draw. On a bitterly cold night, only 22,074 (City's lowest of the season) brave soles ventured out to watch a game that had been in doubt often owing to the icy conditions and bone-hard pitch. For the visitors, Peter Mellor (once an amateur on City's books) in goal had a superb game and had it not been for his countless saves City would have won by the proverbial hatful. With just four minutes left it looked as though Lee's 20-yard first-half strike would be enough to secure the points only for Martin Dobson to equalise from close in on a rare Burnley sortie into Blues' territory.

The draw with Burnley meant City had now gone four games in the League without a win and unfortunately the run was far from over. Tony Book missed the trip to Coventry as well as the 3-0 defeat on a mud-bath pitch. Goals from Neil Martin and John O'Rourke with two made it a convincing scoreline as the home side adapted much better to the conditions than City. It was a game in which Mercer's men tried manfully but could only manage a performance that vied between second and third gears. Poor Joe Corrigan in goal had a dreadful game, being at fault for all three Coventry goals, and appeared to be stuck in first gear all afternoon.

Francis Lee and Colin Bell played for England four days later in a goalless draw with Holland at Wembley. So poor was England's performance that the team was booed from the pitch by the disgruntled spectators at the end of the game. What with City's bad run of late and now this England performance, Messrs. Lee and Bell must have wondered where their next positive review, let alone victory, was going to come from. It wasn't to come in the next League game as Stoke left Maine Road with a 1-0 victory. Mulhearn replaced Corrigan following the youngster's nightmare the previous week at Coventry and despite a solid show, was helpless to prevent Terry Conroy's winner with less than a quarter of an hour left. Gordon Banks in the visitors' goal confirmed that he was still the country's best by producing superb saves from firstly Alan Oakes, and then, in the dying seconds, from Colin Bell. It was another stuttering City performance and hardly what was required as the FA Cup clash with Manchester United loomed into sight.

If they'd been stuttering for weeks, City ground to a complete halt at Old Trafford and surrendered the FA Cup to the old enemy in an unbelievably tame showing. Right from the kick-off the Blues were both nervous and apprehensive and it was amazing that they held out until the 44th minute before falling behind thanks to a Willie Morgan penalty after Bobby Charlton had been fouled by Pardoe. Brian Kidd scored twice in 11 minutes in the second-half to complete the scoring and give the Stretford End a rare opportunity to mock Allison. As if to make things worse, Summerbee injured a knee and would miss the next three League games. Tony Towers came on as a substitute for Summerbee and hit the underside of the bar in the dying minutes. Had it gone in, it would have improved the scoreline, but certainly not the performance. Joe Mercer was understandably subdued afterwards: "They were easily the better side. Could we possibly have played worse? It's a great disappointment but one we must

124

get over quickly. There is no question of a crisis even though this was the worst performance by any City side in the five years since I came here."

There seemed to be no way to stop City's progress down the slippery slope. At West Bromwich they failed to find the net for the fourth consecutive game. When this happens, teams invariably lose and this is exactly what happened, City again conceding three times. Thanks to goals by Colin Suggett and Jeff Astle, the home side led at the interval and even when their goalkeeper John Osborne left the field for ten minutes following a collision with Doyle, City were still unable get themselves back in the game. A badly limping Osborne returned for the second-half following a pain-killing injection to his bruised hip but City were in such generous mood that they rarely troubled him. With ten minutes left Asa Hartford completed another disappointing Saturday afternoon for Manchester City when he made it 3-0. If City were to have any chance of lifting the League Cup against this same team, they would have to produce considerably more of everything than this showing.

Joe Mercer and Malcolm Allison missed the defeat at The Hawthorns as they were away in Portugal watching City's next opponents in the European Cup-winners' Cup. Academica de Coimbra lost 2-0 to Championship rivals Benfica although by all accounts should have won. Malcolm Allison: " They could cause some trouble for us. They are full of skill, strong in midfield and a team to be respected. They should have murdered Benfica; it seemed they beat themselves. They appeared unable to believe that they had the beating so easily of the top club in Portugal." On City's most recent performance he went on to say: "We gather we didn't play too well again, but it's just a temporary inconvenience. All great teams go through these patches."

Glyn Pardoe was City's latest casualty with an ankle injury and Arthur Mann returned to first-team duties against Notts. Forest after a gap of ten months. The day before the game, newspapers reported on City's abortive bid to lure Jimmy Greaves away from Tottenham and bring his obvious goalscoring talents to the barren wastes of Maine Road. Someone had to break the Blues' lean spell and the honour fell to Mike Doyle who struck the ball between Alan Hill's legs in the Forest goal after Bowyer had headed down Young's corner. Coming in the 16th minute it was just the sort of start City wanted. However they were unable to increase their lead and with six minutes left fell victim to a lack of concentration at the back that enabled Dave Hilley to grab an equaliser. Tony Book had earlier left the field with an ankle heavily strapped to give Willie Donachie his first taste of senior football. The young Scottish full-back watched as City failed to convert wave after wave of chances, he himself going close at the end with a dipping shot into the arms of Hill. Their inability to score meant City had won just once – at Hull in the FA Cup – in their last ten games. In those ten games the Blues scored five times. Whilst Notts. Forest were carrying out their 'smash and grab' at Maine Road, George Best was scoring six times on his own in an amazing 8-2 FA Cup win at Northampton. Kim Book, the brother of Tony, had the misfortune to be in goal for Northampton.

The cold weather made an unwelcome return and decimated football on Saturday, 12 February 1970. Six of the 11 First Division games – including City's at Sheffield Wednesday

– were postponed due to varying states of frost and ice. The delay gave the Blues an extra few days to try and work out a plan of action in readiness for the midweek visit of Arsenal. One major change was the debut on the right-wing of the former Altrincham player Frank Carrodus who lined up against a solid-looking Gunners' rearguard just hours after sitting his engineering exams at college. The weekend's ice had now melted and turned the Maine Road pitch into a surface more suitable for growing rice than for playing football. Arsenal brought with them their well-known capacity for rugged defence and bore little threat to Mulhearn's goal until the last 20 minutes. Bowyer, wearing number nine and leading the attack, had given the Blues the lead in the 40th minute, and City, with Carrodus doing well on his debut, and Mann looking comfortable again, looked well placed for their first League win in two months. Unfortunately Arsenal levelled the game in the 86th minute when George Graham finished off a fine move involving Peter Marinello, John Radford and Jon Sammels. Once again City's inability to kill off a side with a crucial second goal had cost them dearly. Ken Mulhearn, Ian Bowyer and Neil Young were all found guilty and dropped for the next League game at Molineux.

The so-called 'fans' that had deluged the club with abusive letters in recent weeks must have been eating their words when the Blues appeared to have finally turned the corner. After a first-half of supreme dullness (and no goals) City produced arguably their best football of the season to win 3-1. Mike Summerbee was back in the side after his injury and playing at centre-forward led the attack superbly, scoring two goals into the bargain. City's other goal came from Colin Bell but such was the confident showing in the second-half, the Blues could still afford to squander enough chances to have doubled the score, and let Les Wilson pull one back for Wolves as well as allowing Lee the rare privilege of missing a penalty. The much talked-about (and needed) shake-up appeared to have paid dividends. Even one of those dropped, Neil Young, was philosophical about the changes, asking the management to play him in the reserves in an attempt to regain his confidence.

Neil Young remembers

The team was on a bit of a bad run and so was I personally. I'd not been playing too well and asked to be dropped into the reserves for a couple of games to try and get my form and confidence back. It seemed to do the job for me and I was back in the first team for the trip to Portugal. We didn't know a great deal about Academica but we soon found out they were a very dirty side. Everyone one of them would run past you and spit at you in an attempt to get you riled. I didn't play too well myself over there. I had a bit of a niggling injury and wasn't 100 per cent fit and probably shouldn't have played but I just wanted to. I used to love playing in Europe.

Not surprisingly City named an unchanged side for the visit of Ipswich Town. With Carrodus and Pardoe playing as wingers, the Blues managed to win 1-0 thanks to a Lee penalty, although the game was less than inspiring with a difficult trip to Portugal and the League Cup Final inside the next seven days. With Carrodus in particular playing poorly, Mercer and Allison took their side to Coimbra still with selection problems but delighted by the news that the opposition's star-striker, Manuel Antonio, had ruled himself out of the game due to a leg injury.

City encamped at a monastic retreat high in the hills that was once a palace for the Kings of Portugal. A 16-mile bus ride was required to transport the players and staff to the Municipal Stadium and a disappointingly small crowd of 8,000 owing to match being televised. As was the custom, City had to wait until 9.45 pm local time for the kick-off. Coimbra took to the pitch wearing a menacing all-black kit and their early tackles – Lee was a particular target – gave the impression that the students had taken up the wrong game. With the game of such importance to both sides, it soon became apparent that it would be a very cagey night, one of few clear-cut chances. Coimbra missed their regular centre-forward whilst City's most positive attacker, Lee, was limited to long-range efforts. Both sides' frustration at being unable to break the deadlock saw an outbreak of some over-enthusiastic tackles towards the end but City were the most satisfied with a 0-0 draw. Joe Mercer certainly was: "Perhaps both teams were a bit frightened of each other, but it is still a very pleasing result for us. I know it wasn't a classic, but we got what we wanted." Ten minutes into the second-half City's trainer Dave Ewing was dismissed from his seat on the bench: "The referee said it was because I shouted at the players. It hasn't happened to me before." Perhaps Ewing had been taking lessons from Allison although no one would ever believe he could shout at the players!

Neil Young remembers

When we got back from Portugal it was just a few days before the League Cup Final. Malcolm took me to one side and told me I wouldn't be playing at Wembley. He said to me: "You're struggling with this injury, your not really fit so I'm not going to play you." At the time I could have hit him but I knew, deep down, that he was probably right with the decision and I understood his thinking behind it. I came back home and didn't watch the game because I'm a lousy spectator. It was a funny situation – especially after the previous year against Leicester – and although I was disappointed, I understood the situation. I wouldn't have liked to have played and not done well. Even though we'd had a good result in Portugal, I knew I'd not done that well and I suppose I was half-expecting to miss the Final. My wife gave birth to our daughter, Melissa Jane, on the Friday night before the game on Saturday so my mind was on other things as well!

The result in Portugal gave heart for West Bromwich Albion and the League Cup Final. Once the travelling problems of fog and snow had been alleviated, Joe Mercer announced his team for Wembley. Although he'd been given a recall in Portugal, Neil Young had had a relatively quiet game and was dropped for the Final, his place taken by George Heslop in a new look (for City at least) 4-3-3 formation. Last year's Wembley winner couldn't even find a place on the bench; that honour went to Ian Bowyer. Young consoled himself with the arrival of a new daughter, Melissa Jane.

The idea of playing Heslop alongside Tommy Booth at the back was to counter the obvious aerial threat of West Brom's Jeff Astle. After five minutes the plan looked to have backfired in the worst possible way. Corrigan waited for Bobby Hope's cross to drop, Astle didn't and City were a goal down. The goal seemed to inspire the Blues more than the Midlanders and for the next 20 minutes it was constant City pressure. The Blues made of a mockery of a dreadful Wembley surface (thanks to the Horse of the Year Show that had recently been held on it) to produce some terrific play, the likes of which their supporters had been starved of in recent times. Lee in particular was outstanding, many saying that this was his finest performance in a City shirt, but for all their pressure and chances, they were unable to find the elusive equaliser until the 59th minute. Summerbee, hobbling on one leg after a crunching tackle by Ray Wilson, managed to hook Pardoe's corner into a crowded goalmouth. Bell back-headed it into the path of Doyle who drove home. It was no more than City deserved and surely now it was just a matter of time before they got the winner. Summerbee's contribution to the goal was his last kick of the game. He left the field immediately to be replaced by Bowyer and was later diagnosed as having a hairline fracture of the left leg.

Malcolm Allison remembers

Francis Lee was a tremendous player for Manchester City. He was very intelligent, and for me, played in the wrong era because I always felt he was ahead of his time. He had many great games for us and some say his best was in the League Cup Final against West Brom. I remember talking to the players at the end of the 90 minutes, the usual stuff, do this, try that, sort of thing. Francis said: "Never mind all that Mal, just give me the fucking ball; I'll win the game for us." He'd played against Leicester in the FA Cup Final the year and was disappointed with his performance. Now was his chance for redemption and he took it.

Tony Book remembers

The pitch at Wembley was awful; Joe Mercer described it as a "cabbage patch". We'd had some trouble flying back from Portugal and were transferred to Birmingham and had to get a coach down to London. I'd turned an ankle in Portugal and I managed to get into Highbury on the Thursday and Friday before the Final for a bit of treatment. The ankle wasn't 100 per cent but with Glyn playing in midfield and Arthur Mann already included I thought we might struggle for defenders so I gave it a go. We didn't start too well. I remember someone getting a cross in from my side early on and Joe should have come for it but he didn't and they went in front. Fortunately Mike Doyle and Glyn scored for us and we were back in Europe again. Even though we'd won the League Cup we were still up for the Cup-winners' Cup games. I always felt we were a better Cup side. We had a decent squad and if we ever had any injuries there was always someone else good enough to come in. I know the game's different today but back then Joe and Malcolm never rotated the squad like they do nowadays. Joe used to say: "I'll always pick my best team." That's how it was; if you were fit you played. We didn't use too many players but we had good fringe players who could come in and do a good job for us. Players like Dave Connor, Tony Towers and Derek Jeffries could all hold their own.

With the score level after 90 minutes neither side looked forward to another half hour on the heavy, bog-like surface. It was now that City showed their remarkable fitness and strength, legacies of all the hard work Allison had put them through on the training ground. In the 101st minute Lee on the right-wing chipped the ball to Bell. He in turned found Pardoe who just managed to reach the ball before goalkeeper John Osborne and defender Doug Fraser and hook it ball into the net. What a time to score your one and only goal of the season! Tony Book played through the pain of an injured ankle to collect the League Cup from Sir Stanley Rous. Wembley's new £30,000 electronic scoreboard proclaimed Manchester City as winners of the 1970 Football League Cup, the first north-west side to achieve this feat, and it guaranteed European football in Moss Side again next season no matter what happened in this.

Despite constant moans nowadays, successful sides have always had problems with fixture pile-ups at the end of seasons. It is the nature of the beast and has to be more appealing to everyone rather than having an end of season dance in January. City had just three days to come down from the highs of Wembley when they played hosts to Crystal Palace. It was the Blues' fourth game in 12 days and perhaps not surprisingly was one game too far. Still suffering from a Wembley 'hangover', City succumbed to a defensive, second bottom Crystal Palace side who were delighted to celebrate their first away win of the season thanks to a lacklustre City performance and Gerry Queen's second-half 20-yarder.

With the FA Cup semi-finals taking place the following Saturday, City took advantage of a few days break to recharge their batteries as well as allowing Bobby Owen to join Swansea on loan for the remainder of the season. Academica de Coimbra were their next opponents, another team capable of providing tough opposition and another game that would require a gruelling 30 minutes extra-time. The Portuguese once again displayed their ability to frustrate City by a series of niggling fouls and general gamesmanship not often seen in England at that time. Young returned to the starting line-up but any hopes the Blues had of an easy passage to the semis were not helped by injuries to Heslop, Doyle and Bell, all of which contributed to City's frustration as they struggled to break through. Chris Glennon, 20, was given his debut as Bell's replacement but it was to be another young substitute, Tony Towers, who was the hero on the night. In the very last minute of extra-time, Young's cross from the left was half-cleared to Towers on the edge of the penalty area. The 17-year-old pounced on the ball and hammered it through a crowd of players and high into the net to send the majority of the 36,338 spectators home happy, even if some had left their fingernails behind. It had been a

Tony Book remembers

Coimbra were a strong side who could play a bit when they put their minds to it. The game at Maine Road against them was very difficult and went into extra-time like the League Cup Final did. One of the reasons we were so successful was because we were so fit, probably one of the fittest teams around at the time. We used to have an athletics regime every Monday. Derek Ibbotson, Joe Lancaster and Danny Herman – one was a distance runner, one a middle-distance and the other a sprinter – used to put us through our paces. It was hard work but it certainly paid off.

very difficult night's work but City had made it to the final four of the European Cup-winners' Cup. To progress further they would have to overcome FC Schalke 04 from Germany. The other semi-final saw Roma paired with Polish side Gornik Zabrze.

West Ham arrived at Maine Road with Jimmy Greaves (a City target not too long ago) but without Martin Peters, the two players swapping clubs earlier in the week just five hours before the transfer deadline. Greaves had a habit of scoring on his debut for his new club and unfortunately maintained this record with two at Maine Road. In heavy rain and on a flooded pitch, West Ham ran out 5-1 winners having lead 3-1 at half-time. Lee equalised Greaves' first goal, only for the prolific marksman to add a second in the 36th minute and then Geoff Hurst's diving header made it 3-1 a minute before the break. The visitors went further ahead in the 82nd minute with a most bizarre goal. Corrigan cleared the ball from his hands on the corner of the penalty area and began to jog back to his goal without looking at the destination of the kick. Meanwhile, waiting in the centre-circle was Ronnie Boyce who volleyed it straight back into an empty net. No one in the partially-drowned crowd of 25,381 could believe it, least of all a dumbstruck Corrigan. With three minutes left Hurst completed a sad day for City who ironically, had not played nearly as badly as the result suggests.

Schalke coach Rudi Gutendorf was in the stands at Maine Road to see City yet again slump to a home defeat, this time against a Derby County side without Dave Mackay but chasing a place in Europe for next season. Derby's 1-0 win (thanks to Roy McFarland's header in the 18th minute) made it one home League match win in the last ten attempts for City. There was little Good about this Friday game; only Book, Jeffries and Booth earned any praise as the German returned home full of optimism for the semi-final clash in a fortnight.

If City had been playing poorly, losing more than they'd been winning and struggling to find the net, where would be the best place to go and forget about their troubles? That's right, Old Trafford. Twenty-fours hour after the defeat by Derby, ten of the same players – but a completely different side as far as performance goes – won 2-1 to erase memories of the FA Cup defeat. Lee again saved his best for the Reds and opened the scoring in the 10th minute from the penalty-spot after Alex Stepney had brought down Young. Six minutes later Corrigan failed to hold to a hard, low cross from Willie Morgan and Brian Kidd was on hand to equalise. Doyle then restored the Blues' lead, taking advantage of David Sadler's error on the edge of the box to drive the ball past

130

Stepney. Not surprisingly United were looking for excuses, saying that their three FA Cup semi-final battles with Leeds United had taken their toll on the players. Mike Doyle was less sympathetic: "This must surely prove we're the top side in Manchester. If we'd have had a full side out today, we'd have pulverised United. They've beaten us just once in the last ten games between us. I wanted to take the penalty today but Francis Lee wouldn't let me. The only thing that could have given me greater pleasure than scoring the winner was scoring the other one as well." Malcolm Allison, never one normally to be short of a few words, simply said: "It was inevitable we would win." It is not known whether or not scouts from Schalke witnessed this performance. Never mind, the Germans would find out first-hand in a few days time. They'd also get a chance to see Summerbee and Bell, both of whom were back from injury.

Despite their success at Old Trafford, City appeared to save their best performances for Cup-ties, and the Cup-winners' Cup semi-final first-leg proved no exception. Showing commendable skill and spirit, City withstood the Germans until the 78th minute when their captain Libuda beat Corrigan with a well-placed shot just inside the post. It was the only goal of the game and City returned from Gelsenkirchen confident of victory at home and a place in the final in Vienna. Joe Mercer: "I was disappointed with the result but very satisfied with the performance. Libuda scored a good goal, but it was hard on us after we had done so much. This tie is far from over yet. We can do it at home. Summerbee and Bell did a good job for us even though they weren't 100 per cent fit. Oakes, Jeffries and Corrigan all played splendidly." Malcolm Allison: "We can win the semi-final at Maine Road if we attack but we need the right atmosphere. All of us want our supporters to roll up and back our efforts."

Tony Book remembers

The 1-0 defeat away to Schalke was a great result for us. We knew if we could get teams back to Maine Road with that sort of scoreline we'd have a great chance. The atmosphere in the return leg was brilliant. The 'house full' signs were up, the lads were raring to go and the whole place was buzzing. It was a fantastic night, in fact all the European games under floodlights were great games to play in.

As if the League-Cup theory needed any more proof after Wednesday, City once again came down to earth with a bump on the Saturday. Sunderland, desperate for points at the bottom of the table snatched a thoroughly undeserved win thanks to Dennis Tueart's solitary strike in the 65th minute. City were without all of the famous Lee-Bell-Summerbee triumvirate, their places taken by Glennon, Jeffries and Carrodus, although it wasn't for the want of trying, and pressure, that City failed to score again. With only Doyle showing any sort of determination, the game was just another example of City's lack of consistency and they were unable to break down a very poor Sunderland side who restricted their efforts to one in each half.

The Blues' next opponents were Crystal Palace, a side just two places and two points above Sunderland. Once again the result was the same; Manchester City lost 1-0. The Blues now had another young face in the team, Willie Donachie unusually wearing the number eight shirt, and it was he who nearly won the game with a scorching shot that goalkeeper John Jackson did well to turn away. Roger Hoy scored the all-important goal for the home side, one that meant they stayed in the First Division. Palace fans celebrated as though they'd won the FA Cup. City were described in the *Daily Express* as "a team that tosses League points away like confetti".

Because of their ability to donate points willingly to teams at the bottom, City had been christened "the struggling club's best friend" by some sections of the media. Southampton played host to the Blues just a week before the crucial second leg of the Cup-winners' Cup semi-final. The Saints were hoping for some more generosity from City (as they too could still mathematically at least be relegated) who for their part were looking for some improvement bearing in mind the imminent arrival of Schalke. In the end a goalless draw satisfied neither side completely, Southampton ruing several missed chances whilst City's most active moment came when Booth, Doyle and Summerbee were all involved in 'an unpleasant scene' towards the end.

Neil Young remembers

I can remember almost every minute of the game against Schalke. It was one of the most memorable games of my whole career. I scored twice at Maine Road, and maybe because I'd missed a few games, I was that bit more determined. Possibly Malcolm knew this and thought: "I'll just leave him out for a couple of games to see if it gets him going again". He had a lot of confidence in my ability to score goals and, looking back, maybe it was the right thing to do.

The Leeds-Chelsea FA Cup Final finished 2-2 on Saturday, 11 April 1970. City meanwhile were preparing themselves for one of the biggest games in their history. The Leeds-Chelsea replay would coincide with the Final of the European Cup-winners' Cup and would feature significantly in City's history 18 days later.

Trailing by one goal from the first-leg, the Blues obeyed Allison's instructions to the letter and attacked Schalke from the outset. In the 8th minute Doyle had levelled the tie and by half-time Young had scored two trademark left-footers to give City a 3-0 lead on the night. Lee and Bell scored goals four and five before Libuda stabbed home a consolation goal in the last minute. Corrigan had broken his nose in a training accident earlier in the day and apart from picking the ball out of the net right at the end, had little to do apart from stand back and watch as his team-mates destroyed Schalke with one of the greatest attacking displays ever seen in European football. Quite simply on the night, City were awesome and thoroughly deserved the standing ovation they got at the end.

There was no hiding the satisfaction of City's management. Joe Mercer: "A great performance – it really was thrilling to watch. They played as Malcolm Allison and I wanted them too – full of flair, drive and imagination – and tore Schalke apart. We can talk tactics all the week, but the players have to go out and do the job. They did so admirably." Malcolm Allison: "We are not worried whether it is Gornik or Roma in the final. Both are good sides but we fear no one. We shall try and have a look at next week's play-off. Football teams are rather like racehorses – you train them to reach their peak on special occasions – and we want to produce our top performances when it counts, in Cup football." Even the shell-shocked Schalke coach, Rudi Gutendorf, was honest in his assessment: "We are shattered. Manchester City kept coming at us and we could do nothing about it. I'm sure they will win the Cup-winners' Cup now."

Malcolm Allison remembers

I suppose, looking back, I was, like Joe, a bit disappointed with the result in the first-leg against Schalke. Again, like Joe, I wasn't disappointed with the performance. We'd played really well against a good side in a tough game. Back at Maine Road we played brilliantly, one of the greatest nights of my life. I remember their coach (I think he was Germany's Coach of the Year) shaking his head afterwards saying: "I've never played against anything like in my life." Francis Lee suggested we went out for a drink after the game to a restaurant I part-owned with Freddie Pye in city centre Manchester. We had a good meal and two or three bottles of champagne. The following day Freddie Pye goes in and says to one of the staff: "How much did we take last night?" The reply was: "£390 Mr. Pye". Freddie was pleased: "£390, good. Who was in then?" "Malcolm was in," said the member of staff. "Malcolm eh," says Freddie. "How much was his bill?" "£340" came the reply! "Did he pay you?" said Freddie. The lad said: "No he signed it!"

Leeds United, a team like City with their minds on a Cup Final at the end of the month, were next to feel some of the power unleashed on the Germans in midweek. City exacted revenge for the controversial defeat at Maine Road back in November with a convincing 3-1 victory. For City it was good to see Harry Dowd once again back between the posts but perhaps the biggest plus factor was the continued good form of Neil Young in attack. Young opened City's account with a stunning 30-yard drive that went in via the underside of the bar. It was the only goal of a first-half that had started with the nice (if somewhat un-Leeds-like) gesture of the Yorkshire side lining up on the pitch to applaud City for reaching the final of the Cup-winners' Cup. Their kind sentiments, although greatly appreciated, did little to moisten Blue eyes as City continued their good work in the second-half. Bell made it 2-0 after 50 minutes and could have made it three moments later when his long-range effort struck a post. City didn't have long to wait before Towers did increase the lead before Rod Belfitt scored for Leeds towards the end of a game entirely dominated by City. The Blues managed three goals at Elland Road without the services of Francis Lee. He was busy scoring for England in a 1-1 draw with Wales in Cardiff.

And so to Sheffield Wednesday on Wednesday, 22 April, for the last League game of another remarkable season. If Sheffield Wednesday had won, they'd have stayed in the First Division at the expense of Crystal Palace on goal difference. Unfortunately they encountered a City side who by now had decided against helping out any more charitable causes and lost 2-1 to be relegated after 11 seasons. Already without Corrigan, Bell and Lee, City lost Summerbee in the 22nd minute with a recurrence of his leg injury sustained at Wembley. He was immediately declared doubtful for the final against Gornik. Summerbee's replacement, Bowyer, had been on the field for less than ten minutes when he scored with a left-foot volley after good work by Oakes and Young. This goal came shortly after Doyle had contrived to smash his penalty-kick straight at Peter Grummitt in the Sheffield goal. Former City favourite Tony Coleman levelled the scores in the 65th minute and City (with their minds no doubt on other things) appeared to have settled for a point until Bowyer (apparently no one had told him) headed home Young's cross in the 90th minute to condemn Wednesday to the Second Division.

Summerbee was still a doubt as City flew out to Vienna on Tuesday, 28 April for the biggest game in the club's history, the European Cup-winners' Cup Final at the Prater Stadium. Another doubt was the size of City's following prompting secretary Walter Griffiths to say: "We just don't know how many are going. Fourteen 'planes, dozens of cars and coaches and goodness knows how many travelling by rail and sea are making the trip."

In the end, Heslop played at the expense of Summerbee, who was fit enough to take his place amongst the five named substitutes. As for supporters it was estimated that some 4,000 had made finally made the trip to the rain-soaked open-air stadium. The game was televised live on Austrian television, and this, coupled with the dreadful weather, produced a disappointing crowd estimated to be in the region of 15,000. Unfortunately, the game was not broadcast back home, the pride of place being given to the FA Cup Final replay between Leeds United and Chelsea at Old Trafford. Imagine an English club today reaching the final of a European tournament and the game not being show. It just would not happen.

But for all the complaints about the weather, the crowd and the lack of television coverage, the game itself brought huge delight to anyone connected with Manchester City Football Club. The Blues won 2-1 to lift their first European trophy and became the first English club ever to win both a domestic and European trophy in the same season. Neil Young and Francis Lee scored the goals that enabled the players to share a win bonus of £32,000 between them. In the 12th minute Lee cut in from the left and fired a skidding shot across Kostka in the Gornik goal. The goalkeeper could only parry the greasy ball into the path of Young who gratefully accepted the offer. Three minutes before the interval, Young was again involved in the thick of the action. Having collected a through ball, he was in the process of rounding the stranded Kostka when he was unceremoniously body-checked inside the penalty-area. The power of Lee's resulting kick took the ball through the legs of the goalkeeper and City went into the break with a two-goal cushion but without Mike Doyle who'd earlier dislocated a knee.

Neil Young remembers

I've never seen rain like the downpour we had in Vienna. I think it was the last time they've played a European Final in an uncovered stadium. Everybody was absolutely drenched and I honestly didn't think we'd finish the game. I was at a dinner with Frannie not so long ago and he told me he thought that the Final was our best performance in Europe. I was involved in both goals, scoring the first after the goalkeeper had blocked Frannie's shot. For the second, I was trying to take the ball around the goalkeeper and he just went for me. I don't even think he was looking at the ball; he just made a beeline for me and Frannie scored the penalty. It was fantastic achievement and it meant that Manchester City was a name on everyone's lips and was a force in Europe.

With nothing to lose, the Poles came out for the second-half with all guns blazing and in the 69th minute captain Ozlizlo pulled a goal back. The goal set up a furious last 20 minutes but in the end the Blues held firm, indeed when substitute Bowyer missed a great chance at the end, City could have won by a bigger margin. Tony Book yet again collected a piece of silverware and was hoisted high into the rainy Vienna skies by his delighted team-mates. It was becoming quite a habit for the 'old man'.

Tony Book remembers

And then Vienna! It was amazing if for no other reason than the weather. It was a great day with the sun shining and I can remember going outside for a walk and it was glorious. As soon as we got to the stadium the bloody heavens opened! What few fans were there were all huddled together and it just poured down for the whole 90 minutes. But what another Cup performance! When I looked round the stadium and saw the small crowd I thought "this is a bit disappointing for a Final". It just wouldn't happen today. Wherever the game would be played you'd be guaranteed a full house. Despite the heavy rain it dampen our performance or our spirits afterwards. I remember going back to the hotel for a party and there's Harry Godwin playing the piano with Francis Lee – dressed in just his underpants – singing and dancing on top. What a night!

If there was only one drawback on a memorable evening, it was the absence of chairman Albert Alexander. The little man who'd done so much to restore the fortunes of Manchester City missed their greatest achievement as he was recovering from an operation in a Manchester hospital. The first thing Joe Mercer and Malcolm Allison did on their return was to take the trophy round to the hospital. Joe Mercer later told Peter Gardner of the *Manchester Evening News*: "You should have seen his eyes sparkle when he saw it. I only wished he could have been there to see us win it."

Malcolm Allison remembers

It wasn't the first time I'd been to the Prater Stadium. I'd done my National Service in Austria, in Vienna, and I'd seen Austria against Italy there and I'd also played on the pitch in an army game. It was in Austria that I first got the taste for training and coaching. I picked up things over there that I brought back with me to England. I could never have believed at the time that some 20 years later I'd be coaching a side there that had just won the European Cup-winners' Cup. Me, a lad from Bexleyheath in Kent: it really was amazing. The weather on the night was awful. I could never understand the stadium there with no roof on it. In the south of France or Portugal, somewhere like that then OK, but not in Austria, mind you if United had have been playing you could have guaranteed a beautiful night! I was so proud of all of the players. When I think of them, how'd they come through, come up, and worked and worked and worked, it was a credit to them. A lot of them had been with the side in the Second Division days. There were also a lot of local lads, in fact, the sides that won the Championship, the FA Cup and the European Cup-winners' Cup were made up entirely of Englishmen, something that could not possibly happen today. We'd finally conquered Europe, a bit later than I'd initially predicted, but nevertheless we'd done it.

1970-71
Another One for the Injured List

WHAT with the injuries and gunshots experienced in America last summer, City decided to try somewhere else for their pre-season tour this time around. On 10 May they drew 1-1 with a Western Australia side in Perth. It was the first of seven games played in 20 days and the only one in which City failed to win. On the return journey from Sydney to Fiji, City were joined on board their aircraft by comedian Jimmy Edwards who no doubt continued to put a smile on the faces of some already very happy footballers.

Tony Book remembers

The tour to Australia will live with me forever. Not just the footballing side, although we did manage to win a few games, but it was just a great place to go to. Like the rest of the players, I'd never been there before and it was just a fantastic place. The other thing I remember is how well we were treated. The sponsors of the tour were Wills the tobacco people and everywhere we went we had first-class accommodation. Everything was right about the tour. I'll always remember Mike Summerbee on that tour. Even though he had a broken leg – which was in plaster – he still came on the trip and everyone took it in turns wheeling him around the place!

With five trophies – including the First Division Championship and the European Cup-winners' Cup – in five years, Manchester City were on top of the world, a major footballing force both at home and in Europe. And yet, as the saying goes "all good things come to an end", although as the 1970-71 season began, little did anyone know how quickly those halcyon days would be over.

Although they'd finish the season comfortably placed in a mid-table 11th position and reach the semi-finals of the European Cup-winners' Cup, based on the high standards they'd set themselves, the season would be one of great disappointment.

If the club wasn't helped by a string of long-term injuries to key players on the pitch, it certainly wasn't helped by the boardroom unrest off it. Malcolm Allison in particular was angered by the apparent reluctance of some who thought City were still a 'small club' in spite of their recent remarkable successes. He was also frustrated by the fact that he was unable to take over as manager from Joe Mercer. The story goes that when Mercer and Allison first got together in the summer of 1965, Joe is alleged to have said: "Just give me two years Malcolm, then it's all yours." However Mercer could not possibly have known the scale of what was to come and understandably wanted to continue. It began to put pressure on the close working relationship of Joe Mercer and Malcolm Allison.

The injuries and boardroom activities were some way in the future as City opened the season on 15 August with a 1-1 draw at Southampton. Mike Summerbee had the unfortunate pleasure of being the first player anywhere to be sent off in the season when he was dismissed in the 86th minute for allegedly head-butting Saints' David Walker. So bizarre was the decision (both players had collided going for a loose ball) that even Walker's team-mates were amazed by the referee's actions. As the teams walked off at the end of the game, Francis Lee had a few words with Walker in the tunnel over his 'gamesmanship'. Colin Bell had earlier scored City's goal in the 24th minute following Summerbee's free-kick, only for Ron Davies to head home an equaliser with just over a quarter of an hour left. In the end a draw was fair to both sides and it began a run of eight games before the Blues' first defeat. Four days later Alan Oakes provided the only goal of the game (with City's first shot on target) at Crystal Palace in front of 33,000. Palace had a goal disallowed for offside and in John Jackson, had by far, the lesser occupied of the two goalkeepers. It was a game many felt, including some honest Blues, the best team on the night lost.

Without both Booth and Young for the first two games, it had been a good start. Booth's replacement was the ever-dependable George Heslop but Young's was a new face in City's colours. Freddie Hill had been a £10,000 May signing from Halifax Town and brought with him no shortage of skill as well as 13 years professional experience, 12 of which were spent at Bolton where he was a team-mate of Francis Lee. It was Hill's jinking run and cross that enabled Oakes to score the winner at Crystal Palace.

The first home game of the season was played in front of 36,599 spectators, uncomfortably squashed into three sides of the ground owing to the Scoreboard End being demolished to make way for the new, covered North Stand. Burnley provided the opposition but unfortunately neither side could provide a goal. Towers played as a sweeper, a strategy that enabled six City players to attack at any one time, but unfortunately they constantly ran into a well-organised Burnley defence, behind which Tony Waiters in goal was outstanding. The game against Burnley was the first of 12 home fixtures in 38 days, a fact which no doubt kept the administration staff on their toes!

Two thousand more fans watched City's next game against another Lancashire neighbour, Blackpool. Captained by the immensely experienced Jimmy Armfield playing in his 600th League game, the Seasiders returned home empty-handed thanks to first-half goals from Lee (24 minutes) and Bell eight minutes later. Lee even managed to miss a penalty; his effort saved by Harry Thomson. Interestingly enough the referee for this game was a gentleman by the name of Mr Fussey. Can anyone remember whether or not he lived up to his name? Young and Booth were both back in the side for the game against Blackpool and it was the first time that season that Mercer and Allison could name their strongest forward line. Because of the severity of the injuries, the names Summerbee, Bell, Lee and Young would only appear together 11 times during the whole campaign. Another statistic confirms that of those 11 games, seven were won, three drawn and only one lost.

A trip to Harry Catterick's Goodison Park was always difficult back in those days. However City maintained their terrific run of League form and thanks to Bell's fifth-minute header, they came away with both points to disappoint the large majority of the 50,000 crowd. Had City's finishing been better on the day the scoreline could easily have been five, and according to the *Daily Telegraph*, Everton were "outplayed, outclassed and tactically bewildered".

Before City's next League game, players and staff enjoyed a few days break as they travelled to Italy for their first (and only) excursion into the Anglo-Italian Cup. As League Cup holders they'd been invited to take part in the two-legged tournament and played Bologna, Italy's current Cup holders. To take advantage of some late summer sunshine, City based themselves in Rimini on the Italian Riviera, some 80 miles from Bologna itself. It was a tournament City treated almost like a serious training session and despite fielding a full-strength team, they lost the first-leg by a solitary goal on an oppressively hot night. Italian international Franco Rizzo scored after just three minutes, and apart from Lee, Doyle and Towers, City generally underperformed in the Stadio Comunale.

Bell was enjoying some of his best football in a City shirt and he continued his goalscoring efforts with two more in a 4-1 win at West Bromwich, this after City had gone behind thanks to a goal by Bobby Hope. Summerbee (helping in Young's shot) and Lee (from an acute angle) scored the others and, had two claims for penalties been awarded, the winning margin could have been more and still would not have been unfair to the home side. Such was City's attacking prowess on the day, it was difficult to see if any defence could have withstood it. That win at The Hawthorns moved the Blues into second place behind Leeds United with the newspapers regularly praising their performances. Along with Bell, another individual was also earning great praise. 18-year-old Tony Towers, already an England Youth international was being tipped by many as a player capable of going on to great things.

The first major disappointment of the season came at Second Division Carlisle United in the second round of the League Cup. The Blues turned in a poor performance, lost 2-1, and with it the defence of one of their trophies at the first attempt. Only Lee's 60th minute equaliser provided any consolation on a bleak, wet and windy night and it was a sad way to lose a cup they'd fought so hard for last time out. The Blues defence faltered regularly under constant pressure and to make things worse also lost Doyle when he was carried off near the end with a badly bruised thigh. Malcolm Allison remarked City made more mistakes in that one game than they'd made so far in the whole season. For the record, Carlisle's scorers were Dennis Martin and the prolific (and much-travelled) Bob Hatton.

139

Neil Young remembers

We played poorly at Carlisle and got exactly what we deserved. The conditions were terrible and of course the result meant we'd lost one of our trophies at the first attempt. What was more disappointing for me was that we were going well in the League but against Carlisle we were shocking. I'd already missed the start of the season because of an injury I'd picked up on the tour to Australia. I got a cut on my left leg that got infected and took ages to clear up. Everyone was sick about the defeat at Carlisle.

The disappointment of Carlisle seemed to have no bearing in what, at least up until then, had been an excellent League campaign. When Notts. Forest visited Maine Road three days later, the sides were separated by the fully-recovered Mike Doyle's 25-yarder, one that won the game and kept City up with the First Division leaders. Overall it was a largely defensive game and it was the fourth consecutive one in which Forest had failed to score.

City's defence of their second trophy, the European Cup-winners' Cup began on 16 September against the Irish part-timers, Linfield. For the first time since Fenerbahce, City's name came out of the hat first thereby forcing them to play the first-leg at home. Once again, City struggled against a side – on paper at least – they should have beaten easily and had it not been for Colin Bell's 83rd-minute goal (a close in effort after McAllister in the Linfield goal had misjudged Oakes' cross) they'd have travelled to Belfast two weeks later with no advantage at all. Linfield, managed by the former Everton player Billy Bingham, had certainly done their homework on City and were unlucky not to return to the Emerald Isle with at least a draw. The Blues found it difficult to break down a massed midfield which in turn restricted the number of scoring opportunities. The whole manner of City's play seemed to have shifted alarmingly in just a couple of months. For the last two seasons they'd saved their best performances for the Cup competitions whilst the League appeared to be of secondary importance. This time out though it was the complete opposite. They were playing some great football in the League and were right up at the top whereas they'd played poorly in two cup-ties, losing one and being very fortunate in the other. The pattern would change again before the season was out.

Neil Young remembers

I think the game with Linfield was very similar to the one with Fenerbahce in as much as I don't think Malcolm had them watched. We all thought it was going to be an easy game, no problem. However we'd got to the point when there were no easy games anymore. They had one or two useful players and the whole side played above themselves but overall we played badly. Had it not been for the away goal rule we'd have gone out of the European Cup-winners' Cup at the first time of asking as well.

Stoke City were brushed aside at Maine Road less than 72 hours after the difficulties encountered against Linfield. City won easily 4-1 against a side that had won the previous week against League leaders Leeds United, with goals from Book (his first for three seasons), Young and Lee, and, unusually, a Gordon Banks own goal, but the game was perhaps indicative of the entire campaign. Certainly no one who saw it could be prepared for what was to follow. Neil Young's goal was his first of the season in the League. For the man who'd scored many crucial goals over the past few seasons, amazingly it proved to be his last. Tommy Booth was carried off in the first-half with an injured knee, tests later revealing he'd need a cartilage surgically removing. He did not play another League game until 12 December. In a terrible season, Booth was the first of seven first-team players to be struck down by long-term injuries. Summerbee also injured a knee in the game (this time ligaments) and with City down to ten men in the last few minutes, Mike Bernard pulled a goal back for the well-beaten visitors.

Once again George Heslop deputised for Booth and managed to score a rare goal in the 2-2 return draw with Bologna in the Anglo-Italian Cup. Unfortunately the result meant City's attempt to bring more silverware to Maine Road had failed, although the game did entertain more than 25,000 people and provided the opportunity to see Freddie Hill back in the first team and Francis Lee score his fifth goal of the season. In a bruising game, City created four times as many chances as the Italians but still managed to trail twice thanks to goals from Perani and Savoldi. Interestingly Heslop scored with his left foot whilst Lee's goal came from a header.

City's terrific run in the League came to an abrupt end at White Hart Lane in a 2-0 defeat. Having disposed of Coventry and Blackpool in their previous two home games – both without conceding a goal – Spurs inflicted the same on City thanks to goals from Martin Chivers and Alan Gilzean, one in each half. It was Tottenham's fourth consecutive win in the League and was inspired by the performance in midfield of Alan Mullery, a man criticised by Allison during the recent World Cup in Mexico. If he was trying to prove a point, he certainly managed it.

The Blues then travelled to Belfast for the return game against Linfield with injury doubts over the scorers against Bologna, Heslop and Lee. Both players were given stern tests prior to the game and in the end it was Lee who was passed fit with Heslop eventually being replaced by the maturing Derek Jeffries. The work put into getting Lee fit paid off when he scored for City after six minutes, his goal in reply to Millen's shock strike two minutes earlier. Lee's goal proved crucial as Linfield produced more of the same form showed at Maine Road and rallied magnificently to take a 2-1 lead thanks once again to Millen. The second goal came from a free-kick after Book had bitterly complained following an incident when Corrigan was struck on the leg by a missile thrown from the terraces. Linfield could so easily have won the tie in the dying minutes but in the end City – having shown temporary glimpses of their true form – hung on, and, somewhat fortuitously, progressed to the next round where the opponents were one of the greatest European sides of the 1950s, Honved of Hungary. Despite the defeat, the Irish had every right to feel proud of both their performances against the current holders of the European Cup Winner's Cup. One critic told Peter Gardner of the *Manchester Evening News*: "Linfield are out, but this is one of the greatest moments in the footballing history of this country."

Of City's 13 games played so far, they'd only managed to score more than one on four occasions, with one of those games being against Bologna. They were unable to improve on this in the next game against Newcastle United at Maine Road. City were yet again out of sorts whereas Newcastle were regularly performing better away from home, the theory being that there was less pressure and expectations away from St.James' Park. Thanks to a 76th minute headed goal by Doyle, the match finished 1-1 after David Ford had opened the scoring for the Geordies. Corrigan in goal was having a bad run of form and he was responsible for Newcastle's goal when he allowed Wyn Davies' looping header to evade him and drop into Ford's path. As an aftermath to the game, City's playing staff were instructed to report to the ground on Monday to be examined in an all-out attempt to combat the stomach virus that had affected them all week. Firstly Summerbee and then Book (who missed the Newcastle game) contracted it, with Doyle, Bell and Oakes all ordered home to bed straight after the game.

Nearly 52,000 witnessed another 1-1 scoreline at Stamford Bridge seven days later. Bell scored his sixth League goal of the season (a stunning volley from Oakes' long cross in the 21st minute) only for Keith Weller to equalise for Chelsea five minutes before the break. The home side then had two goals disallowed but with Corrigan back on song in goal, a draw was no more than City deserved.

Anyone doing the pools regularly that season must have loved City. For the third successive Saturday they played out a 1-1 draw, this time against Southampton. The Saints played their usual no-nonsense style of punishing tackles and trying to stifle their opponents, but despite these methods City played their best football for some time although they still remained guilty of being unable to convert several clear-cut chances. In a largely one-sided affair, Ron Davies had given Southampton the lead with a left-foot shot after half an hour, an incident Peter Fitton of *The Sun* described as: "an act of sheer piracy". City's equaliser came in the 73rd minute when Lee rose above Southampton's back four (christened 'The Wild Bunch' in the press) to head home Hill's delicate chip.

Neil Young had not featured in the first team since the defeat at Tottenham three weeks earlier. In an attempt to regain both form and fitness he played (if that's the right word) in a 4-3 win for the reserves at Huddersfield on the same day as Southampton were 'stealing' a point at Maine Road. In the very first minute of the game at Leeds Road, Young collected an injury that would keep him out of the game for seven weeks. He suffered a 12-inch gash on the inside of the shin which, when coupled with the severe bruising and swelling, would have done justice to Hollywood's finest make-up men. Ironically he never touched the ball before the tackle took it out of play for a throw-in. The injury prevented him from walking for five days and with goals currently in short supply, it could not have come at a worse time.

Neil Young remembers

I got an absolutely shocking injury in the reserves at Huddersfield. I still wasn't quite right and Joe played me in the reserves to try and get back to full fitness. We'd just kicked off and I hadn't even touched the ball when I went running towards it along with their full-back. I think he was under orders to nail me early one because he never went near the ball; he just went straight for me and I ended up in the second row of the stand. There was blood everywhere; my leg was in a right mess. Joe went berserk at their manager Ian Greaves afterwards and I was out of action for weeks.

There were also injury doubts about Book, Towers and Oakes in preparation for the European Cup-winners' Cup. All three had suffered an assortment of bruises against Southampton but in the end it was only Oakes who missed out. On the BEA charter flight the day before the game, physio Peter Blakey now had seven players under treatment.

Contemporary reports put the crowd anywhere between 6,000 and 14,000 at The Kispest Stadium in Hungary for City's game with Honved, the Blues' first-ever competitive game behind the Iron Curtain. Either way it was a disappointing turn-out for a European clash and the fact that the game was both an afternoon kick-off and shown live on national television appear to be the main reasons for the apparent lack of support. Both sides were currently third in their respective Leagues but the Hungarian Cup holders provided little concern to a City side returning to top form and with Lee again on target in Europe after a well-worked free-kick by Bell and Summerbee. So superior was City's performance that they were reported to have created 15 clear-cut chances with one newspaper saying the 1-0 win "could easily have been 5-0". Nevertheless City had once again shown their preference for playing the away leg first and had a vital away goal to show for their efforts. Honved had beaten Aberdeen in the first round but found City a completely different proposition. The Blues stroll in the park suffered one minor setback when Colin Bell was kicked in the head, the injury requiring two stitches and an x-ray.

Derek Jeffries still replaced Oakes as City slumped to their heaviest defeat of the season so far, a 3-0 defeat at Wolves on October 24. Only Bell played to anything like his true form although both Lee and Summerbee threatened occasionally, especially when Summerbee hit a post. Despite Bell grazing the top of the crossbar in another rare attack, the home side were far more productive and thanks to two goals from Bobby Gould and Jimmy McCalliog's penalty, they ran out easy winners on the day. In a nutshell, Wolves defended much the better of the two sides and were well worth the two points.

Tony Book remembers

We'd already lost our League Cup when we didn't play at all well against Carlisle. We then played the Irish part-timers of Linfield in the European Cup-winners' Cup and we nearly slipped up there as well. They did ever so well in both legs, especially at Maine Road to keep us to a 1-0 win. We were getting used to the European stuff by the time we played Honved. We'd had some difficult games and travelled to some difficult places – Fenerbahce for instance – but we understood that that was their way of life and we had to get accustomed to it. You come to live with it. When we played Honved back here it poured down with rain all night but bad as it was, we used to really like playing in those sorts of conditions. Whatever type of conditions we used to come up against we could always adapt to them better than the opposition and I felt that was one of the strengths of the team. When I think of some of the surfaces we played on back then, and the pitches today, well there's no comparison. I see a lot of grounds nowadays that are as good at the end of the season as they are at the start. The quality of pitches today, what with all the new technology and science, has been a huge improvement in the game as far as I'm concerned.

By the time Ipswich Town visited Maine Road on 31 October, City had slipped to seventh place in the First Division, admittedly not a complete disaster but a position that still concerned Joe Mercer. "What's missing is primarily a few goals and I thought we looked a bit jaded at Wolves last week," were his comments in the matchday programme. The game against Ipswich – a side that had not won away in more than a year – provided a perfect tonic for Joe. City won 2-0 with a fierce left-footer from Lee, and Bell with four minutes to go, supplying the goals. It was the ideal preparation for the return leg with Honved.

In conditions not too dissimilar from the great night in Vienna just over six months earlier, the Blues adapted better than the Hungarians and won comfortably 2-0 to progress further in Europe. If Towers had been brilliant in the first leg, tonight was Bell's turn. The England midfielder was outstanding despite being injured and being forced to leave the field in the first-half. He returned to the action for the start of the second-half to a huge reception from the fans and with a new, dry, numberless shirt. Bell had already opened the scoring after 17 minutes with a well-struck shot after a typical burst through the Honved defence. Oakes then had a goal disallowed before Lee clinched the game with a deflected shot in the 67th minute. The result didn't really confirm the Blues' superiority; Corrigan cutting a lonely figure standing the heavy rain. Joe Mercer commented after the game: "There is no doubt that the ground conditions saved them from a heavy defeat." Honved's manager, Kalman Preiner was also impressed with City: "If they continue to play like that, they must surely win the trophy again." City had to wait until March the following year to see if his comments would prove to be true. Old adversaries Gornik stood next in their way.

With Book missing because of a groin strain (and with him a huge calming influence on the side) another trip to the Midlands proved fruitless for the Blues as they went down 2-1 at Coventry. For the neutral it was a great game to watch with both sides producing some fine football and chances at either end. Unfortunately for City they ran into Bill Glazier in the Coventry goal who turned in an inspired performance and stopped almost everything City could throw at him. Bell, Towers, Lee and Bowyer in particular were all denied until Bell finally managed to pierce his defences in the 75th minute after good work by Oakes. Obviously still inspired by a Fairs Cup win over Bayern Munich four days earlier, Coventry's goals came courtesy of Mike Doyle in only the 2nd minute and Willie Carr 15 minutes later. Bearing in mind the old saying 'football is all about opinions', the *Daily Mail* commented: "A 5-1 scoreline to Coventry would have been appropriate". Meanwhile a series of corners and heavy City pressure in the final minutes prompted the *Daily Mirror* to pen: "How desperately close City came to saving this match".

Before the next League game, the Blues took the short trip across Manchester to take part in a testimonial game for United's long-serving centre-half Bill Foulkes. The gesture to appear was the only generous point of the whole affair as a determined City romped home 3-0 in front of 26,000 with Mike Doyle gleefully ramming home a penalty.

Two home games in a week preceded arguably the biggest incident of the season at Maine Road. The Blues hosted firstly Derby County and then West Ham prior to huge press coverage and speculation concerning a proposed takeover of the club.

Having replaced Book at Coventry, Arthur Mann then took over from Pardoe against a Derby County side that took the lead in the first-half through John O'Hare. Colin Bell equalised in the 75th minute when he out-jumped both goalkeeper Les Green and Roy McFarland to power home a header from Summerbee's cross. It was Bell's fourth goal in as many games and City were now 6th, seven points behind Leeds. Against West Ham, it was now Hill's turn to miss out. He had to watch from the sidelines as Mann – after 'gathering dust' for months at full-back in the reserves – unusually played outside-left and turned in an outstanding performance causing many to think he was better suited as an attacking player. Lee rediscovered his goalscoring touch with a goal in each half in the 2-0 win against some erratic defending. Once again Corrigan was a spectator, not having a shot to save until an hour into the game.

By this stage of the season, Malcolm Allison had now reached the end of his tether. Still angered at "constantly being patted on the head" he wanted sole control of the team and set about getting it. He'd heard that vice-chairman Frank Johnson was interested in selling a vast amount of his shares (rumoured to be more than 500) for £100,000. If Allison could come up with this amount of cash he'd get his wish. In turn, Allison then contacted Ian Niven, a lifelong City fan and publican, and a man who would later find himself on the board, to explain the situation. Niven suggested that a man by the name of Joe Smith, a double-glazing tycoon from Oldham, might have both the interest and necessary cash to be just what Allison was looking for.

Smith was indeed interested and on the morning of Monday, 23 November, he was at the house of chairman Albert Alexander with a proposal. So early was Smith's unexpected call, that the chairman hadn't yet had time to change out of his pyjamas. Smith had certainly done his homework very quickly as he knew the state of play at the club. He knew that there were currently 2,000 shares in Manchester City, and told Alexander that with Johnson's shares providing the bulk, he was confident in obtaining the sufficient majority holding very quickly. Smith also had the support of Ian Niven, Simon Cussons of the famous soap-making family, former City director Chris Muir and Manchester-based solicitor Michael Horwich.

The national newspapers picked up the story very quickly and within a few hours it was front-page news. A board meeting was arranged 24 hours after Smith had visited Alexander's house. Allison was promised the full support of the new board (should of course there actually be one) as well as a 20-year contract. It was just what he wanted to hear. Albert Alexander on the other hand – a determined little man and Blue to the core – felt differently about any changes, as did Joe Mercer. It was clear to see that there was now an obvious division within the club, with two crucial people – Mercer and Allison – on opposite sides.

Malcolm Allison remembers

Whatever you want to call it, whether it be ambition or ego, it finally reached the point when I wanted to be called team manager. I felt I could still work with Joe but now it would be me having the final say so. I wasn't bothered what title they gave Joe. Another thing that really got to me was the apparent small-mindedness of some of the directors. I'd helped to make Manchester City one of the top sides in the country and these men were still concerned about the size of hotel bills for away games. These were the reasons behind me organising a takeover of the club. I knew that vice-chairman Frank Johnson was ready to sell a large amount of shares for £100,000. With that in mind I got in touch with Ian Niven, a staunch City supporter, to see if he knew someone who could come up with that sort of money. He recommended a double-glazing tycoon from Oldham by the name of Joe Smith. Smith was keen to get involved, even to the tune of offering me a 20-year contract, and I left for a few days break in London whilst all the paperwork was sorted out. When I got back I learned that it wasn't going to be that easy and I was going to be sacked after a game at Leeds. It was then that Joe saved me by saying that if that was the case, then he'd go as well. I was grateful to Joe for giving me his backing but as he'd already said he fully supported the existing board, I began to have doubts whether or not our relationship would ever be the same again. Eventually changes were made on the board and I finally got my wish, although my new contract was nowhere near 20 years and was so full of holes even my solicitor couldn't get it right despite months of hard work. In turn Joe was never really happy with his title of simply 'Manager' so I suppose you could say the new board proved to be no good for either of us.

Not surprisingly the board meeting produced some heated debate. It also produced a change of mind for vice-chairman Frank Johnson. Once he knew who supported Smith's bid – especially Chris Muir and Michael Horwich – he felt he'd been misled and he promptly withdrew his shares from sale and gave his full support to the current board. With Allison being so supportive of the new regime, it became obvious that his place at the club was now in jeopardy. He was even challenged by Messrs. Lee, Bell and Summerbee who told him in no uncertain terms to leave things alone.

Francis Lee escaped all the unrest – at least for a while – whilst on England duty. He scored the first goal in England's 3-1 win against East Germany at Wembley and won the plaudits of all the newspapers with a man of the match showing. When Lee opened the scoring, it was England's first goal since the 3-2 defeat by West Germany in the Mexico World Cup some five months earlier. On the same night, an Australian X1 played at Maine Road as part of a European tour. Mercer and Allison saw the game as an opportunity to blood some of the younger players – eight in all – who proved more than a match for the visitors in a 2-0 win;

Paul Smith and Mike Brennan scoring the goals that meant the Aussies lost their hitherto unbeaten run.

Tony Book remembers

All the talks of take-overs and the like made it a trying time for the club but from the players point of view we made sure we didn't get involved. There's a lot of politics in the game and that's one aspect of football I've never enjoyed, even though I've also been through it as a manager. But as a player, I didn't even think about it. As far as I was concerned the players were there to play. I'm of the opinion that if someone has got something to say to you then they say it face to face and don't say it through the media. They should be able to look you in they eye and tell you what's going on. If things like this go on for too long then it can affect the players, especially if the results start to go wrong. People start looking for excuses and that's what they hang their hat on. As a club we'd had a lot of success and could well have done without this sort of distraction. Joe and Malcolm were a fantastic team; Joe was the great PR man and calming influence and Malcolm was the one who did all the work with the players. Not surprisingly both of them wanted the title of manager and you can't blame either of them for that. Malcolm felt because of his efforts he'd earned it but then, human nature being what it is, Joe didn't want to give it up either. It really got to be a no-win situation. Can you blame anyone for not wanting to let go of anything that's been so successful?

The situation off the pitch simmered away all week and on the Friday before the game with Leeds at Elland Road, Allison was taking a training session on the Maine Road pitch. Joe Mercer came out and told him the directors wanted to see him, adding: "You're on your own now, Malcolm." Allison went to the boardroom expecting the inevitable, namely the sack. He was asked to explain why he felt all these changes were necessary but the meeting broke up with Allison still an employee of Manchester City and with the game at Leeds to look forward to. On the coach journey to Yorkshire there was another change of heart, this time by Joe Mercer, the man who's job seemed the most precarious should Joe Smith take control.

According to Gary James' authorised biography of Joe Mercer, *Football With a Smile*, Mercer told Allison: "Son, I have thought it over and it's you and me together. We are this bloody club." Perhaps not too surprisingly City lost 1-0 to a Leeds side who welcomed back after four matches, the influential Scottish duo of Billy Bremner and Eddie Gray. Johnny Giles missed a penalty and Peter Lorimer hit a post before Allan Clarke scored the decisive goal eight minutes into the second-half. City could not get going, especially in midfield and even a change of referee could not help them. Maybe the players weren't as focussed on the game as much as they should have been, but who could blame them? Don Revie provided scant consolation when he said: "It was our best display at home all season." After the game Albert Alexander met both Mercer and Allison in a corridor under the stands at Elland Road. Alexander told Allison his services were no longer required and he was to be sacked with immediate effect. It was now that Mercer was true to his word when he said: "If he goes, I go." Mercer's decision prevented the distribution of the prepared press statement and kept the relationship together at least for the near future although it was perhaps never exactly the same again. The irony of the whole situation though was that both men wanted Manchester City to be a great club, but came at it from totally opposite directions. Of course there is a strong case saying that they were already a great club.

Neil Young remembers

There was a lot of talk going on about the boardroom changes and I think it all got a bit too much in the end. I thought it would have been better all round if it could have been kept a bit quieter. Because of my leg injury – I was just really hobbling about, nowhere near fit – and the fact that I don't like watching, I just stayed away from the ground whilst a lot of this was going on. I read a lot in the papers and there was an air of uncertainty around the place and I'm sure in the end some of it rubbed off on the players although really we were just the same bunch of lads. Malcolm wanted to be called 'manager'. As far as the players were concerned Joe would always be 'boss' and Malcolm would always be coach. Looking back I suppose if Malcolm felt so strongly then maybe he should have gone somewhere else at the time, but who can blame him for wanting the job at City? By the same argument, who can blame Joe for wanting to stay on? Not long after Joe had gone to Coventry, Malcolm moved on as well, so in the end all the changes made no difference. In fact they just spoiled things for everyone.

The following week, Arsenal, a side City had not beaten since returning to the First Division in 1966, were keen to extend that run to nine games and did so with a 2-0 win. City played Jeffries alongside Heslop in a new formation at the back but it made no difference as City lost their unbeaten home record and any Championship aspirations they might have had in the Maine Road mud. The new formation lasted just five minutes when Heslop left the field with a dislocated shoulder. Doyle followed not long afterwards and with Towers limping through most of the second-half, nine-man City hung on until the 75th minute when George Armstrong broke the deadlock. Up until then Bob Wilson had been much the busier of the two goalkeepers. In the very last minute John Radford scored Arsenal's second to seal the victory and City dropped to ninth in the League, still four points and five places above their next opponents, Manchester United.

If Arsenal were keen not to lose their record against City, then the same could also be said for the Blues against their oldest rivals. With Booth and Young welcomed back into first-team action after similar two-month absences, City once again destroyed the Reds in their own backyard, the 4-1 scoreline kept to reasonably manageable proportions only by the sterling work of Jimmy Rimmer in United's goal. City's fourth successive League victory at Old Trafford was inspired by a 17 minute Francis Lee hat-trick. Doyle (17) and Lee (42) gave City a 2-0 lead by half-time but saw team-mate Glyn Pardoe stretchered from the pitch midway through the half with a badly broken leg after a collision with George Best. In the second-half of a fiercely competitive game – Lee, Best and John Fitzpatrick were all booked – City continued to rip United's defence to pieces as Lee completed his hat-trick with a 53rd-minute shot and a header five minutes later. Corrigan had spent most of the afternoon avoiding a shower of missiles hurled at him by the distraught United followers and did not have a shot to save until Brian Kidd beat him with one in the 74th minute. The severity of Pardoe's injury – he wouldn't play again for nearly two years – took the edge off another Old Trafford triumph.

Neil Young remembers

I was really close to Glyn when George Best tackled him. I can still remember his leg going up somewhere near his neck. Glyn was in a terrible state. I don't think there was any malice in it. There will always be bad tackles but players don't deliberately go out of their way to injure another one. These things happen in football and unfortunately that was the outcome of it.

Tony Book remembers

I went to see Glyn the day after the injury and he really was in a bad way, so much so that Joe put an embargo on any of the players talking to the press about it. That embargo then caused a problem between Joe and me. A journalist found out I'd seen Glyn and got on to me to ask if he bore any malice. I innocently said no, it was just an accident and one of those things. That's what I said and as far as I was concerned was the end of it. Anyway the next day when the papers came out, he's printed an exclusive article that was a completely made up story, nothing like what I'd said to him. It was the only problem I ever had with Joe during all my time at Maine Road. George simply let the situation get away from him and he tried to retrieve the ball. I've seen him go in like that lots of times before and get away with it but unfortunately for Glyn this time he didn't. It was a terrible tackle and Glyn nearly lost his leg. I've always been a bit of coward with things like that but because I'd seen injuries before, as well as pictures, I knew straight away it was very, very bad one. I've always said that Manchester City would have won more trophies had it not been for the injuries to Glyn and Colin Bell. They were both great players, both very fit and could easily have gone on playing well into their 30s.

When City travelled to Burnley's Turf Moor ground seven days later, it was almost as though there had been no break in the play from Old Trafford. Once again the Blues were in rampant form and once again scored four, this time without reply. With Doyle and Oakes supporting the attack throughout, City constantly pressured the Burnley goal with up to seven forwards. Young made two goals for Bell whilst Doyle was the provider of the other two, firstly for Lee and then Summerbee. Things got worse for Burnley when – at 4-0 down already – Dave Thomas blasted a penalty over the bar after Oakes had been adjudged to have handled.

There was a definite shortage of the Christmas spirit at Maine Road on Boxing Day when City battled out a 1-1 draw with Huddersfield Town in a game constantly disrupted by fouls

149

Neil Young remembers

I wasn't finding the net a lot myself during this time but I was creating a lot for others, two for Colin Bell at Burnley spring to mind. I suppose I could have been a victim of my own success really. Once you start knocking a few goals in you get a bit of a reputation from other managers who tell their defenders to stick close to you. I never got any space at all around the box, I was always really tightly marked. To try and combat this Malcolm started to play me a bit deeper to try and give me more space and in the end I started making more than I was scoring.

and raised fists. The final result could have been a lot different had Young's shot not struck a post after just 50 seconds. The best crowd of the season so far – 40,091 – watched Book mis-kick a clearance past Corrigan to give the Yorkshire side the lead two minutes into the second-half. Fortunately, three minutes later, Bell was alert enough to intercept a backpass and levelled the score.

Northern Premier League side (and part-timers) Wigan Athletic were City's opponents in the third round of the FA Cup. Last week's record crowd was beaten by 6,000 as City, always on a hiding to nothing, took far too long to find any rhythm and consequently struggled for victory. Against a side containing player-manager Gordon Milne and former Everton player and Wembley winner Derek Temple, it took City more than 70 minutes to break the deadlock; Bell finally slipping the ball past Reeves in the Wigan goal. As with Linfield earlier in the season, City almost slipped up against a side supposedly of far less quality, however it should be said that overall Wigan matched the Blues on the day and most certainly enhanced their claims for League status.

Tony Book remembers

I always felt the game with Wigan would be a difficult one. Because I'd been in exactly the same position myself as a non-League player, I knew they'd raise their game against a big side that was going well. A non-League side going to a League side in the Cup is always a great leveller because they've got nothing to lose. A shock result is always a possibility; it's happened so many times and will still go on happening.

Back in the League, City then took on Crystal Palace without Lee whose recurring thigh injury had forced him to limp out of the Wigan game. Without him and with Young and Bell looking unusually out of sorts, Palace had little trouble in holding City's attacks at bay. Until that is, the 71st minute. It was then that the Londoners failed to clear a Hill free-kick completely and in the ensuing scramble, Book – an unlikely but nevertheless welcome source – tapped home what turned out to be the winning goal from close range.

City were now unbeaten in their last five games and seemed to have put all the boardroom wranglings behind them, at least on match days. It was at this time, with control discussions still going on off the pitch, that captain Book pledged the full support of all the players to the existing board. Fans (and players) just wanted a quick and amicable conclusion as soon as possible, one that would allow people to talk once again about City's ability with a football and not with a balance sheet.

Malcolm Allison remembers

The contrasts between Joe Mercer and myself couldn't have been any further apart. I was always jumping into situations and really aggressive with my comments. Joe on the other hand was calmness personified, forever pouring oil on the torrents of water I'd stirred up. When I joined him at Maine Road we both felt we had something to prove although everyone knew he was the boss. He knew what I could offer both him and the club, and as long as we were winning, he'd let me get on with things – on and off the pitch – my way. He also knew my one burning ambition, namely to be in sole charge of a successful side. I think most City fans know the story of our trip to Middlesbrough on the opening day of the 1965-66 season. This was when Joe told me: "Two years will do." By the time two years were up we'd won promotion and had almost finished rebuilding a side that was capable of winning the First Division. Not surprisingly Joe wanted to stay on. Hard as it was for me, I didn't – couldn't – blame him either then or now. With hindsight, if Joe hadn't said anything on the bus to Middlesbrough then things might have turned out differently in the end.

The unbeaten run continued in a goalless stalemate at Anfield. Two strong defences determined the outcome and the game evolved into a series of personal battles with neither side being able to create a clear-cut chance. City came closest when Hill shaved a post in the 35th minute and could have won the game with Bell's header right at the death but a win by either side was not truly deserved.

A visit to Blackpool in January could test even the hardiest of football supporters although on this occasion they were warmed by a free-flowing, attacking game, and one that provided six goals. After 62 consecutive games, Blackpool's Tommy Hutchison (later of course a Maine Road favourite) was left out by manager Bob Stokoe at his own request. Hutchison witnessed an amazing start when John Craven gave the home side the lead in the very first minute. Ten minutes later Fred Pickering, Hutchison's replacement, doubled their advantage. Another player with Maine Road connections, Tony Coleman, was the cause of a booking for Doyle and City were not really in the game until the 43rd minute when Summerbee flicked home Bell's cross. Pickering restored Blackpool's two-goal advantage 17 minutes into the second-half and then, with cries of "Easy, Easy" from the home supporters, City began to take control against a tiring opposition. Bell collided with a post whilst sweeping home City's second and then, with five minutes left, Summerbee crowned a fine personal performance with a looping header for the equaliser.

For the past few weeks Lee had been battling against an assortment of niggling injuries and was hindered even further by a kick on the hip at Blackpool on his return to the first team.

In order to get him fit for the fourth round FA Cup clash at Chelsea, he was given a solo, one-hour fitness test 48 hours before the game. Unfortunately it proved to no avail and he – along with Young who was dropped to the bench – missed the convincing 3-0 win for City. Bowyer and Heslop were the replacements as Bell's two goals in as many minutes in the first-half put the game out of Chelsea's reach. When Summerbee broke a bone in his right foot (an injury that would force him to miss the next four League games) it only added to Peter Blakey's already extensive workload. With five minutes remaining, Bowyer scored City's third goal from close range to crown a fine victory.

Leeds United maintained their position at the top of the First Division when they won 2-0 at Maine Road on 30 January. It was a game Joe Corrigan will want to forget as both Leeds goals were down to errors by the big City goalkeeper. In the 12th minute he dropped Terry Cooper's cross into the path of Alan Clarke and then 16 minutes later, mis-punched Johnny Giles' corner straight to a waiting Jack Charlton. Even without Billy Bremner and Peter Lorimer in the side, Leeds, with Norman Hunter outstanding, turned in a very professional performance that was just too good for the Blues. Over a post-match drink, Malcolm Allison admitted that Leeds were the best team in the country. The win put Leeds 12 points in front of City who slipped from third to seventh place.

Having just played the top team, City then travelled to second-placed Arsenal seven days later. Book missed the game with a back strain but travelled with the party and watched the game from the directors' box, his brief being to analyse the Blues' next opponents in the FA Cup. Book couldn't have seen much as it was generally a poor game that gave the impression neither side wanted to give too many secrets away. There was very little action at either end until the 84th minute when Bell's shot had 'goal' written all over it only for Bob Wilson to produce a magnificent flying save. Sixty seconds later Corrigan was at fault for the second week running when he failed to hang on to a shot from Peter Simpson and John Radford followed up to score the only goal of the game.

The fifth round FA Cup clash between the sides had to be postponed when heavy rain caused the Maine Road pitch to be waterlogged. The delay of four days gave Summerbee the opportunity to have the plaster removed and recover from his broken foot, but despite spending six hours at the Burnley home of physio Peter Blakey (along with some heat treatment equipment borrowed from the ground) he still couldn't make it. Further rain during the game made conditions even worse and it was Arsenal who adapted the better to win a lot more convincingly than the 2-1 scoreline suggests. Charlie George scored in each half for the visitors whilst Bell gave false hope to City supporters with a goal five minutes from time. As sporting as ever, Joe Mercer went into the Arsenal dressing-room after the game and said: "Well done lads, you deserved to win." The Gunners had not won the FA Cup since 1950; they'd not won the League since 1953. In just over three months, Bertie Mee's side would win them both again.

Jimmy Greaves celebrated his 31st birthday but had to contend with a point as City held West Ham to a goalless draw at Upton Park three days after the defeat by Arsenal. West Ham had not won at home since 31 October and as City were missing both Bell and Summerbee, the game had all the hallmarks of a nil-nil even before kick-off. The normally prolific Geoff Hurst and Francis Lee (playing as a lone striker) failed to convert clear chances with Lee coming the closest when his shot hit the bar.

Because of the Aston Villa-Tottenham League Cup Final being played on a Saturday, City made the long trip to Ipswich for an evening kick-off the day before. With the European Cup-winners' Cup clash with Gornik just two weeks away, Ronnie Healey (who would be travelling to Poland as Corrigan's understudy) was given his first opportunity in the League, Allison commenting: "He needs the experience." Ipswich played much better than their lowly League status implied although it was City who nearly took the lead in the 18th minute when a shot from Young was deflected by Mick Mills forcing Laurie Sivell to make a diving save. If Ipswich raised their game on the night then City lowered theirs, their performance causing the *Daily Telegraph* to note: "City did not look like a team that had won four trophies in three years." Future City player Colin Viljoen scored for the home side on the half-hour and the game was sealed when Frank Clarke made it 2-0 in the 61st minute.

At Wolves on 6 March City still missed Bell and with neither side at their best, particularly in attack, the game produced little action and no goals. Young had the best chance to break the deadlock but after collecting Lee's through ball, the photographers were in more danger than Phil Parkes in the Wolves goal. After going nine games unbeaten, City had now not won in their last six outings. Hardly the ideal preparation for a trip to Poland and the most crucial game of the season.

The Blues landed in Kracow some 70 miles from Katowice the day before the vital European Cup-winners' Cup clash with Gornik Zabrze to be greeted with literally mountains of piled high snow and frost and a temperature of minus 12 degrees. There was no snow on the Chorzow Stadium pitch at kick-off, although large parts of the playing surface were still frozen solid, and the temperature had 'risen' to the dizzy heights of minus seven. Not surprisingly the home side – searching for revenge after last year's Final defeat by the Blues in Vienna – were more accustomed to the conditions (even to the tune of wearing tights and polo-neck sweaters under their kit) and adapted much better. Despite City wearing special leather studs brought in from Germany, they found the surface very difficult and spent long periods slipping and sliding all over the place. The huge crowd of 100,000 (with nearly every one of them having access to either a hooter or a claxon) made a cacophony of noise and urged the Poles to a 2-0 win. Lubanski, Gornik's star player, was back from injury and opened the scoring after 55 minutes with a glorious left-foot shot from just inside the area after a superb move had opened up City's defence. Five minutes later, Wilczek made it 2-0 after Corrigan had blocked his first shot. Allison was disappointed about the result claiming over the past few games City had simply stopped running. He went on to say: "We were all right at the back but produced nothing up front." Mercer accepted the fact that City were down, but not yet out: "We can't complain about that; it was a fair result. But I've not given up on this one yet. Let's see what we can do at Maine Road." City would have to perform much better if they wanted to keep both hands on their European Cup-winners' Cup.

The following League game with Derby County continued in the same pattern as a lot of City's games so far this season, namely no goals but more injuries. Corrigan's elbow injury gave Healey another opportunity, whilst in the game itself, Summerbee broke his left leg just above the ankle (his third break in 12 months), Book dislocated a shoulder (out of action for a month) and Oakes' damaged cartilage would force him to miss the rest of the season. With nine fit men and a limping passenger, the Blues did well in the end to hold the home side who felt robbed in the last minute when John O'Hare's 'goal' was disallowed for pushing. Before City's next game, Malcolm Allison was 'invited' to the FA headquarters to explain remarks he allegedly made to the referee during the 4-0 win against Burnley back in December. He would hear the decision of the meeting a two weeks time.

With four teenagers in the side and an average age of 24, City's next opponents were Coventry. For the second time this season, Bill Glazier in the Coventry goal was the difference between the two sides, one particular save from Young proving exceptional. John O'Rourke had given the visitors the lead in the 31st minute and despite all the pressure, City had to wait until the 85th minute for an equaliser. Even then it came from a twice-taken penalty after Glazier had been adjudged to have moved whilst saving Lee's first effort.

One of the younger players drafted into the side was Ian Mellor, a tall, gangling winger and the replacement for Mike Summerbee. He proved an influential figure in the return game with Gornik at a swamp-like Maine Road on 24 March. If the snow and ice had favoured Gornik at home, they could not handle the heavy Manchester rain as well as a rampaging City side who attacked them form the first whistle. Against a Gornik side containing seven internationals and playing their 11th consecutive season in Europe, City hit the woodwork three times before Mellor finally headed in Donachie's cross four minutes before half-time to give the Blues a real chance. There was more of the same in the second-half. Mellor put Doyle through on goal in the 67th minute only for the midfielder's shot to bounce back off goalkeeper Gomola. Doyle responded quicker than anyone to head the ball home and level the tie. In the final minute City could have won when Bowyer's shot was controversially kicked off the line by a player who seconds earlier had been receiving treatment by the physio at the side of the goal. It was undoubtedly a tremendous performance by City, especially after the recent poor showings in the League and the terrible run of injuries, with 12 of the 20 first-team players used saying it was the side's best showing of the season. City and Gornik would need to be separated by a third game with neutral Copenhagen chosen as the venue.

27 March, FA Cup semi-final day, a visit to West Bromwich Albion and another goalless draw (their fifth) in the League. Only Bell seemed untroubled by the exertions of the win over Gornik and if Mellor had done well on Wednesday, the same couldn't be said on the Saturday. He missed three glorious opportunities, including an open goal, to win the game for City.

Albion had at least 90 per cent of the attacks but came up against Healey who was once again in fine form standing in for the injured Corrigan.

Forty-eight hours after coming away with a fortunate point from The Hawthorns, Malcolm Allison received his sentence from the FA. He was to be banned from all footballing activities at Maine Road for two months, the ban coming into force the following Monday. The ban really did mean everything; he couldn't even watch games at home, although the FA did concede that they could not prevent him travelling to away games purely as a spectator. Allison's crime was 'bringing the game into disrepute' following remarks made to referee Bob Matthewson during City's 4-0 win over Burnley on 19 December. City's flamboyant and outspoken coach was livid with the decision saying that its severity was purely because it was given against him. "Anyone else would have got away with it", he argued.

The growing confidence of the youngsters would undoubtedly cause selection problems in the future but for the time being, Mercer and Allison had no other option but to play four of them – Healey, Donachie, Towers and Jeffries in the replay with Gornik. On a cold, wet night, 12,000 saw City win 3-1 in the Idraetspark Stadium in Copenhagen. When Young fastened on to a pass from Lee and drilled a low shot past Kostka it was the first time in 229 minutes that City had led in the tie. With seven minutes to go until half-time, Booth headed in Towers' free-kick to double the Blues' advantage. In the 57th minute Lubanski pulled a goal back for Gornik and City then had Healey to thank for a point-blank save from Skowronek as the Poles pressed hard for an equaliser. Lee clinched the tie with City's third goal when Bell's shot had been partially saved by the diving Kostka in the Gornik goal. City had overcome a highly talented Gornik side under difficult circumstances to progress once again to the semi-finals of the European Cup-winners' Cup. Their opponents would be the English Cup holders Chelsea, although their visit to Copenhagen wasn't quite over. Surprised by the fitness levels of the City players, Gornik President Ernest Wyra demanded a drugs test, with Bell's, Connor's and Jeffries' names being the ones drawn from the hat. Not surprisingly after their efforts, none of the players could provide the necessary sample despite the offer of orange juice (which was taken) and Allison's champagne (which wasn't). It came as no surprise to anyone – except possibly a still angered Gornik President – that when tests were finally taken, the results proved negative. It was a farcical end to another great European night for Manchester City.

Neil Young remembers

It was absolutely freezing in Poland and it was the first time I'd ever seen footballers wearing women's tights! We lost over there and won at Maine Road to set up a replay on a neutral ground. We played well in Copenhagen, I scored one and I think I had a hand in one as well. I remember their captain, Lubanski (who'd also played in the Final against us) came to see me after the game and said he'd warned his team-mates to 'keep an eye on that Neil Young' which I thought was a nice compliment. Then of course we had the saga of the drug tests. It took the lads about three hours to have a pee!

Alf Ramsey was at Maine Road for the last game (at least for time being) in which Allison could have any bearing, a 3-0 win against Everton. Continuing their efforts from Copenhagen, Ramsey was impressed by the youngsters as City outplayed the visitors who were without the influential Colin Harvey in midfield. Doyle, Hill and Booth all scored in the first-half to give City an easy victory. Another home game followed on Good Friday against Notts. Forest although there was nothing good about the outcome. Forest won 3-1 with Healey and Jeffries adding their names to the apparently never-ending casualty list. Healey dislocated a finger to be replaced in goal by Doyle, a man who always fancied himself as a bit of a goalkeeper, and when Jeffries tore ankle ligaments, it gave substitute Book his first game in a month. Before deputising in goal, Doyle had equalised 20-year-old Duncan McKenzie's opener but in the second-half, Tommy Jackson and McKenzie again (in only his second League appearance) secured the points.

Twenty-four hours later, City welcomed back Corrigan but lost 1-0 at Huddersfield in what was generally thought of as a negative performance, at least as far as City were concerned. A confident Huddersfield side turned in one of their best performances of the season but despite long periods of possession were unable to convert their superiority into goals. They had to wait until the 79th minute when Trevor Cherry headed home a free-kick to decide the outcome.

As far as the League standing was concerned, the trip to Newcastle on Easter Monday was really a meaningless game. The only good thing was the result, a 0-0 draw, usually not thought of as a classic but with Newcastle having taken nine points from their previous six matches, it was a well-earned point. City gave debuts to two 17-year-olds, Jeff Johnson and Steve Carter, a young midfielder who nearly won the game for City when, with Liam McFaul in goal beaten, Bobby Moncur hooked his shot off the line. However the game also produced three more serious injuries, all of which were completely unwelcome with the first leg of the European Cup-winners' Cup semi-final with Chelsea just two days away. Corrigan turned in a sparkling performance despite losing the sight of one eye after a kick in the face; Doyle collided with Newcastle centre-half David Young and left the field with knee damage, followed in the 75th minute by Colin Bell with a similar injury. Despite being officially banned from all footballing activities, Allison had contacted Mercer prior to the Newcastle game and suggested strongly that both Doyle and Bell should be given a day off. When Mercer played them both, and then both got injured, Allison was livid. He described it as "the blackest moment".

Whilst Mercer and Allison were disagreeing, City's injury list was seemingly never-ending and there was still some disharmony off the pitch, Altrincham-based businessman and City supporter Peter Swales went out for a quiet drink in a pub in Hale Barns. Also in the pub were directors Sidney Rose (the club doctor) and John Humphreys. Never one to miss an opportunity, Swales went over to them and offered his services as a peacemaker. Even by his own admittance, Swales wasn't sure exactly what he could or would do to remedy the situation in the Maine Road boardroom. Whatever he said or promised certainly impressed Albert

Maine Road to Wembley!

F.A. CUP FINAL, 1969
Manchester City Players'
Official Souvenir

2/6

The City players produced their own souvenir brochure for the 1969 FA Cup Final.

Cup-winning City players are greeted by their fans back in Manchester's Albert Square.

Joe Mercer holds aloft the FA Cup to ecstatic City supporters after the 1-0 Wembley victory over Leicester City.

1969 F.A. CUP FINAL

MATCH COMMENTARY
HIGHLIGHTS

By arrangement with
BBC RADIO ENTERPRISES

MANCHESTER CITY 1

LEICESTER CITY 0

No videos or DVDs in those days but in 1969 City supporters could buy a 12-inch LP and relive the BBC wireless commentary of their side's FA Cup Final victory.

Still showing off that FA Cup. This time Joe Mercer is joined by a triumphant Malcolm Allison.

The ball used in the 1969 FA Cup Final, shown here on display at Maine Road.

Alan Oakes heads clear at Turf Moor in August 1969 as Joe Corrigan watches. Ian Bowyer scored for City in the 1-1 draw.

Colin Bell heads City's second goal against Atletico Bilbao in the Cup-winner's Cup first round second-leg match at Maine Road in October 1969.

City pictured in July 1969. Back row (left to right): Alan Oakes, Colin Bell, Mike Doyle, Glyn Pardoe, Tony Book. Middle row: Malcolm Allison, Arthur Mann, Tommy Booth. Joe Corrigan, Harry Dowd, George Heslop, Dave Ewing. Front row: Ian Bowyer, Bobby Owen, Neil Young, Tony Coleman, Francis Lee, Mike Summerbee, Dave Connor.

A young Joe Corrigan finally established himself in the City first team in 1969-70 and went on to make a remarkable 604 senior appearances and win nine England caps.

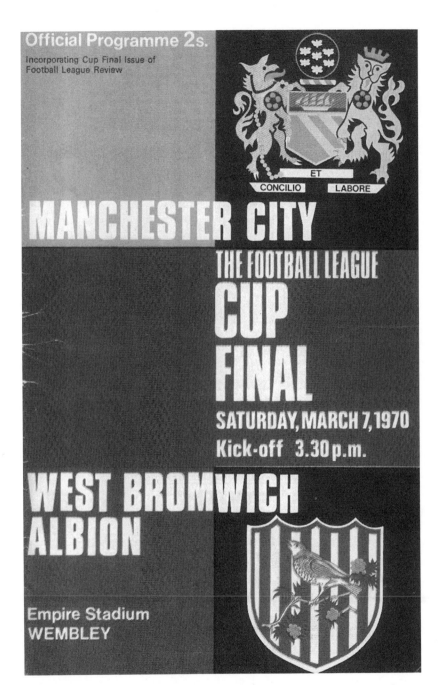

MANCHESTER CITY

THE FOOTBALL LEAGUE
CUP
FINAL

SATURDAY, MARCH 7, 1970
Kick-off 3.30 p.m.

WEST BROMWICH ALBION

ET
CONCILIO   LABORE

Empire Stadium
WEMBLEY

In March 1970, City returned to Wembley to meet West Bromwich Albion in the Football
League Cup Final.

163

Tony Book is chaired by his team-mates and Francis Lee takes an imaginary sip of champagne from his tankard. City have just won the League Cup with an extra-time victory over West Brom.

Ticket for the 1970 European Cup-winners' Cup Final between Manchester City and Gornik Zabrze on a rainy night in Vienna.

GRATIS

**29. APRIL 1970
EUROPACUP-FINALSPIEL
DER POKALSIEGER**

MANCHESTER CITY – GORNIK-ZABRZE

HERAUSGEGEBEN
VOM ÖSTERREICHISCHEN FUSSBALL-BUND
IM AUFTRAG DER U. E. F. A.

Programme for the 1970 European Cup-winners' Cup Final between Manchester City and Gornik Zabrze.

It's becoming a familiar pose as City skipper Tony Book is chaired by his team-mates, this time with the European Cup-winners' Cup.

Manchester City's playing and coaching staff at Maine Road before the start of the 1970-71 season, with the European Cup-winners' Cup and the Football League Cup.

Francis Lee (far left) beats England World Cup goalkeeper Gordon Banks to score in City's 4-1 win over Stoke City at Maine Road in September 1970.

City's George Heslop gets in a tackle on Spurs' Alan Mullery at White Hart Lane in September 1970. City lost 2-0.

Mike Summerbee dives in to score in City's 4-0 win at Burnley in December 1970. The Clarets' goalkeeper is Peter Mellor. Colin Bell and Colin Waldron look on.

Francis Lee gets up high for a header at Upton Park in February 1971 watched by teammates Mike Doyle (far right), Tommy Booth (left) and Ian Bowyer. The Hammers players are Bobby Moore (6) and Peter Eustace. The game ended 0-0.

City pictured in August 1971. Back row (left to right): Peter Blakey (physiotherapist), Willie Donachie, Mike Doyle, Tommy Booth, Glyn Pardoe, Ron Healey, Joe Corrigan, George Heslop, Tony Towers, Alan Oakes, Derek Jeffries, Malcolm Allison. Front row: Colin Bell, Wyn Davies, Freddie Hill, Tony Book, Francis Lee, Ian Mellor, Mike Summerbee, Neil Young, Dave Connor.

Back room boys in August 1971. Ken Barnes, Joe Mercer, Harry Godwin and Johnny Hart.

Willie Donachie finally established himself in the City team in 1971-72 after first getting his chance when Glyn Pardoe suffered a broken leg. He went on to become one of the best full-backs in the First Division in the 1970s and was capped 35 times for Scotland.

Francis Lee made his League debut at 16 against Manchester City before he went to Maine Road as a 23-year-old for £60,000 in October 1967. He went on to make 328 appearances for City, scoring 148 goals, many of them from the penalty spot. He won a host of club honours and 27 England caps. In 1971-72 he scored a club record 15 penalties for City.

Looking forward... City's first-team squad in August 1972. Back row (left to right): Willie Donachie, Mike Doyle, Tommy Booth, Joe Corrigan, Tony Book, Tony Towers, Derek Jeffries. Front row: Rodney Marsh, Francis Lee, Colin Bell, Mike Summerbee, Wyn Davies, Ian Mellor.

And finally... September 1973 and Francis Lee is still smashing them home from the penalty spot. This time Chelsea goalkeeper Peter Bonetti stands no chance at Maine Road, where City eventually won 3-2.

Mike Doyle missed only one League game in 1971-72 to continue a remarkable City career that had begun back in the pre-Mercer-Allison days of 1963-64. By the time he left for Stoke City in June 1978, Doyle had made 565 senior appearances for City and won five full England caps.

The great entertainer Rodney Marsh was signed from QPR for £200,000 in March 1972. Opinion was then divided, many feeling that his style had disrupted that of the current City side.

Alexander's side of the table and Joe Smith's as within a few short weeks Swales found himself a director of Manchester City Football Club. In October 1973, just two and a half years later, he had progressed to chairman. By the start of the 1971-72 season Joe Smith and Simon Cussons were also on the board, with Chris Muir and Ian Niven both following within 12 months. It seemed that Peter Swales had indeed delivered on his promise as harmony was returned, and football itself, at least for the time being, became the number one priority.

City went into their biggest game of the 1970/71 season without the services of Doyle, Oakes, Summerbee and Bell. Even with those four stalwarts in the side, the European Cup-winners' Cup semi-final, first leg, at Chelsea would always be a difficult game. The Blues' line-up contained 17-year-old Jeff Johnson for only his second senior outing and Joe Corrigan, still with one eye partially closed after the kick received at Newcastle. Up front, Lee tried manfully to keep the Chelsea defence occupied with his usual forceful running, but with City mounting a rearguard action for most of the evening, he was left on his own for long periods. Despite his injury, Corrigan's handling was excellent and some fine defending from the back four supported him. After a goalless first-half, City went behind to a goal a minute after the break scored by Chelsea's South African-born inside-forward Derek Smethurst. It was the only goal of the game and could prove crucial over the two legs. Joe Mercer was delighted with the result adding a cautious: "Of course we still have to win the second-leg." So too was Tony Book: "It was fantastic performance. We're not going to give the Cup up easily."

By a strange quirk of fate, City's next opponents in the League, three days later, were Chelsea, this time at Maine Road. Once again the Blues had little option but to play their by now reasonably experienced youngsters, whereas Chelsea made eight changes from the side named in the programme. It was obvious where their priorities lay. In the 56th minute, Keith Weller intercepted a mis-directed pass from Mann to race through and beat Corrigan. With ten minutes left on the clock, Lee rose above the Londoners' defence to head home Young's free-kick for the equaliser. A draw was a fair result but had Chelsea been sharper up front, they could have stretched City's inexperience to the limit. The match programme for the Chelsea game gave an up-to-date list of City's casualties: Bell-cartilage, Doyle-knee ligaments, Corrigan-eye, Bowyer-as Doyle, Jeffries-ankle, Healey-dislocated finger, Pardoe-broken leg, Summerbee-as Pardoe, Oakes-knee, Carrodus-ankle and reserve team player John Gannon-as Carrodus and Jeffries. Even the secretary Walter Griffiths had been in hospital with a back injury. But the most serious injury belonged to Paul Smith, a young, skilful midfield player who'd fallen through a roof on an out-building whilst training behind the Platt Lane Stand. He'd gone on to the roof to reclaim a lost ball and suffered severe head injuries as a result of the fall. He was unconscious for two and a half days and advised not to head the ball again. Regrettably the injuries prevented him from ever playing in the first team; something everyone at the club was certain he would achieve.

With the exception of Lee who put himself about with his customary gusto, everyone else in the side seemed content on avoiding injury at Stoke in the 2-0 defeat on 24 April. With that in mind, it is perhaps surprising that it took the home side until the second-half – thanks to John Ritchie and John Mahoney – to decide the issue. 'Banks of England' in the Stoke goal remained untroubled all afternoon.

With a line up of Healey, Towers, Donachie; Heslop, Booth, White; Carrodus, Johnson, Bowyer, Mann and Carter, (eight under 20) a 2-2 draw against Liverpool in the next game was a remarkable result. What made it even more remarkable was that Booth was replaced after 11 minutes with an injured knee, and 17-year-old debutant Howard White broke an ankle four minutes later but played on until half-time. Liverpool – with one eye on the FA Cup Final with Arsenal in less than a fortnight – featured a good number of reserves in their side as well and twice took the lead through Bobby Graham. City's first equaliser came when substitute Mellor's cross was headed into his own goal by Liverpool's centre-half Ian Ross, just one of three goals coming in as many minutes around the half-hour mark. In the 84th minute Carrodus was hauled down in the penalty area, giving Steve Carter the opportunity to convert the resulting spot-kick 'like an old-timer' and give City a deserved share of the points.

Corrigan had recovered completely from his eye injury only then to be struck down by a boil on his knee. The timing couldn't have been worse, coming on the same day as the return leg with Chelsea in the semi-final of the European Cup-winners' Cup. Once again Healey deputised, this time with unfortunate, and costly, repercussions. Summerbee was back in the side for his first game in six weeks but with six regular first-teamers still missing, the task of ruffling the feathers of a calm Chelsea defence was once again left to the solitary (albeit imposing) figure of Lee. Chelsea took control of the midfield very early on, and in the wizardry of Charlie Cooke they possessed not only the most influential player of the game, but also one of the most skilful of his era. Two minutes before the break Keith Weller's inswinging free-kick brushed Connor's back on its way towards goal. Healey misjudged the ball and could only help it into the net by his near post. It was the only goal of the night; Chelsea had won the tie 2-0 on aggregate and had reached a European Final for the first time in their history. Scant consolation for City was that Chelsea went on to beat Real Madrid in the Final so at least the trophy stayed in England. After the game Joe Mercer commented to reporters: "We can't argue about that – they played very well. We didn't get into the game at all in the first-half. We didn't even throw the ball forward and although we played a lot better after half-time, we couldn't break through. Full marks to Chelsea; they deserved it."

Neil Young remembers

We did really well at Chelsea and I thought the 1-0 defeat was a good result for us because of all the injuries we'd had. I thought we had a great chance at Maine Road but it just wasn't to be. We did everything that night apart from score. It only takes a couple of injuries and a couple of players off form to disrupt a side. We had far too many injuries, none of them were minor either, they were all long-term, and in the end it just proved too much for us.

Although the season finished with two home League games – against glamorous opposition in the shapes of Tottenham and Manchester United – the defeat by Chelsea really did put a dampener on things. Even Bell decided to miss the Spurs game; he'd gone into hospital the night before to have his cartilage operation. The 1-0 defeat had all the hallmarks of a typical end of season game even down to the crowd; only 19,674 bothered to turn up. Spurs' next game – just 48 hours later at home to Arsenal – was the Championship decider, and, despite what manager Bill Nicholson said, their players appeared to treat the game at Maine Road as no more than a training session in readiness for the vital clash. The visitors' style of play seemed to encourage City to do the same and a generally weary, sad and depleted Blues even managed to concede a bizarre, decisive goal. In the 44th minute a shot from Alan Gilzean beat Healey but was headed off the line by Towers. Steve Perryman tried again with the rebound, only to see the ball hit Healey's body, then Towers' toe and then a post before finally sneaking into the net. Although primarily a midfielder, Perryman did exactly what all top goalscorers would do; he claimed the goal.

For the visit of Manchester United on Wednesday, 5 May, the crowd had swelled to 43,636 and witnessed the proverbial 'seven-goal thriller', although as far as City were concerned, the goals weren't shared out as they'd have liked. It was to be Matt Busby's last game in charge of the Old Trafford side – including their fairly useful triumvirate of Best, Law and Charlton – and his players were determined to put on a show for him. Both teams lined up and welcomed Busby on to the pitch, as did another surprise guest; Eamon Andrews and his 'big red book' invited him to be a guest on *This Is Your Life*. As for the football itself, City were 3-0 down at half-time, with Charlton opening the scoring after 14 minutes, then Law and Best adding two more in a minute shortly before half-time. Two minutes after the break Hill pulled a goal back before Best scored his second in the 72nd minute to restore United's three-goal lead. Lee on 79 and Mellor 85 gave City fans a glimmer of hope for an astonishing draw but in the end it just wasn't enough. The two points earned by United leapfrogged them over City in the final standings; City finished 11th with 41 points whilst United (who were 12th on goal average before kick-off) finished 8th with 43 points. If 'typical end of season game' had been directed at the Tottenham match, then the same could certainly be said about this one.

Tony Book remembers

Because of the shoulder injury I got at Derby I missed the two other games with Gornik, the return at Maine Road and the replay in Copenhagen. I was back for the Chelsea games in the semi-final when we had to play a lot of the youngsters because of all the injuries we had. We fought really hard in both those games but unfortunately lost by a single goal both times. One thing those injuries did though was to give opportunities for the young players to see how they stood up to the first-team. We had the likes of Derek Jeffries, Willie Donachie and Tony Towers who were all very good players and the fact that they'd come through was typical of the kind of structure in place at City during all my time there. There was always a nucleus of good young players – a lot of them local – on the outskirts of the team. Even if you look at our successful sides, there were people like Mike Doyle, Glyn Pardoe, Alan Oakes and Neil Young, all terrific players who'd come through the ranks. For a long time this seemed not to apply any longer at City although I am delighted to say that in recent times there have been some really terrific youngsters coming through.

Joe Mercer summed up the season in the programme for the United game: "It's difficult to be constructive about this season, in terms of hard results. Whatever we say it will sound like excuses – which I don't like. It began well. We were second from the top with a game in hand and not even playing as well as we should have been. Since then, apart from a few bad results, we have had to reconstitute the side so many times that what the scoresheet says hasn't revealed half the story. We've won nothing in terms of silverware. But we have greatly improved the depth of our first team pool; a lot of young players who were quietly and efficiently learning their profession now know much more about what is required of them. All the world knows about our injuries. It's been a particularly hard season for those players. It's been hard too for the fit ones. It's not easy playing in a constantly changing side. It's been equally frustrating for the spectators. I shall be pleased to see the back of this season – and that's something I never thought I could say. I believe a lot of our supporters will feel the same. But the prospects for next season must be good…plenty of players, plenty of experience. It's a racing certainty that in a few weeks we shall be aching to get back, fit and raring to go. And I'm sure our supporters will feel the same."

1971-72
Lee One Pen

THE previous summer tours were greatly reduced this time as City travelled to Chester, Port Vale and Doncaster at the end of July, registering three wins, seven goals and three clean sheets on the way. Two 1-0 defeats followed on a short tour to Germany, one of the sides, Hertha B.S.C. being invited back to Maine Road for a return game in September.

There were lots of things new at Maine Road prior to the season's opening game with Leeds on 14 August. One new face belonged to the towering figure of Wyn Davies, the Welsh centre-forward signed from Newcastle United for £52,500 on 2 August. Davies had long been admired by both Mercer and Allison and would prove the ideal foil for his former Bolton team-mate Francis Lee in the months to come. Something else new on the playing side was the pitch itself. Stan Gibson had overseen major work done both below and on top of a playing surface that had come in for some criticism on occasion last year. Although with nearly six inches of rain recorded in Manchester in November last year, some of that criticism may have seemed harsh. Under Allison's instructions, Gibson had also made the pitch two yards wider. There were also new names, if not unfamiliar ones, on the board of directors. Joe Smith, Simon Cussons, Peter Swales and Reuben Harris, the joint assistant manager of Great Universal Stores, all found their names listed in the programme. The new North Stand was open for public use after two years under construction although the likes of turnstiles and bars would not be completed for a few months yet. Pride of place in the new stand went to a state-of-the art electronic scoreboard. At a cost of £11,000 and 90ft in length, it was supplied by a Bolton-based company who also made the one currently in use at Wembley and had already secured the order for the one to be used in the 1972 Munich Olympic Games. Fans would no longer have the pleasure of gazing up in wonderment on the sight of A2-1 going up at half-time. The last new thing was Allison's idea for training. He reckoned that team's were conditioned to be 100 per cent fit from the start of the season, thereby running out of steam in the cold of December and January. His new emphasis would be getting the Blues at the peak of fitness at Christmas, in readiness for (hopefully) an attack on the Championship again. Francis Lee had missed a lot of these changes. He'd played five games in as many weeks for Cape Town City in South Africa. Although he took his wife and family with him, it must certainly have been a (most enjoyable) busman's holiday for the England player.

When the football did finally begin (with City at only 90 per cent fitness) they were still without Bell, Towers, Jeffries and Hill, legacies from the end of last year's horrendous injury crisis. They did, however, give Wyn Davies his League debut, who impressed despite losing the services of Summerbee from the wing when he left the field with a groin strain. Both goalkeepers were in fine form but it was the formidable Leeds trio of Billy Bremner, Johnny Giles and Paul Madeley that took control of the middle of the pitch and with it the game. Doyle, Lee, Jack Charlton and Norman Hunter all found their names into referee Clive Thomas's notebook in the usual hard-fought game between these sides. The odds on those four being booked must have been very short although there were plenty of other names (on both teams) more than capable of joining them. One single goal was always going to decide the outcome and unfortunately for the Blues it went the way of the visitors. In the 71st minute, Peter Lorimer broke through and fired a shot across Corrigan. The City goalkeeper got a good hand to it but could only palm it straight into Tony Book's body as he was desperately trying to get back.

Tony Book remembers

I said at the start of the season that I felt we had a good chance of winning things again and I really meant it. Because of all the injuries last season we'd played a lot of youngsters and it was great to see them coming through. Apart from Colin Bell we were also over the injury problems we'd had with the seniors and we'd just signed Wyn Davies. Even though Wyn was a traditional target man, we never altered the way we played. We'd always had good players so no matter who was up front, that was our target. It was never our intention to look for Wyn all the time; if we could pick him out then we did. Wyn was a good player in his own right but was terrific for Francis Lee. Frannie lived off Wyn all season. Wyn did very well all season then went to United at the end in what I thought was a strange decision.

City had just four days to forget about the defeat by Leeds as Crystal Palace travelled north for a Wednesday night fixture. On a lovely summer's evening, City really did go for a 'stroll in the park' and brushed aside the visitors 4-0. Lee opened the scoring with a 9th minute penalty after John McCormack had fouled the same player. City's lead increased in the 25th and 31st minute when first Lee, and then Booth headed in Young's crosses. On the rare occasions when Palace did threaten, they found Corrigan in impeccable form. Meanwhile, his opposite number, John Jackson, was constantly under siege and had a torrid night. The second-half had 'the atmosphere of a pre-season friendly' according to the *Daily Telegraph* with no further goals until the 89th minute when Wyn Davies got his first in City's colours.

City's next game was at Chelsea, a side with star player Peter Osgood in the line-up despite recently being put on the transfer list because of 'unsatisfactory performances'. Unfortunately for City he did not have one of his off days on 21 August. He made two goals – for Tommy Baldwin and Keith Weller – and City were up against it after just 25 minutes. Six minutes after the break, Lee won and converted a dubious penalty and then equalised after being put through on goal by Mellor's decisive pass. Donachie replaced the injured Book in the 67th minute and as City pressed for the winner, Chelsea's beleaguered defence held out for a draw in a game they must have thought they'd won at 3.30.

City then lost 2-1 at Wolves in a game they should have won easily. They made enough chances to win at least half a dozen games but gave such an erratic performance in front of goal, their only reward was an 87th minute penalty, scored yet again by Lee. Captaining the side for the first time in Book's absence, on this occasion Lee did not win the penalty himself; the honour fell to Mellor who was brought down by full-back Bernard Shaw. Wolves' first win of the season was earned by a goal in each half. After 20 minutes Kenny Hibbitt curled the ball round Corrigan following a cross by former City favourite David Wagstaffe and then in the 75th minute, Jim McCalliog clinched the points with a 20-yarder. City dropped to 11th in the League with Wolves now overtaking them. The surprise leaders were newly-promoted Sheffield United with a maximum eight points from the first four matches.

The Blues welcomed back Colin Bell (still, in his own words "only 80 per cent fit") against a hitherto unbeaten Spurs for the fifth game of the season. After just six minutes Bell gave City the lead but for some reason, Allison's men then sat back and let the visitors take control of the game. A series of corners put Corrigan's goal under pressure and then, in the 44th minute, and completely against the run of play, Summerbee scored a fine opportunist goal to double City's advantage. Allison had plenty to say in the dressing-room about such a disjointed first-half showing, his message obviously getting through as City were much more composed after the break. In the 58th minute Davies headed in Summerbee's cross for City's third goal and his second in five League games for City. He had now scored as many as he did in the whole of last season for Newcastle. Lee completed the scoring after 77 minutes when his 25-yard shot deflected off Terry Naylor before beating Pat Jennings.

Next up was a hard-fought clash with Liverpool, a game that remained goalless until the 49th minute. It was then that Davies headed down Summerbee's corner for Mellor to beat Ray Clemence with a dipping shot. With Larry Lloyd, Tommy Smith and Alec Lindsay in defence, Liverpool were in no mood to take any prisoners although when Connor was forced to leave the field with a damaged right ankle the offending player was the mild-mannered Peter Thompson. Never could this fast, direct winger be classed in any way a dirty player and after the game he publicly apologised to Connor for the accident. Connor meantime had his leg in plaster and would be out of action for three weeks. With Liverpool only showing an inclination to attack in the last 15 minutes, the 1-0 victory was no more than City deserved.

Neil Young remembers

I never really got into the side this season, one that turned out to be my last. I knew Malcolm had wanted to sign Rodney Marsh for a long time and the only way he could afford him was by selling me. Ian Mellor came into the side on the left so I knew my days were numbered from early on in the season. Looking back I'm sure we'd have won the League that year had we have not bought Rodney. No disrespect to Rodney, he was a great player, but he just didn't fit in with our style of play at that time. He disrupted the way we'd been playing for the last five or six years.

After convincing wins against two of the country's top sides, City then played out a dour, goalless draw at Leicester. Once again Davies had the beating in the air of the opposition defence but this time failed to create much panic owing to the lack of service. Lee came closest to scoring when he hit a post and later forced Peter Shilton into a terrific diving save. The point was City's eighth and moved them up to sixth spot, five behind the still unbeaten Sheffield United.

A break from the rigours of the League came in one of the most attractive League Cup-ties in the trophy's 11-year history. In a wonderful attacking game, City found themselves twice two goals behind but managed to finally overcome Wolves by a 4-3 margin. Wolves led 2-0 thanks to John McAlle (22) and Danny Hegan (25) but Davies managed to give City some hope when his header pulled a goal back five minutes before half-time. In the second-half Derek Parkin restored the visitors' lead from the penalty-spot and there were no further goals until the 78th minute. That was the moment when a still not fully-fit Bell converted an overhead-kick, the first of three City goals in a six-minute spell. Lee earned and scored a penalty after being floored by Mike Bailey and then got the winner from close range after a cross from Davies. City's reward for a terrific comeback in a terrific match was a trip to Bolton in round three.

Tony Book remembers

As we got into the season we began to score a few goals. Once we got all the forwards fit, we always fancied our chances of scoring. It was simply the way we played. Even though Neil Young wasn't in the side much – he'd been terrific for us over the last few years – we still had a lot of power up front. Ian Mellor had come in as Youngie's replacement and although he didn't look too much like a professional footballer, he had what I call, a 'good gate' on him. He could easily stride past people and developed into a good player.

Malcolm Allison's name was linked with the vacant manager's job of the Scottish national side as preparations were under way for the home game with Newcastle. Although it was another win in the League, the 2-1 scoreline hides the fact that yet again City failed to convert the proverbial hat-full of chances. On a day when the forwards tried to take one touch too many, the Blues managed to find themselves a goal behind thanks to the £180,000 Malcolm Macdonald. Bell equalised on the stroke of half-time when he realised only one touch was required to beat Iam McFaul in the Newcastle goal. Having found it hard going against his former team-mates in the centre, Davies tried his luck out on the wing and in the 77th minute his cross found its way to Lee who scored the winner with his left foot from a narrow angle.

The Blues then took part in the 16-team Texaco Cup, a competition pitting together sides from England, Scotland and Ireland and which Wolves had won the previous season. There

180

was £1,000 per team on offer with City being drawn against Airdrie, the first-leg of the tie being played at Maine Road on 15 September. The Blues rested both Lee and Bell and took the lead twice but could only manage a 2-2 draw against a team of part-timers from just outside Glasgow. Davies was fouled by Sam Goodwin (a car salesman by profession) to give Doyle a rare chance from the penalty-spot in the 27th minute only for the same player to equalise eight minutes later. Mellor made it 2-1 shortly before the interval and when Drew Busby levelled again in the 67th minute, the scoring was over for the evening.

With referees following orders to be stricter when penalising defenders tackles, the season was already becoming one of dubious penalty decisions. City's next game at Notts. Forest did little to buck the trend, with both sides scoring one each although City felt hardly done by when Ian Moore's 76th minute spot-kick robbed them of their first away win for nine months. Once again, the young Duncan McKenzie showed his liking for City when he gave the home side the lead in the 54th minute only for Lee to equalise (from the penalty-spot) a minute later. Davies gave City the advantage nine minutes later, and with Corrigan in commanding form, the points looked set for Maine Road before referee Mr. Nicholls and Moore decided otherwise.

Three days later, City entertained Hertha B.S.C. in the return friendly, with chairman Albert Alexander hoping to return some of the hospitality City received in the Olympic Stadium in the summer. Unusually for a friendly, the Berliners seemed not at all interested in attack and it therefore came as a surprise to City – without Lee, Bell and Summerbee – when they opened the scoring in the 74th minute through centre-forward Hans-Jurgen Sperlich. Neil Young, for so long a hero at Maine Road but nowadays seemingly confined forever in the reserves, was given a rare first-team outing and scored City's equaliser. With just five minutes to go, his corner was punched to Hill by goalkeeper Volkmar Gross. Hill laid the ball back to Young who cut in and his trusty left-foot did the rest. Unfortunately many of the 5,775 fans who'd paid to watch the game had been so disappointed by the negative Germans that they'd already gone home and missed what turned out to be Young's final goal in the first team.

Southampton came to Maine Road one point and two places behind City although at five o'clock the gap between the sides appeared to have been much bigger. Eric Martin was kept busy in the Saints' goal all afternoon and although City won easily in the end thanks to three well-worked goals, they were once again guilty of missing many more chances. City lost Davies in the game's first attack when he left the field to have four stitches inserted into a hand wound. However the Welshman was soon back in action and laid on City's first two goals, for Lee and then Bell. Just after an hour's play, Davies was rewarded with a goal of his own, a sliding left-foot shot that went under Martin's body. With City moving to fourth place, Joe Mercer said: "It was our best all-round performance of the season."

Broomfield Park, Airdrie, was City's next port of call, and the return-leg of the Texaco Cup, More than 20,000 watched the game, the outcome of which obviously didn't concern Mercer and Allison too much; only Donachie and Jeffries of the starting line-up had played

181

against Southampton two days earlier. Healey had a good game in goal but could not keep out two goals in a minute in the second-half, firstly from Drew Busby and then Derek Whiteford. City's reluctance to field anything like a first-team cost them their £1,000 appearance and a ban from playing in the tournament for the next two seasons.

With Connor and Towers replacing Mellor and Bell, City played a 4-3-3 formation at The Hawthorns against a West Brom. side that had scored just once in their previous seven games, and that from the penalty-spot. The Baggies' League standing (they were just one point off the bottom) held true and the game, as a contest, was over after just 13 minutes. By then City had taken control of the game and led 2-0 with Lee and Connor getting the goals. Jim Cumbes in the West Brom. net was left completely stranded each time by his poor defence. The same could not be said about City's defence. Book in particular was in fine form and twice came to the rescue when he cleared off the line.

Any confidence in the team at present was swiftly knocked out at Burnden Park in the League Cup. With Lee, Davies and Hill in the side, City's highly experienced Bolton contingent was put to the sword by the home side's 20-year-old Burnage-born centre-forward Gary Jones. A header in the 16th minute was followed by a 68th minute lob and finally an 80th minute penalty, all these efforts in reply to a City side that fired blanks all evening. Joe Mercer was once again honest with his opinions: "They ran us off our feet", was his summary after the game.

Two days after the defeat at Bolton, a board meeting was held at Maine Road where the club directors appointed Malcolm Allison team manager in a reallocation of duties. After the three-hour meeting secretary Walter Griffiths read out a prepared statement: "The board is pleased to announce the appointment of Malcolm Allison to the position of team manager with full responsibilities to the board for all team management. Mr Joe Mercer will continue as manager of the club." Mercer, who earlier expressed his approval of the proposed moves said: "It's only right that Malcolm should get the recognition after all the fine work he has done, and I am delighted for him. He has done this job splendidly for the last six years, when we have worked together to bring Manchester City a lot of success, and now it is simply a matter of him getting the right title. But I still believe I have a lot to offer. I must stay in football or I'll die and now it's a case of adapting. Malcolm will call me 'Joe' instead of 'Boss', but I'll still advise him from time to time. They can call me what they like. I've always encouraged Malcolm being in charge of the team anyway. I'm a tactician not an administrator and don't really see myself as a general manager. Still, any move that keeps us together should be satisfactory. At least it will make Malcolm less vulnerable to other offers." A delighted Allison kept his comments somewhat shorter: "I'm very pleased with the appointment as I have wanted a job like this since I was a lad. I'll see how the results go before I start predicting, but it will be nice to think of walking out at Wembley with a Cup Final side."

Allison's first game in sole charge was a 1-0 win against Everton on 19 October. Interestingly enough the programme printers had either finished their job early or had not been informed of the changes; Joe Mercer's name was still listed as team manager. Everton

Tony Book remembers

When they made the changes with Joe and Malcolm it didn't really change things in my eyes. I still looked on Malcolm as the coach because that what he was; that was his strength. There were no differences as far as the players were concerned. Malcolm was still out on the training pitch with them every day. There was no way he'd ever miss a session. I assume there were some subtle differences with Malcolm though as he'd now have to sit in on board meetings, would discuss more about which players were coming and going and he'd have access to the money.

were without their much-lauded midfield of Howard Kendall, Alan Ball and Colin Harvey and should have provided less of an obstacle but came up against a City side that was well out of sorts with itself. Young was back in the side as a replacement for the injured Davies and earned a 62nd minute penalty which Lee put away for his sixth success of the season. Everton centre-half Roger Kenyon was not impressed with referee Gordon Hill's decision: "Young just fell over my leg", he said afterwards. It was a scrappy way to win a scrappy game with Everton being unfortunate to travel back along the East Lancs. Road empty-handed. It wasn't the most convincing of starts to Allison's managerial career.

Neither was the trip to Leeds seven days later. Bell, who hadn't kicked a ball for three weeks failed a late fitness test and missed the 3-0 defeat, a result that gave the Yorkshire side the double over City that season. With Davies fit again, Young dropped to the subs' bench; it was the final time his name appeared on a senior first-class line-up. Allan Clarke beat Corrigan from a tight angle to open the scoring in the 13th minute and was later livid when he saw Book clearly handle a goal-bound effort off the line. Fortunately for City the referee didn't see the incident although when Mick Jones scored Leeds' second goal in the 68th minute from an obvious offside position, some justice was seen to be done. Peter Lorimer completed the scoring with a trademark 25-yarder, the overall performance convincing neutrals that maybe Don Revie's men had finally turned a corner after a recent bad run of form.

Neil Young remembers

My last start for City was against Everton in October although I was sub the week after at Leeds. That was it as far as playing for City was concerned. In January 1972 I moved to Preston North End along with Dave Connor. Malcolm knew I'd been a professional at Maine Road for the best part of 11 years and I knew he was still desperate to buy Rodney Marsh. With this in mind I went to see Malcolm in the boardroom. He said: "I know what you're going to say. If you sign for Preston I promise you we'll play a testimonial game for you. I'll take a side up to Deepdale for you." Naturally I agreed to the deal and I also know this conversation is actually written down somewhere in the minutes at the club. So I went to Preston, waited a while and then went to see their manager Alan Ball senior. He said not to worry about it, it was going to take place and then he got the sack. Not long afterwards Malcolm left City so I went to see the new Preston manager Bobby Charlton. He told me bluntly: "You shouldn't be in the game for money." So that was the end of it for me with Preston, then I had a few weeks at Rochdale before retiring. I was so sick about it at the time because I'd been promised this game more than once but then nothing ever came of it. I didn't even go near the ground until Francis Lee (as chairman) invited me back in 1994. The fans have been great to me in recent times and have really put a lot of work in to trying to remedy this situation but it was a sad way to end the relationship. If I have one particular highlight of my time with City it has to be the Championship decider at Newcastle. It was a real end-to-end game, goals going in left, right and centre and was fantastic to play in. I also managed to score a couple as well which helped!

Alan Oakes returned to first team duties against the early pacesetters Sheffield United for his first League game since August. Bell also returned – and took over the captaincy from Book – and Lee played despite a groin strain suffered at Elland Road. The wheels had come off the Sheffield bandwagon recently (they'd lost their last three games although they were still second) and they were determined to stop the rot at Maine Road. In polite terms, the visitors 'put themselves about' and at the end of the game Davies had four stitches in a head wound, Bell two in a knee and Summerbee had a foot x-rayed. When Lee was ordered to bed for 48 hours with bronchitis, it had been quite a price to pay for both points in a 2-1 win. All three goals came in the space of five minutes in the second-half. Firstly Doyle scored a controversial opener in the 52nd minute only for Bill Dearden to equalise 60 seconds later. Lee forgot about his chest troubles in the 57th minute when he decided the outcome with a stunning shot from the edge of the box.

At Huddersfield, the match report was an all too familiar one: "City were unable to translate their superiority into goals". Summerbee and Davies had by now begun to link well together but despite being in control of the game, they once again managed to concede the first goal. When outside-left David Smith beat Corrigan, it was Huddersfield's first League goal for three weeks. Although they were much the superior side, City struggled to get that elusive equaliser and when Summerbee and Bell both had 'goals' disallowed for offside, their patience snapped. Lee in particular was so outraged by Bell's disallowed effort that he was booked for arguing. Having recently been fined £150 by the FA, this new booking also cost Lee the £50 he'd promised to charity should he be booked again. Carter replaced Mellor after 65 minutes, a wise move by Allison, as it was Carter who finally managed the equaliser. With Huddersfield fourth from bottom and City third from top, it was really a game City should have won.

On 6 November, the day after Bonfire Night, there were still plenty of fireworks left at Maine Road. The occasion was the 85th Manchester 'derby'. After a few days break in Blackpool, Bell had spent 48 hours in hospital as a precaution following his knee injury. He left the hospital just three hours before kick-off to play in one of the most eventful 'derbies' of all time. For United, Denis Law missed the game, his place taken by 17-year-old Sammy McIlroy for his debut. And what a debut it turned out to be for the young Irishman – and of course future City player. After surviving early City pressure (again), it was McIlroy who gave the Reds first blood in the 39th minute. In a game of countless fierce challenges, United then lost the services of full-back Tony Dunne to a particularly heavy one from Summerbee right on half-time. McIlroy's goal separated the sides until two minutes into the second-half when another Irishman, one George Best, made it 2-0. Lee's determination then took him into a scramble in United's penalty area only to be tripped by Tommy O'Neill; the obvious result giving City a lifeline after 57 minutes. Seven minutes later Bell dribbled round Alex Stepney to roll the ball into an empty net and send the Blue half of Manchester wild with delight. However their joy was short-lived; three minutes to be exact. The Blues found themselves behind again when substitute John Aston's shot took a deflection off team-mate Alan Gowling before flying past the helpless Corrigan. In a game of so many twists and turns already, it was hard to see where another one could come from. With less than three minutes to go an exhausted Summerbee thought he'd levelled the game again but his 30-yard shot was tipped over by the acrobatic flying Alex Stepney. So tired was Summerbee that he didn't even have the energy to take the ensuing corner. It turned out be very fortunate for City. After a superb save, Stepney then managed to drop what appeared to be a relatively simple Lee corner and Summerbee found just enough energy to smash the ball into the roof of the net and end a marvellous afternoon's entertainment.

Summerbee was on the scoresheet again four days later, this time in the white shirt of England. His header at Wembley (his only international goal) earned England a 1-1 draw with Switzerland in a European Championship game. Team-mate Francis Lee was once again getting himself into trouble with a referee. His booking was his third in 12 days and he joked about getting the rest of the team on a sponsored walk just to pay off all of his £50 promises.

Arsenal had proved to be a bit of a bogey side for City, indeed the Blues hadn't beaten them since 1963. That all changed with a 2-1 win at Highbury in what was generally a poor game with countless mis-directed passes going astray from both sides. Once again City had to rally after conceding the first goal when Arsenal full-back Sammy Nelson beat City's attempt at an offside trap to slot the ball past Corrigan in the 71st minute. This time though the Blues showed more resilience and when Mellor collected McLintock's headed clearance, the equaliser had been just four minutes in coming. Keen to regain their lead, Arsenal left themselves wide open at the back, a perfect invitation for Bell with only six minutes left, to inflict the third defeat in eight days for the Gunners.

Two days after the sterling win at Highbury, City made good their promise to take part in a testimonial game for Preston's captain Alan Spavin. More than 14,000 turned out at Deepdale and witnessed a 3-2 win for the Blues and exactly the kind of football and spirit that should dominate these sort of games. Meanwhile back at Maine Road, changes were being made in the boardroom. Albert Alexander, the 79-year-old chairman, was handing over the reigns to his son Eric, making Eric the youngest chairman in the First Division. Albert was given the title of president whilst new leading shareholder Joe Smith replaced Sydney Rose as vice-chairman. Mr Rose remained on the board but had asked to step down owing to his medical commitments. One of the first tasks the new board discussed was a ten-year (at £12,000 a year) contract for Malcolm Allison.

Another trip to the capital, this time to West Ham, proved another success, courtesy of a 2-0 win. The vastly more experienced Davies gave West Ham's young centre-half Tommy Taylor a torrid time, culminating in literally a long-running tussle that ended only when Taylor pulled Davies to the ground. Despite the home team's protests that the final act was outside the area, Lee knocked in another penalty (albeit via the bar and post) to give City a deserved lead. Davies later doubled City's lead and then, with the tussle still going on, got himself booked for a foul on Taylor. With Manchester United beating Leicester and Derby beating Sheffield United, the win at West Ham was vital as it meant only three points separated the top three sides.

With City going so well in the League (currently lying third) it was somewhat of a disappointment that only 31,003 turned up to watch the game with Coventry. Although it is fair to say that Coventry have never been one of the biggest draws in English football, those that did bother to turn up saw Allison's side easily shrug aside the one of his old team-mate Noel Cantwell. Coventry played with a lot of spirit but a distinct lack of skill and were no match for a City side that scored four times whilst keeping a clean sheet. Davies led the attack having recovered from a burst blood vessel in his stomach but the goals were shared evenly between Bell and Lee. When Lee's glancing header beat the harassed Bill Glazier for City's final goal of the afternoon, it was the England man's 16th goal of the season. Amazingly he still hadn't reached half of his year-end's total.

When the second and third-placed teams in the First Division (or Premier League in today's language) meet, you know you are in for a *Match of the Day*. Unfortunately when City travelled to Derby on 4 December, only Corrigan and Lee performed anywhere near their best, and it was third-placed Derby who looked the likeliest Championship contenders. Alan Hinton (he of the famous-infamous white boots once described by Stuart Hall as 'a runaway wardrobe') was on prime form on Derby's left. In the 22nd minute he scored a penalty after Mellor had brought down John McGovern, and then planted crosses on the unmarked heads of Ron Webster (36) and Alan Durban (38) to give the home side an unassailable 3-0 lead at the interval. In the 65th minute John Robson fouled Summerbee to give Lee the opportunity to restore some pride and to convert his ninth penalty of the season. Lapses at the back in the first-half had cost City both the game and second spot in the Division.

If December had started badly, then November, with three wins and a draw, had been a great month as City maintained their challenge at the top. As a way of recognising this, Malcolm Allison, after his first full month in charge, was presented with a gallon of whisky and a cheque for £100 and was named Bell's Manager of the Month for November. The presentation was made prior to kick-off against Ipswich Town at Maine Road and the Blues responded with a 4-0 win in a most one-sided game. Admittedly he was up against some poor defending, but nevertheless Davies missed just one header all afternoon and opened City's account in the fourth minute with a well-placed back one. Another Davies header enabled Mellor to make it 2-0 and in the 42nd minute yet another one (from Lee's cross) found Bell for the third. Three minutes on to the second-half Lee beat three men before firing a low cross-shot past a shell-shocked Laurie Sivell in the Ipswich goal. According to one contemporary newspaper report: "at this point City declared". With Derby losing 3-2 at Liverpool, the win moved City back into second place.

Immediately after beating Ipswich, 16 players left Manchester Airport for a four-day trip to Malta, the idea being to take a break from some of the stamina and strength training and to try out some new tactics in conditions more conducive to, in Allison's words: "standing around whilst I sort things out". On the last day of the trip, City played out a goalless draw against the part-timers of Floriana at the Gzira Stadium. On a sandy pitch, Young limped off with an injured ankle, his replacement Connor following shortly afterwards. Despite these injuries, Allison described the trip as "a satisfactory workout".

Whatever new tactics had been worked on in the Mediterranean certainly weren't put to good use in the next home game, against Leicester. The Blues struggled all afternoon to break down a packed Leicester defence and had to rely on Lee's 66th minute penalty (his tenth of the season) to earn a share of the spoils. Leicester had taken the lead as early as the 7th minute when a mis-placed backpass by Book was intercepted and then converted by Keith Weller, the former Chelsea player, a man who seemingly loved to score against City. The goal inspired the visitors to some resolute defending (often with eight men behind the ball) but had it not been for Bell's shot being kicked off the line and Booth hitting the bar, the outcome could have been much different. Despite all City's efforts, it was home point they could ill afford to drop in the battle at the top.

At Stoke on 27 December, the withdrawal shortly before kick-off of centre-forward John Ritchie seemed to confuse the home team so much that they decided not to attack at all and concentrated their efforts solely in the middle of the pitch. Before saving a shot from former City player Peter Dobing in the 75th minute, Corrigan had hardly touched the ball, such was City's dominance and Stoke's rather bizarre tactics. With Lee, Bell and Summerbee all in top form, Towers surprisingly scored the opening goal when he headed in (via the bar) Summerbee's cross after 15 minutes. It took until the 83rd minute before Book increased the lead, and with Lee adding a third on 86, and Dennis Smith, back after a three-week suspension, getting a goal back for the home side in the 90th, the last seven minutes were by far the most interesting of the afternoon.

The first game of the New Year, 1972, saw Notts. Forest visit Maine Road. Forest had not collected an away point for more than two months so who better, even today, to stop a run like that than Manchester City. True to form City obliged with a share of the points in a 2-2 draw. Another valuable home point dropped in another erratic showing, one that yet again had the critics querying City's chances of maintaining a challenge on the Championship. In a scrappy game, Paul Richardson's diving header had given Forest the lead in the 43rd minute before Lee was tripped by Tommy Jackson; the last kick of the half (and his 11th penalty of the season) levelling the scores. The penalty equalled the record jointly set back in the 1932-33 season by Messrs. Evans of Spurs and Ball of Sheffield Wednesday. Three minutes into the second-half Neil Martin restored Forest's lead when his shot hit both the referee and a Blue shirt before finally beating Corrigan. Lee laid on City's second equaliser for Davies ten minutes later but manager Allison left Maine Road pondering, not for the first time this season, about City's lack of penetration in front of goal.

City fans had lost count of the number of times their side had conceded the first goal this season. At Tottenham they did it again, the seventh-minute header by Martin Peters being his 100th League goal. On a heavy pitch, equally made up of sand and mud, Spurs controlled the first-half but tired dramatically in the second. After the break, a much fitter and stronger City raised their game with the inevitable equaliser coming in the 76th minute when Spurs failed to clear the ball properly and Davies poked home from close range.

Before the FA Cup third round against Middlesbrough, City learnt of the sudden death of director Frank Johnson, a major figure in the takeover dealings of the previous year. The 67-year-old former solicitor, who'd been on the board for the past 13 years, died at his home in Cheadle. Also in the news, and in the wars, was Neil Young. Young's ankle injury sustained in Malta had not responded to treatment and it was encased in plaster. Within a week he had the chance to recover properly at his new club Preston North End.

A draw at Maine Road would mean the cancellation of a proposed friendly with Rangers at Ibrox. In the end that's exactly what happened as City equalised with an 86th minute penalty and saved the tie by the skin of their teeth. Middlesbrough's route one tactics spelt trouble all day for the struggling Tommy Booth at the heart of City's defence. However the Blues seemed to have mastered this style of play when, after 42 minutes, Middlesbrough, for the first time, changed it and scored the opening goal. Nobby Stiles (booed constantly for fouling Summerbee constantly) found John Hickton who in turn picked out David Mills for a well-worked goal. The singing Middlesbrough fans were silenced when Lee raced on to to Davies's header before being hauled down by Jim Platt in the visitors' goal. This record-breaking penalty-kick meant the Blues were still in the FA Cup, although only for three more days.

Middlesbrough won the replay at Ayresome Park 1-0 thanks to a fiercely disputed goal, scored by John Hickton. With the linesman frantically waving his flag for offside, the referee over-ruled him, saying the unfortunate Towers was playing Hickton on. On a snow-covered pitch topped up by an occasional blizzard, City felt further aggrieved when Doyle had what appeared to be a perfectly good 'goal' disallowed for offside, this time the referee, Mr Corbett from Wolverhampton, upholding the linesman's flag. Second Division Middlesbrough had knocked Manchester United out of the FA Cup at the same stage last season and City's defeat left a bad taste in captain Bell's mouth: "We feel sick about both decisions that went against us", he said after the game.

188

On Friday, 22 January, Neil Young and David Connor, both outstanding servants of the club who'd given more than 22 years combined service, moved to Preston in a joint deal said to be worth in the region of £40,000. Many supporters felt that the money received from the Deepdale club was being put towards the purchase of a new striker as City had been linked with both Ian Storey-Moore of Nottingham Forest and, not for the first time, Queen's Park Rangers' flamboyant Rodney Marsh.

Joe Mercer meanwhile was far from happy with his new role at the club. Instead of the 'job for life' that had once been promised, Mercer now found himself looking at a three-year contract and a cut in pay. He felt (as did many supporters) that the new board didn't really know what to do with him, let alone what to call him. A very proud man had had his pride hurt. It was later damaged beyond repair when he had his car-park space taken away from him. For all his troubles with the board, Mercer never once had any trouble with Allison. In fact the same could be also said in turn about Allison. He too was showing some dissatisfaction with the new board, saying: "The new board failed to please either me or Joe and my new contract was full of loopholes".

The disappointments of the FA Cup were left behind when a 2-1 win at Crystal Palace maintained City's unbeaten run in London that season. The home side began well and took the lead in the 10th minute when Corrigan failed to keep out a well-struck shot by Bobby Tambling. Once again City's overall superiority began to take control and they were rewarded with a 40th minute equaliser when Lee headed in Bell's cross. Midway through the second-half constant City pressure finally provided the winner although when Summerbee's shot took a fierce deflection off Mel Blyth it was perhaps a rather fortunate way of clinching the points. Overall City had deserved their victory with a fine all-round performance, one that prompted Crystal Palace manager Bert Head to comment: "Man for man, City are probably the most gifted side in the country."

City and Wolves had shared a seven-goal thriller in the League Cup back in September at Maine Road and were to do so again, this time though City's winning margin would be more convincing. Wolves could simply not contain a rampant City side who's attacking performance brought back many happy memories of the 1968 Championship season. Lee's hat-trick took his tally for the season so far to 26 and with Booth and Towers also finding the back of the net, the two efforts from Derek Dougan made little difference to the result. City's 5-2 win took them two points clear at the top of the table from both Leeds and Derby. Manchester United, a side that had not won since 4 December, were fourth, a point further behind.

Having had the rare privilege of a weekend off, City travelled across the Pennines on 12 February to face a Sheffield United side who had slipped down the table to seventh place after losing their last three games. Like City, they too had had a few days off, but whereas City's players had largely spent their free time at home, Sheffield United paid to a visit to Tel Aviv and a game against the Israeli National team. At Bramall Lane, City led 2-0 but then, due to poor marking and conceding a penalty, managed to find themselves 3-2 down, before Lee levelled from the penalty spot after Mike Speight had handled. Things had started well for the Blues when Lee's 21st minute free-kick somehow found its way through the Sheffield wall and inside the post. This was followed ten minutes later when Bell converted Summerbee's cross to give City a two-goal cushion. Billy Dearden pulled a goal back for the home side and after Trevor Hockey had left the field with a broken leg following a collision with Summerbee, Alan Woodward levelled the game with a penalty. Things got worse when Tony Currie headed in Sheffield's second unchallenged header of the game, leaving Allison furious with the marking, but later grateful yet again for Lee's ability from the penalty spot. City had dropped a valuable point in a game they should really have won, particularly after leading 2-0.

It was another Lancashire-Yorkshire clash seven days later when City hosted third from bottom Huddersfield, a position underlined by the fact that the visitors had scored in just two of their last nine games. City were grateful for a 1-0 win in the battle for points at the top, but their overall performance in what was a scrappy game, gave further indication of their inabilities to break down the poorer opposition. The decisive goal came five minutes after the half-time break when Hill's corner was hooked on by Lee before Booth scored at the far post with an overhead kick. Had Doyle not headed a rare Huddersfield attack off his own line the scoreline could have been different but nevertheless two vital points had been secured.

Unbeaten in their last nine League games and knowing that a win would open up a four-point lead at the top, it was a confident City side that visited Anfield on 26 February. Unfortunately it was a hugely disappointed group of players and staff that left Liverpool after suffering a 3-0 defeat. The Blues had looked very good for the first half an hour and had displayed Championship form on more than one occasion. However things changed in the 38th minute. It was then that Liverpool's centre-half Larry Lloyd scored the first goal of the game, one that was hotly disputed by City after Lloyd appeared to be in an offside position. After the break the wheels came off in a big way, especially at the back, and despite Corrigan being in fine form, he could not prevent a brilliant diving header from man of the match Kevin Keegan and a third goal from Bobby Graham.

After missing the last two games because of ankle ligament problems, Bell returned to the side for the Wednesday afternoon game with West Bromwich Albion. Only 25,677 managed to get to the game and even then they found themselves disrupted because of a bomb scare in the main stand. After Bell had given City the lead in the fifth minute, West Brom. then proved difficult to break down, in fact it wasn't until the 72nd minute when the same player finally increased City's lead with a header after good work by Summerbee and Hill. With West Brom. seemingly more intent on defence, Corrigan was hardly troubled all afternoon, although when Doyle handled the ball, he was beaten by Tony Brown from the penalty spot. A 2-1 scoreline gives a false impression of City's superiority although the edge was taken off the victory (and the crucial two points) when Booth left the action with a broken nose.

On League Cup Final day (Stoke 2 Chelsea 1), Arsenal's run of 16 unbeaten games came to an end at Maine Road. With Doyle playing centre-half instead of the injured Booth, City missed his tenacity in midfield, but with Lee up front scoring twice in the 2-0 win, City managed to beat a sixth-placed Arsenal side with some style. Lee's first goal in the 34th minute was his 14th penalty of the season, whilst his second after 56 minutes, came from typical determination after his first effort had been blocked. As for bookings, they finished three each, a figure that equalled the League record, in a game that could hardly have been described as physical. The win confirmed City's Championship aspirations; they were now four points clear of Leeds although the Yorkshire side did have two games in hand. Before City's next game at Everton, Allison made a signing that many thought proved costly to those aspirations.

When Rodney Marsh signed on 8 March 1972, his transfer fee of £200,000 smashed the previous record at Maine Road. Allison had long been an admirer of the Queen's Park Rangers' star striker and was convinced that the signing would be crucial in lifting the title. Even today City fans have mixed feelings about his decision. Certainly no one could argue about Marsh's ability with a football; what concerned City supporters was the way he played the game.

It is now a well-known fact that when Marsh signed he was totally unfit. Because of this he would have to wait a week for his City debut as City took an unchanged team to Goodison Park, hoping for a more successful trip to Merseyside than the game at Anfield a couple of weeks earlier. Against Everton, Allison could not have hoped for a better start. After just 32 seconds, Everton's Tommy Wright headed in Book's free-kick to give City the lead. Twenty minutes later Lee's shot was only partially cleared by Howard Kendall and Hill had the simplest of tap-ins from three yards. Three minutes into the second-half, City's generous defending yet again gave too much space to one of the opposition – this time Mick Lyons – and the home side were back in the game. The majority of the remainder of the game saw Everton desperately pushing for an equaliser but City's defence, despite a few worries, this time held firm. City fans were delighted with the two points but had reservations about the defence.

More than 53,000 saw the game with Chelsea at Maine Road, and with it the debut of Rodney Marsh. Although Towers had been playing exceptionally in recent games, it was he who found himself relegated to the subs' bench in order to accommodate Allison's new signing. Still overweight and obviously not match-fit, Marsh had a good first-half and showed some of the skills and touches the fans expected. Allison later said of him: "I think he's at least six pounds overweight and at least a third under full fitness." Nevertheless he did manage to hit the bar and miss two excellent chances before he tired, not surprisingly, as the game wore on. Towers replaced him with just four minutes to go, Marsh later citing nervous tension to go alongside his other worries. By now City had the best attacking forward line in the country and it was perhaps surprising therefore that the only goal of the game – in the 24th minute – came from a header by centre-half Booth, back in the side after his broken nose. A satisfied Malcolm Allison enjoyed the game from the stands smoking one of his trademark huge cigars.

Marsh kept his place in the side in City's next game, a goalless draw at Newcastle. With Healey taking over in goal from Corrigan who had a bad back, and Summerbee unusually playing in midfield, Marsh looked and played slower than even his critics first thought. Apart from a goal-line clearance at each end and Lee and Marsh both having shots saved, neither side offered much in what was generally a poor game. A classy City encountered a resolute Newcastle and in the end a draw was a fair result as neither side deserved to win. City were now three points clear of Derby County but had played a game more.

Football songs sung by the players themselves were currently in vogue as Easter 1972 came into view and City were no different. With the talents of 10 CC's Godley and Crème, City burst forth with a cheery little ditty entitled *The Boys in Blue*, and considering the general nature of footballing records, is by no means the worst song ever recorded. It was launched in readiness for the visit of Stoke City on 1 April and the lyrics were printed in full the matchday programme. Unfortunately at five o'clock City fans weren't in a singing mood.

Heavy rain all day made the Maine Road surface extremely heavy but it wasn't the conditions that cost City both the game and crucial ground in the title race. The game was won and lost by the antics of just one player; England's Gordon Banks in the Stoke goal. His side had not won in the League since 22 January and had six chances all afternoon in reply to City's 26. Banks stopped everything with a wonderful performance, the highlight being a spectacular save via a post from Lee's header. The conditions were hardly conducive to the touches preferred by Marsh although even without them, City still held the upper hand all day. Amazingly and completely against the run of play, Stoke took the lead in the 35th minute when Healey was beaten by John Ritchie's shot which was deflected by Doyle's face. Perhaps then the writing was on the wall. City's reply was swift, coming just 60 seconds later. Marsh leapt over Bell's cross to give Lee the chance to score his 30th goal of the season and equal Derek Kevan's post-war League record for the club. The second-half mirrored the first with Ritchie scoring his second goal of the game in the 62nd minute, Banks constantly denying City, only this time no equaliser was coming. Heads of fans and players alike were shook violently at the end of a game no one could believe City had lost.

The following Tuesday at The Dell, City's title hopes took another battering. Southampton – a side not for the first or last time worried by relegation – eased their present troubles thanks to a goal in each half by centre-forward Ron Davies. City came nearest to scoring when Lee hit the bar as the Blues were frustrated by a side that played as though they were much higher in the League than fourth from bottom. City had now slipped to third place, the same points as Liverpool, both in turn one behind the leaders Derby. All three teams had five games left.

The Blues got back to winning ways in their next game, a 3-1 home win against West Ham. Marsh got his name on the scoresheet for the first time in City's colours, his two goals being quite simple close-in efforts, but both showed all the hallmarks of great anticipation against a frozen West Ham defence. Marsh also had a hand in City's second goal when his 30-yard pass found Bell before the England midfielder slid the ball home. There was little threat from the visitors in attack and apart from when Harry Redknapp hit the bar early on, their only other effort came when Geoff Hurst beat a limping Healey for a consolation goal in the 82nd minute.

Although Marsh was by now showing increased levels of fitness and had managed to score a couple of goals in his last game, he was relegated to substitute for the trip to Old Trafford. A largely forgettable first-half that was littered with fouls and poor distribution by both sides was brought to life by three goals in seven minutes. In the 54th minute, against the run of play, Martin Buchan opened the scoring for United after Booth had failed to clear Alan Gowling's cross properly. The goal was fatal for United as it forced City into action. Within a minute, Lee had back-headed Donachie's cross past John Connaughton in the United goal to silence the singing Stretford End. Five minutes later Summerbee's free-kick was headed down by Bell and there was Lee to volley home his 32nd League goal of the season, and with it a new club record. Marsh came on as a replacement for Doyle and it was he who confirmed City's superiority with City's third goal in the 85th minute, a cool finish after good work by Bell. Not for the first time, Bell was outstanding at Old Trafford. Lee too confirmed his liking for the place; he'd now scored seven times in City's last five games there.

Tony Book remembers

A lot of people said that when Malcolm signed Rodney Marsh it cost us the League. All I would say is that when Rodney came to Maine Road I don't think he'd played much recently and he was very unfit. We, on the other hand, were 'fit as butcher's dogs', and it showed on Rodney. Tony Towers was in the side then, playing out of his skin, really well, and, like managers do, Malcolm changed it round a bit to accommodate the new signing. I think that was one of the reasons we let the League slip away from us. None of us doubted Rodney's ability – he was a terrific player – and he would easily have come into the side next season when he'd had a chance to get fit. It was simply the fact that we changed the team around when we were going so well. Rodney also played a different style to the way we did. He always wanted a couple of touches on the ball whereas we used to just move it about. But like I say, managers have got to make decisions. I had a similar one to make when I was in charge and we had Kazzy Deyna so I know exactly what it's like.

Unusually for any City side of the Mercer-Allison era, their caution at Coventry was thought to have cost them a point. The home side offered little threat to City's rearguard until Towers gave the Blues the lead three minutes after the break. Doyle's long throw was headed on by Davies for Towers to shoot through a crowd of players. It was then that Summerbee was brought back into midfield, a move that left just Lee and Davies up front, and the move took some pressure off the Coventry defence. In the 77th minute, the home side cleared a City corner, and the resulting quick break found Dennis Mortimore who scored a fine equaliser. Doyle had a goal ruled out for offside but after two successive (and convincing) wins, a point dropped at Highfield Road was not what was required.

In the summer months that followed, City fans analysed the events at the end of a most eventful season. Some said they shouldn't have signed Marsh, some said despite Banks, they should have beaten Stoke. Others talked about the goings-on at Ipswich on a Tuesday night. It was a night of missed chances by the Blues (especially by Lee and Marsh), bizarre refereeing decisions and a 2-1 win for the home side, all of which combined to leave Allison speechless afterwards. Healey had been the busier of the two goalkeepers but held firm until the 34th minute when Trevor Whymark finally beat him with an overhead kick. Summerbee equalised nine minutes into the second-half after he'd converted Book's corner despite heated protests from the home side about the treatment of goalkeeper Laurie Sivell. In the 63rd minute Ipswich full-back Colin Harper scored what turned out to be the decisive goal of the night when his header flew past Healey. To compound City's troubles further, Davies then left the field to have stitches in an eye wound after a collision with, of all people, Summerbee. However the biggest and most controversial talking point of the night happened when Bell beat Sivell with a shot only to see Harper palm the ball deliberately on to the crossbar and safety. Unbelievable the referee claimed never to have seen the incident. This decision cost City the game on the night and ultimately the Championship. Although mathematically they could still win it, the bookmakers now rated their chances as 100 to 1.

Tony Book remembers

We lost 2-1 at Ipswich in the second to last game of the season and ultimately it cost us the League. I remember Colin Bell had a blatant penalty refused and it got Wyn Davies and me into trouble afterwards. I reacted badly towards the referee and got suspended for a couple of weeks at the start of the following season. Wyn got away with it though. He'd got a bang on the head during the game and was replaced by Alan Oakes. He got off the treatment table to have a go at the ref with me although later at the hearing, he got away with it because they said he was suffering with concussion at the time. Even today I can still remember the referee's name; Homewood.

The last game of the season – played on 22 April – pitted second-placed City against the leaders Derby County at Maine Road. Although there was only one point dividing the two teams, on the day there might as well have been 20 as City turned in a magnificent performance. Marsh was outstanding, showing the 55,000 crowd the type of play that Allison had always known he was capable of. He scored City's first goal and played a key part in the second in a game that finished 2-0 but could, and should, have been won by a bigger margin. In the 24th minute, Marsh picked the ball up wide on the right, cut in towards goal, nut-megged Roy McFarland and then crashed the ball across Colin Boulton and inside the far post. The crowd loved it. Midway through the second-half, with Derby attacking in search of an equaliser, Marsh found himself for once in space as his marker Colin Todd was up with his forwards. His run into the penalty-area was blocked by substitute Terry Hennessey's obvious body-check. The result was City's second goal of the afternoon, Lee's 15th penalty and 33rd goal of the season. It was a terrific way to end a season but was also a bittersweet victory.

City finished the season with 57 points and stayed top of the League for a little more than a week. Liverpool had two games left (one point behind), as did Leeds (two points behind), whilst Derby had just one left and were one point behind. It was too much to expect that all three teams would slip up. In the end, City finished fourth, the same number of points as both Liverpool and Leeds, with Brian Clough's Derby County lifting the Championship by a single point.

For all the talk of signing Marsh, the display by Gordon Banks and the defeat at Ipswich, the main reason for City's failure to clinch the title must surely be a statistical one. In April, they dropped seven points in seven games. Just think what a difference that could have made.

Joe Mercer left Maine Road in June 1972 to become general manager with Coventry City. The partnership was then well and truly over. Many felt that the board could have done more to keep Mercer and Allison together in some sort of working capacity and that Mercer had been treated poorly after all his sterling work. What was clear was the fact that it wasn't Joe Mercer who had made Manchester City once again a force in British and European football. It was also clear that it wasn't Malcolm Allison. What it was, was the partnership. Joe Mercer and Malcolm Allison together made Manchester City.

Malcolm Allison remembers

When Joe left Manchester City in the summer of 1972, I was thousands of miles away in South Africa. I'd been asked by the directors of Cape Town City to spend a few weeks out there, organising and running half a dozen football clinics. Looking back, I'm glad I was nowhere near Maine Road at the time. I had some 'phone calls in South Africa from the press back here asking for my reactions but in all honesty I just wanted out of it. I'd had enough of politics over the last nine months or so. Anyway, there was nothing I wanted to say that hadn't been said all ready.

In March 1973, just days after Joe Mercer had returned to Maine Road with what turned out to be a victorious Coventry side, Allison considered his future and decided a move to Crystal Palace was beneficial. Apart from a brief spell in the mid to late 1970s when Tony Book was at the helm, the glory days were now well and truly over with the two men who were so instrumental in bringing them to Moss Side no longer in residence.

Those halcyon days of 1965 to 1972 seem a long time ago. Although for anyone involved with the club at the time, or, who just saw them play, those great memories will never fade away.

Tony Book remembers

It was a sad day for me when the partnership broke up and Joe Mercer left the club. I still feel that when people get to that level they still have something to offer. Clubs can always use that experience, just look at Bobby Charlton at Old Trafford today. I remember when I used to visit Supporters' Clubs with Peter Swales and Ian Niven; we used to travel all over the country. Joe would have been first-rate at doing that kind of ambassadorial work. Also it would have kept him at the club should any future manager need to call on him for a bit of advice. I know when I was in charge I would have loved to have had him still there. He was a players' man and a gentleman. Quite simply they don't come any better in the game.

Malcolm Allison remembers

Joe and I were a perfect partnership and records prove that individually we achieved nowhere near the same level of success. Apart from the tenseness of those last few months, I think we had barely two disagreements in all the time we worked together. I never for one moment regretted working with Joe Mercer, and I know he felt the same way about working with me. We had some fabulous time together and built some fabulous teams. The Mercer-Allison years at Manchester City were the best years of my life. If Joe was still with us today, I think he'd say the same.

Statistics

Bell, Colin

Born Hesleden, County Durham, 26 February 1946.

In a fans' Internet survey conducted in the spring of 2001, Colin Bell was voted as City's greatest-ever player. Quite simply he was the most complete footballer ever to wear the City shirt, with only Peter Doherty in the 1930s coming close. Signed from Bury shortly before the transfer deadline in March 1966, Bell's influence in midfield was an integral part of the great sides built by Joe Mercer and Malcolm Allison. Capped 48 times for England (a club record for any country), only five players have played more games for City, whilst only two have scored more goals. In November 1975, aged just 29, Bell's career was effectively finished when he was badly injured during a League Cup victory over Manchester United. It robbed both City and England of a career many thought could have gone one for at least another six years. Following his eventual retirement from playing in August 1979, Bell joined the youth coaching staff and today is employed by the club's corporate division.

Maine Road Career

League	393(1) appearances	117 goals
FA Cup	33(1) appearances	9 goals
League Cup	40 appearances	18 goals
Other	9 appearances	1 goal
Europe	23(1) appearances	8 goals
Total	498(3) appearances	153 goals

Book, Tony

Born Bath, 4 September 1934.

Although nearly 32 when he joined City, Tony Book became one of the club's most consistent and popular players of all-time. Signed from Plymouth Argyle in 1966, full-back Book played in more than 300 games for the Blues before retiring in 1973. Originally working as assistant to manager Ron Saunders, five months after his retirement Book had taken over completely the reigns of a side he had captained with distinction in the late 1960s and early '70s. He skippered the Blues to all their successes during those halcyon days and was also the joint Footballer of the Year in 1969. Seven years later he managed the side that won the League Cup at Wembley, City's last piece of silverware to date. Book had various backroom jobs in a career spanning thirty years at Maine Road until finally leaving the club in 1996 when new manager Frank Clarke brought about many changes. Today Book is an Honorary President of Manchester City and can be seen regularly at first team home games.

Maine Road Career

League	240(2) appearances	4 goals
FA Cup	28 appearances	
League Cup	18(1) appearances	1 goal
Other	6 appearances	
Europe	17 appearances	
Total	306(3) appearances	5 goals

Booth, Tommy

Born Manchester, 9 November 1949.

Langley-born Tommy Booth made an immediate impression in City's first team after being given his debut in a League Cup tie at Huddersfield in September 1968. Booth had been on City's books, originally as an amateur, since 1965, and his polished performances (with no shortage of skill) would eventually lead him to take over the number five spot from George Heslop on a permanent basis. He is also the holder of four England Under-23 caps and won FA Cup, European Cup Winners' Cup and two League Cup winners' medals in a Maine Road career spanning 16 years. The arrival of Dave Watson in the summer of 1975 saw Booth moving to a midfield role where his experience and ability proved invaluable in a strong City side managed by former captain Tony Book. He scored 36 goals for City, none more important than the last-minute winner against Everton in the 1969 FA Cup semi-final. Booth left Maine Road for Preston North End in October 1981 where he played 84 League games before becoming a television engineer for a large national company. In recent years he has been delivering kitchen accessories for a Chadderton-based firm.

Maine Road Career

League	380(2) appearances	25 goals
FA Cup	27 appearances	5 goals
League Cup	44(2) appearances	3 goals
Other	11 appearances	
Europe	25 appearances	3 goals
Total	487(4) appearances	36 goals

Bowyer, Ian

Born Ellesmere Port, 6 June 1951.

Ian Bowyer was just one of many good young players discovered by City's scouting staff in the mid 1960s. A left-sided attacking player, Bowyer signed apprentice forms for the Blues in the summer of 1966 when he was just 15. He made his debut in a 1-0 defeat at Newcastle in November 1968 and played a part in six games that season. He became a regular member of the first-team squad the following year, taking the place of either Neil Young or Tony Coleman on several occasions. Despite Bowyer's efforts, medals (League Cup and European Cup Winners' Cup) and goals for City, he fell victim to constant barracking from certain sections of the crowd causing his form to suffer. He joined Leyton Orient in June 1971 before playing more than 400 League games in two spells with Notts. Forest where he collected two European Cup Winners' medals under Brian Clough's guidance. After his playing days were over, Bowyer moved into coaching and management and lists Cheltenham Town, Birmingham City, Notts Forest and MK Dons among his employers.

Maine Road Career

League	42(8) appearances	13 goals
FA Cup	4 appearances	1 goal
League Cup	6(2) appearances	2 goals
Europe	5(3) appearances	1 goal
Total	57(13) appearances	17 goals

Coleman, Tony

Born Liverpool, 2 May 1945.

Tony Coleman's tearaway, fire-brand image preceded him to Maine Road in March 1967. His reputation as a potential trouble-maker at first caused Joe Mercer some concern and it was only Malcolm Allison's persuasive abilities that eventually changed Mercer's mind. Allison was adamant that he could harness Coleman's energy for the Manchester City cause and so it proved. Despite playing just over a hundred games for City, Coleman was a huge favourite with the supporters, playing every game with a fierce determination. A £12,350 signing from Doncaster Rovers, Coleman won a First Division Championship and an FA Cup medal during his time at Maine Road before being sold to Sheffield Wednesday in October 1969. He will be forever remembered for his "Give my regards to your mum and dad" remarks to Princess Anne before the 1969 FA Cup Final. Coleman later played for Blackpool, Southport and Stockport County before emigrating to Australia. A more recent sighting put him working behind a bar in Thailand.

Maine Road Career

League	82(1) appearances	12 goals
FA Cup	10 appearances	3 goals
League Cup	7(1) appearances	
Other	1 appearance	
Europe	2 appearances	1 goal
Total	102(2) appearances	16 goals

Connor, David

Born Manchester, 27 October 1945.

The fact that Dave Connor was City's utility player for more than nine professional seasons prevented him from really being able to hold down a regular first-team spot. His ability to play in almost any outfield position, especially full-back, made him a valued squad member and his speciality was the man-to-man marking job, one he carried out to perfection on Everton's Alan Ball in the FA Cup semi-final of 1969. Born in Wythenshawe, Connor made his debut at outside-left against Charlton Athletic on the opening day of the 1964-65 season. Averaging around 15 games a year, Connor unfortunately missed out on all of City's trophy winning sides, indeed he played in only ten games of the 1967-68 Championship winning term. He left Maine Road in January 1972 in a double deal with Neil Young and joined Preston North End. Connor played just 29 League games in three seasons at Deepdale before returning to the reserve side at Maine Road for a spell, later becoming manager at Macclesfield Town. Since 1980 he has been manager of the Mellands Playing Fields complex in Gorton.

Maine Road Career

League	130(11) appearances	10 goals
FA Cup	12(1) appearances	
League Cup	5(1) appearances	
Other	2(1) appearances	
Europe	5 appearances	
Total	154(14) appearances	10 goals

Corrigan, Joe

Born Manchester, 18 November 1948.

Had it not been for the presence of Peter Shilton and Ray Clemence, Joe Corrigan would surely have considerably more than his nine full caps for England. Standing at nearly 6ft 5ins, this giant of a goalkeeper is believed to be the tallest player ever to appear in the first team at Maine Road. Signed from amateur side Sale in September 1966, Corrigan made his debut the following year in a League Cup tie against Blackpool when he had the misfortune to let the ball through his legs for the visitors' goal on the night. Despite being behind both Harry Dowd and Ken Mulhearn in the pecking order, Corrigan worked endlessly at his game alongside Malcolm Allison and would eventually reap the rewards. Only Alan Oakes has played more games for City. Hugely popular with the fans, he won two League Cup winners' medals and a European Cup Winners' Cup medal, and was still between the posts when the Blues lost to Tottenham at Wembley in 1981. He left Maine Road in March 1983, moving to Seattle in the United States before spells with Brighton, Norwich and Stoke. After working with Celtic and Middlesbrough, Corrigan was goalkeeping coach with a host of clubs including Leeds United, Liverpool and West Bromwich Albion.

Maine Road Career

League	476 appearances
FA Cup	37 appearances
League Cup	52 appearances
Other	12(1) appearances
Europe	27 appearances
Total	604(1) appearances

Crossan, Johnny

Born Derry, Northern Ireland, 29 November 1938.

Johnny Crossan was an inspirational midfielder who captained City to the Second Division Championship in 1966. A £40,000 buy from Sunderland in January 1965, the holder of 24 Northern Ireland caps (ten of which were won during his time with City) was the subject of some controversy six years earlier when alleged transfer irregularities led to his move to Bristol City being cancelled. The FA subsequently banned Crossan so leaving him no option but to seek his future in European football. He played for Dutch side Sparta Rotterdam and then Standard Liege in Belgium before the ban was lifted and he came back to the UK with Sunderland in October 1962. Crossan played in 38 League games for City in the 1966-67 season, although he did struggle on occasion to maintain his terrific form of the previous term. At the end of the season City recouped the bulk of their fee when they sold him to Middlesbrough for £34,500 where he played 54(2) League games before retiring and returning to his native Ireland where he ran both a sports shop and an off licence.

Maine Road Career

League	94 appearances	24 goals
FA Cup	14 appearances	3 goals
League Cup	2 appearances	1 goal
Total	110 appearances	28 goals

Davies, Wyn

Born Caernarfon, 20 March 1942.

Although Wyn Davies only played one full season at Maine Road, he'd interested Mercer and Allison for some considerable time prior to his signing in August 1971. A £52,500 capture from Newcastle United, Davies was one of the most powerful headers of ball ever to play League football and he won three of his 34 Welsh caps whilst with City. Prior to Newcastle he'd been at Wrexham and Bolton Wanderers where he played 155 League games, many alongside Francis Lee. At Maine Road they again joined forces, Davies's aerial threat being the perfect foil for Lee enabling the England international to find the net on 35 occasions during the 1971-72 season. Davies himself helped himself to nine goals that term and it surprised many when he was sold to Manchester United after just three games of the following season. Affectionately known to all in the game as 'Wyn the Leap', Davies left Old Trafford in June 1973 for Blackpool, later playing for Crystal Palace and Stockport before finishing his career at Crewe. After his retirement from the game he became a baker in Bolton.

Maine Road Career

League	45 appearances	8 goals
FA Cup	2 appearances	
League Cup	3 appearances	1 goal
Other	2 appearances	
Total	52 appearances	9 goals

Dowd, Harry

Born Manchester, 4 July 1938.

Harry Dowd's name will be forever in the record books. He is one of a rare breed of goalkeepers who've actually managed to score a goal in a competitive match. In February 1964, Dowd broke a finger in a League game against Bury. With Matt Gray deputising in goal, the injured 'keeper returned to the game later with his arm in a sling and scored City's equaliser after Derek Kevan's shot had rebounded off the crossbar. Signed from ICI Blackley in January 1958, Dowd's initial job was to replace the legendary Bert Trautmann. After conceding ten goals in his first two games, Dowd went on to produce many (often unnoticed) fine performances in a Maine Road career lasting twelve years. Having won a Second Division Championship medal in 1966, injury robbed him of a First Division one two years later. Dowd eventually removed Ken Mulhearn from the number one spot to take his place in the victorious 1969 FA Cup winning side. In December 1970, he left Maine Road for Oldham Athletic, playing more than 120 League games before retiring to become a sales representative for a brewery.

Maine Road Career

League	181 appearances	1 goal
FA Cup	22 appearances	
League Cup	16 appearances	
Total	219 appearances	1 goal

Doyle, Mike

Born Stockport, 25 November 1946.

A former Stockport Boys player, Mike Doyle joined City's groundstaff in May 1962 and began his career at right-back, a position he played in as City's youngsters reached the semi-final of the FA Youth Cup in the 1963-64 season. He made his first team debut at wing-half against Cardiff in March 1965, and although he also wore the number nine jersey on several occasions during his early days with the club, Mercer and Allison soon realised his best position was in midfield. A tough-tackling player, Doyle hated to lose, and his dislike of neighbours Manchester United was well chronicled. He was a key player in all the trophy-winning sides of the late 60s and early '70s and scored the equalising goal against West Bromwich Albion in the 1970 League Cup Final. Doyle moved into the back four later in his career, forming a solid partnership with Dave Watson, and captained City to success in the 1976 League Cup Final. The owner of five England caps joined Stoke in June 1978, finishing his career with Bolton and then Rochdale. A keen golfer, Doyle later became sales manager for top sports firm Slazenger. His autobiography was pubilshed in 2004.

Maine Road Career

League	441(7) appearances	32 goals
FA Cup	44 appearances	2 goals
League Cup	43 appearances	4 goals
Other	14 appearances	1 goal
Europe	23 appearances	2 goals
Total	565(7) appearances	41 goals

Heslop, George

Born Wallsend, 1 July 1940.

The career of George Heslop really took off after he signed for City in September 1965. After playing just 27 League games in three years with Newcastle, he managed only ten in the same period at Everton, understudying the seemingly ever-present Brian Labone. Heslop brought much-needed organisation and solidity to City's defence and he picked up a Second Division Championship medal at the end of his first season at Maine Road. In that first season he played just three League games less than he'd played in the previous six. He missed just one game of the 1967-68 Championship season and also collected League and European Cup Winners' Cup medals during his time with City. Heslop eventually lost his regular spot at centre-half to the up-and-coming Tommy Booth, and on Christmas Eve 1971 he moved on loan to Cape Town City in South Africa before a permanent move to Bury in August the following year. After retiring from playing, Heslop took over the manager's role at non-league Northwich for a while, before a career in pub management, one of his pubs being City's old headquarters on Hyde Road. In later years, he earned a living as a social worker in St Anne's. Following a short illness, Heslop sadly passed away on 15 Septmeber 2006.

Maine Road Career

League	159(3) appearances	1 goal
FA Cup	18 appearances	1 goal
League Cup	12 appearances	
Other	2 appearances	1 goal
Europe	7(3) appearances	
Total	198(6) appearances	3 goals

Horne, Stan

Born Clanfield, 17 December 1944.

Will all due respect to Stan Horne, there are many more famous names than his to have worn the City colours through the years. However his importance to the club should not be forgotten as he was a valued member of Mercer and Allison's rejuvenated side, especially during the early days. A tough, no-nonsense half-back, Horne signed for City in September 1965 from Aston Villa and played in 15 League games during his first season, one that saw the Blues win the Second Division Championship. He was initially signed on a one-month trial but after three weeks Joe Mercer had seen enough and signed him permanently. Horne had been at Villa Park for three-and-a-half years, winning a Central League Championship medal, where he played under Mercer, albeit in just a handful of first team games. During his early career, he was diagnosed as suffering from high blood pressure and was advised by doctors to quit the game. However he was as determined off the pitch as on it, and was still playing professional football in the mid 1970s. He left Maine Road for Fulham in February 1969 and later played for Chester before finishing his career with Rochdale. Away from football, Horne worked for many years in the building trade.

Maine Road Career

League	48(2) appearances
FA Cup	11 appearances
League Cup	4(1) appearances
Total	63(3) appearances

Jeffries, Derek

Born Manchester, 22 March 1951.

Longsight-born Derek Jeffries really came to prominence during City's injury-hit 1970-71 season. One of many talented youngsters on the books at the time, Jeffries had been a former Manchester Boy and joined the Blues on apprentice forms in July 1966, turning professional two years later. His first senior appearance came as a substitute for the injured Francis Lee in a 2-1 victory over West Bromwich Albion in October 1969. Jeffries was a skilful defender who appeared to 'switch off' on occasion and could certainly be classed as 'laid-back' even before the phrase entered the language seriously. Unable to hold down the number six position permanently due to the presence of Alan Oakes, Jeffries – always the joker in the pack – moved to Crystal Palace in September 1973. In seven years with City he never managed a single senior goal, although in a 2-1 win against Southampton at Maine Road in December 1972, he did beat Joe Corrigan with a 25-yard blinder of an own goal! He played more than a hundred League games for Palace, had loan spells with Peterborough and Millwall and spent the final four years of his career with Chester.

Maine Road Career

League	64(9) appearances
FA Cup	7 appearances
League Cup	2(1) appearances
Other	2(1) appearances
Europe	9 appearances
Total	84(11) appearances

Kennedy, Bobby

Born Motherwell, 23 June 1937.

Bobby Kennedy played in more than 250 games for City after his arrival from Kilmarnock in July 1961. A £45,000 signing (the money coming from the sale of Denis Law to Torino), Kennedy was a vastly experienced player who'd already won two Cup Finals as well as a Championship runner-up medal during his career north of the border. His debut came in the opening game of the 1961-62 season when the Blues beat Leicester 3-1, the game also marking his first goal for his new club and the first of an ever-present 42 appearances in the League that season. Equally at home at either half-back or full-back, Kennedy was a regular fixture for City during the 'dark days' of the early 60s and was rewarded for his efforts with a Second Division Championship medal in 1966. Unable to hold down a permanent spot owing to the emerging Mike Doyle, Glyn Pardoe and Alan Oakes, and the arrival of Tony Book, Kennedy became player-manager of Grimsby Town in March 1969 where he played 84 League games before his retirement. Since then he has successfully worked alongside his wife in a ladies fashion shop in Hebden Bridge.

Maine Road Career

League	216(3) appearances	9 goals
FA Cup	18 appearances	
League Cup	16 appearances	
Europe	1 appearance	
Total	251(3) appearances	9 goals

Lee, Francis

Born Westhoughton, 29 April 1944.

Described by Joe Mercer as "the final piece in the puzzle", nobody scored more goals for City during the Mercer/Allison years than Francis Lee. In fact, only five have ever scored more in the club's entire history. A record £60,000 signing from Bolton in October 1967, Lee was a critical part of the hugely successful City sides in the late 1960s and early '70s. His goal at Newcastle clinched the title in 1968 whilst his penalty won the European Cup Winners' Cup two years later. Capped 27 times for England during his Maine Road career, Lee also built up a successful waste-paper business, his acumen enabling him to become a wealthy man in the days when footballers were paid 'peanuts' in comparison to today's superstars. His dynamic, bustling style of play made him extremely popular with the fans and also won him his fair share of penalties. In August 1974 he was surprisingly sold to Derby where he played for two seasons, collecting his second Champions' medal on the way. Lee returned to Maine Road (with a massive showing of support from the fans) in 1994 to take over as chairman from the beleaguered Peter Swales. Unfortunately the days on the pitch a second time bore no resemblance to those of the first time and Lee resigned in 1998, having seen a succession of failed managers and imminent relegation to the Second Division. On the positive side though, Lee's chairmanship made the club a more successful business than perhaps it had ever been and his enthusiasm and support for the youth set-up should be applauded. Nowadays Lee can be seen regularly as a spectator at Eastlands as well as at the country's racecourses.

Maine Road Career

League	248(1) appearances	112 goals
FA Cup	24 appearances	7 goals
League Cup	26 appearances	14 goals
Other	8(1) appearances	5 goals
Europe	22 appearances	10 goals
Total	328(2) appearances	148 goals

Mann, Arthur

Born Falkirk, 23 January 1948.
After playing for amateur sides Kinlochleven and his own district Burntisland, Arthur Mann had an unsuccessful trial with Cowdenbeath before signing for Hearts in June 1967. He played just 32 League games for the Edinburgh-based club prior to a move to Maine Road on 25 November the following year. Interestingly Mann's fee was a new club record – £65,000 – and eclipsed by £5,000 the previous record held by Francis Lee. He made his debut in a 2-1 defeat at West Ham fives days after his arrival, but, even by his own admission, found the pace of the English game a lot quicker than he'd been used to in Scotland. A stylish left-back, Mann was unable to hold down a regular first-team spot, although his persistence did earn him a League Cup winners' medal in 1970 and he turned out in more than a hundred games for the reserves, many at outside-left. In July 1972 he joined Notts. County and played in 253 League games before a move to Shrewsbury. After Shrewsbury he played 116 times for Mansfield before retiring and taking up both league and non-league management. Arthur Mann was tragically killed in a fork-lift truck accident in February 1999, ironically the same month as '50s favourite Joe Hayes also passed away.

Maine Road Career

League	32(3) appearances
FA Cup	4 appearances
League Cup	1 appearance
Europe	3(1) appearances
Total	40(3) appearances

Mulhearn, Ken

Born Liverpool, 16 October 1945.
Nine days after putting pen to paper in September 1967, Ken Mulhearn was standing in goal in front of 63,000 people in a Maine Road 'derby'. It was Mulhearn's first taste of top-flight football as for the previous three years he'd been with Stockport County. Not surprisingly he was literally worried sick and Malcolm Allison had to keep him out of sight of the other players prior to kick-off. City lost the game 2-1 but Mulhearn had done enough to earn a regular place (at the expense of Harry Dowd) and won a First Division Championship medal seven months later. Mulhearn had a reputation as being a good shot-stopper and was somewhat unlucky to be made the scapegoat after City's poor showings against Fenerbahce in the European Cup. The defeat against the Turkish champions kept Mulhearn out of the first team for more than twelve months. In March 1971 Joe Corrigan had taken over the number one jersey and Mulhearn moved to Shrewsbury, playing 370 League games in

a nine-year stay. After two years with Crewe, Mulhearn finally called it a day; he'd kept goal in more than 600 League games. He later returned to Shrewsbury where he became a pub landlord.

Maine Road Career

League	50 appearances	
FA Cup	5 appearances	
League Cup	3 appearances	
Other	1 appearance	
Europe	3 appearances	
Total	62 appearances	

Oakes, Alan

Born Winsford, 7 September 1942.

Alan Oakes' contribution to the history of Manchester City Football Club is immeasurable. No one has played more senior games for the club; his first was in 1959, his last in 1976; he played 19 games in his first season, 49 in his last. After schoolboy successes with Mid-Cheshire Boys, Oakes joined the staff at Maine Road as an amateur in April 1958. Just over 12 months later he turned professional, making his debut in a 1-1 draw with Chelsea, the first of an amazing 680 appearances in a sky-blue shirt. He was undoubtedly a mainstay of the successful Mercer/Allison teams and although he didn't get as much of the limelight as some of his team-mates, they knew, as did the crowd, how important he was to the side. During his time at Maine Road, he truly was City's "Mr Dependable", guaranteed every week to give his all for the team. Much respected by players from other clubs, Oakes' only international honour came in 1969 when he turned out for The English League against The Scottish League. Many far inferior players to Oakes have won full caps for England. In the summer of 1976 he moved to Chester as player/manager where this remarkable footballer played more than 200 League games before finishing his career at Port Vale in 1983.

Maine Road Career

League	561(3) appearances	26 goals
FA Cup	41 appearances	2 goals
League Cup	46(1) appearances	5 goals
Other	11 appearances	
Europe	17 appearances	1 goal
Total	676(4) appearances	34 goals

Pardoe, Glyn

Born Winsford, 1 June 1946.

Like his cousin Alan Oakes, Glyn Pardoe followed the same route to footballing success with Manchester City. Another product of Mid-Cheshire Boys, Pardoe signed apprentice forms for City in July 1961 and was still an amateur when he made his debut against Birmingham the following April. If Oakes' appearance record seems as though it will never be broken, then the same could also be said about Pardoe's age on his debut; he was just 15 years and 314 days old, the youngest player ever to appear in City's senior side. In his early days he played regularly as a centre-forward, but he was so comfortable with the ball that he could – and did – play anywhere, with the exception of centre-half and goalkeeper. Mercer and Allison decided his best position was left-back and this is where he turned in his most impressive displays for City. He scored the winning goal in the 1970 League Cup Final only to have his leg badly broken in a tackle with George Best nine months later. He would be out of the game for nearly two years. He retired from playing in 1976 and moved on to City's coaching staff where he remained for 16 years before being replaced in a shake-up instigated by manager Peter Reid. Pardoe never returned to football and for mant years worked in the computer centre of a major UK bank.

Maine Road Career

League	303(2) appearances	17 goals
FA Cup	30 appearances	1 goal
League Cup	26 appearances	4 goals

Other	4 appearances	
Europe	15 appearances	
Total	378(2) appearances	22 goals

Summerbee, Mike

Born Preston, 15 December 1942.

Mike Summerbee is part of not one but two footballing triumvirates. As well as joining Lee and Bell for City, 'Buzzer' also joins father George and son Nick as rare family members, all of whom have played professional football in England. Summerbee had played for non-league Cheltenham Town before joining Swindon in March 1960. After more than 200 League games for the west country club (including the '8,000' game at Maine Road) he signed for City in August 1965 for the what turned out to be bargain price of £35,000, or, £3,500 per season, a figure less than a weekly wage for the majority of today's players. His debut came in the opening game of the 1965-66 season at Middlesbrough; a season in which he played all 42 League games and collected a Second Division Championship medal at the end of. Although he did score some vital goals for the Blues (none more so than at Newcastle in 1968 and at Old Trafford in 1969) his best position was on the right-wing where his direct play and crosses provided plenty of goalscoring opportunities for his hungry colleagues. Capped eight times for England, Summerbee played key roles in all City's trophy-winning sides with the exception of the European Cup Winners' Cup Final, a game he missed through injury. He joined Burnley in 1975, later finishing his career at Stockport as player-manager. Today he runs his own successful bespoke shirt-making company and also works on the club's commercial side.

Maine Road Career

League	355(2) appearances	47 goals
FA Cup	34 appearances	11 goals
League Cup	36 appearances	8 goals
Other	8(1) appearances	1 goal
Europe	16 appearances	1 goal
Total	449(3) appearances	68 goals

Towers, Tony

Born Manchester, 13 April 1952.

Not unlike Derek Jeffries, Tony Towers established himself in City's first team during the 1970-71 season. He was one of several young players blooded as injuries took their toll on the Blues that term and he turned in regular fine performances that belittled both his age and inexperience. Moston-born, Towers joined the Blues in 1969 and made his debut in a 3-0 defeat at Southampton the week before City's successful FA Cup Final against Leicester. An industrious and strong midfield player with an eye for goal, it was substitute Towers' shot that finally beat the Portuguese defences of Academica de Coimbra to win City a place in the European Cup Winners' Cup semi-final of 1970. As a reward for that goal, the 18-year-old played in the Final against Gornik. He was capped by England at Schoolboy, Youth and Under-23 level and would eventually win three full caps with his next club Sunderland. Towers moved to the north-east in March 1974 as part of a deal that saw Dennis Tueart and Mick Horswill travel to Maine Road. After three years with Sunderland, he joined Birmingham and in later years tried his hand in North America with Tacoma and Canadian side Vancouver. Towers currently earns his living as a golf professional.

Maine Road Career

League	117(5) appearances	10 goals
FA Cup	8(1) appearances	1 goal
League Cup	14 appearances	
Other	5 appearances	
Europe	13(2) appearances	1 goal
Total	157(8) appearances	12 goals

Young, Neil

Born Manchester, 17 February 1944.

Once of the most graceful City players of all time, Neil Young was born in Fallowfield and grew up looking at the ground from his bedroom window. A tall, left-sided player, he was a former Manchester Boy and joined City's groundstaff in May 1959. He'd been an outside-left during his younger days, but Mercer and Allison coaxed him into the number ten position, and, aware of his shooting prowess, encouraged him to shoot at any occasion. Young made his first-team debut at Villa Park in a 2-1 defeat in November 1961 but really blossomed under the new managerial partnership. Following orders to the letter, Young did begin to shoot, finding the net with unnerving accuracy and often at crucial times. He scored twice in the Championship decider at Newcastle, and then in the European Cup Winners' Cup Final he scored the first and was then brought down enabling Lee to score the second from the penalty spot. In both the Second and First Division Championship seasons he top scored and for good measure was also on target against Leicester in the 1969 FA Cup Final. After ten seasons of first-team football, Young joined Preston in 1972, finishing his career at Rochdale two years later. Fortunately his dispute with the club regarding his testimonial game appears to have been settled and nowadays Young – a former milkman and tiler – can often be seen at Supporters' Club functions as well as running his own soccer schools.

Maine Road Career

League	332(2) appearances	86 goals
FA Cup	32(1) appearances	10 goals
League Cup	28 appearances	6 goals
Other	4 appearances	1 goal
Europe	17 appearances	5 goals
Total	413(3) appearances	108 goals

Mercer, Joe OBE

Born Ellesmere Port, 9 August 1914.

Joe Mercer was one of football's greatest ever ambassadors; known, loved and respected by everyone in the professional game. In a career spanning more than 50 years, he really had seen and done it all, and yet, such was his modesty, he was never known once to gloat about any of his personal, or his teams' achievements. Mercer's father (also called Joe) had played for both Tranmere Rovers and Notts. Forest, and it is from him that young Joe inherited his talent and enthusiasm. Everton signed him as a 15 year-old schoolboy and in 1938-39 (the last full season before the outbreak of World War Two) Mercer – playing at left-half - was the master tactician of a side that won the First Division Championship. Already the holder of five England Caps, Mercer played 26 Wartime Internationals, many as captain, and, at the grand old age of 32, joined Arsenal in December 1946. Despite his age, he continued playing for a further seven years until his career was finally ended when, in April 1954, he broke a leg in a collision with his Arsenal team-mate Joe Wade. Following his injury, Mercer returned to the Wirral and his grocery business, however the lure of the game proved too much. Sixteen months after his injury, Mercer became manager of Sheffield United. Crowd expectations and a constant lack of money made the job very difficult in Yorkshire and in December 1958 he took over at Villa Park. He guided Aston Villa to promotion from Division Two, a League Cup Final win and to two FA Cup semi-finals. Despite these successes, Mercer found himself eventually in a financial position not too dissimilar to that in Sheffield. In the end the pressures of work proved too much, causing him to suffer a stroke in July 1964. Norah Mercer (one of the game's longest suffering and most resilient 'football wives') at last thought he'd finished with the game. Imagine her shock then, when, just twelve months later, he took the job at Maine Road. It was hardly a 'cushy number'. Manchester City had really trodden on hard times; attendances were very poor (almost as poor as the team) and the club was languishing in the middle of the Second Division, giving constant displays of mediocrity. Mercer was well aware of his health limitations and had the foresight to bring in with him a most brilliant right-hand man, coach Malcolm Allison. Calm, quietly spoken, genial Joe and loud, brash Big Mal, two completely different personalities with football the one binding factor. Both men knew exactly what was required to re-establish Manchester City and set about doing it. The partnership lasted seven years and it produced by far, the most successful period in the club's century- plus long history. Not only were the sides successful, but also their attacking and entertaining style of play actually encouraged non-City fans to want them to do well. A far cry from some teams today! In June 1972 Mercer moved (somewhat reluctantly) to Coventry City as General Manager, a position he'd held at Maine Road for the previous eight months. Malcolm Allison had been given sole responsibility for team matters in October 1971, and it was felt by many that Joe's pride had been hurt and the whole affair had been handled badly. Mercer knew full well of Allison's ambition to want to take over the side (and did not blame him in the least) but felt disappointed that the club now wanted no input from him whatsoever on team affairs. In 1974, following the departure of Sir Alf Ramsey, Joe Mercer became caretaker manager of the England side. His enthusiasm and enjoyment of the game rubbed off on the England players and in his seven games in charge, only one ended in defeat. Two years later, he was awarded the OBE for services to football. Mercer finally retired from the game in 1981, when after six years as a director, he resigned from his post at Highfield Road. Back home on the Wirral, Mercer was a regular follower of Tranmere Rovers and could be seen regularly at home games when his busy after dinner speaking engagements allowed. In later years Joe Mercer became a tragic victim of Alzheimer's disease, and, on his 76th birthday, he passed away peacefully in his favourite armchair. A man who always treated "football with a smile" had gone to rejoin some of the finest names in British football in the great reminiscing room in the sky; he was a friend to every one of them.

Allison, Malcolm

Born Dartford, 5 September 1927.

Many people tend to forget, if they knew at all, that before Malcolm Allison became one of the top three coaches in the world (just ask anyone who worked with him, they'll confirm this) that he did actually play a bit as well. He joined Charlton Athletic in December 1945 from amateur side Erith & Belvedere. In four seasons at The Valley he played in only two League games, but even at such a young age, he knew the training wasn't right and began to develop his own ideas. Whilst doing his National Service in Austria he'd visited the Prater Stadium in Vienna (a ground that featured strongly again in Allison's life many years later) and was immediately influenced by the locals' ability with a football. He followed this with a visit to Wembley in 1953 to witness England's defeat by the fabulous Hungarians. Germs of ideas had been planted firmly in Allison's mind. In February 1951 he joined West Ham and was the regular centre-half for seven years, clocking up 238 League appearances. Even throughout his playing career, Allison was fascinated with training and tactics. When most of the other West Ham players had finished training for the day Allison would stay behind with anyone interested to discuss the game and try out new set plays. One player who stayed behind to learn from Allison was a young Bobby Moore. On rainy days the local café was used with salt and pepper pots replacing the more human defenders. Allison's playing career was terminated in 1958 when a bout of tuberculosis caused the loss of a lung. He spent a year in a sanatorium recuperating from his illness before concentrating full-time on coaching. His successes at Lilleshall gave him an opportunity with Southern League side Bath City, a side that included a certain Tony Book among its ranks. After Cambridge University and Toronto, Allison joined Plymouth Argyle and in the summer of 1965 at the bequest of Joe Mercer, was offered a job at Maine Road. Mercer had seen Allison in action at Lilleshall and knowing what a marvellous football brain he possessed, was convinced he was just what was required at a sleeping Maine Road. Mercer's experience and father-like qualities complemented Allison's ability to get the best out of the players perfectly and so began the greatest period in City's history. Players who'd been at the club for years prior to Mercer and Allison's arrival – such as Doyle, Oakes, Pardoe and Young – developed into some of the best players in the country under their expert guidance and tutelage. Allison instigated training methods until then unknown in the game in England, weightlifting and special diets amongst them, and was one of the first to make use of modern gymnasium equipment. In the words of many of his contemporaries he really was "20 years ahead of his time". Second and First Division Championships, the FA Cup, the League Cup and the European Cup Winners' Cup, the trophies queued up to gain shelf space at Maine Road. Allison took over team affairs solely in October 1971 when Mercer 'moved upstairs' to become General Manager. It marked the end of a great partnership; and that's exactly what it was, a partnership. Neither was as good individually; each needed the other. In March 1973, Allison had got to the point when he felt he could no longer motivate the players and moved to Crystal Palace. Six years later he was back at Maine Road primarily to work alongside his former captain Tony Book. This partnership proved less successful than the previous one. Allison immediately stamped his authority on things and began his much-chronicled clearout. Desperate to believe he could resurrect the past, the board back Allison's spending spree but in the end it was all to no avail and he left for a second time in October 1980, returning to Crystal Palace. He later spent time in Portugal and Kuwait, as well as Bristol and Middlesbrough, settling in the north-east in the 1980s, where for a while, he did some scouting work for Arsenal. He is now back in his beloved Manchester and although troubled by illness still tries to attend as many home games as possible.

1965-66

Appearances (substitute appearances in brackets)

Player	League	FA Cup	L. Cup	Other	Europe	Total
Bacuzzi	15(1)					15(1)
Bell	11					11
Brand	17		1			18
Cheetham	12(3)	2	1			15(3)
Connor	29(1)	8				37(1)
Crossan	40	8	1			49
Dowd	38	8	1			47
Doyle	19(1)	7				26(1)
Gomersall	1					1
Gray	3(3)		1			4(3)
Heslop	34	8	1			43
Horne	15	5	1			21
Kennedy	35	8	2			45
Murray	11		1			12
Oakes	41	8	2			51
Ogley	4		1			5
Pardoe	40(1)	8	2			50(1)
Sear	19	3	2			24
Summerbee	42	8	2			52
Wood	1(1)		1			2(1)
Young	35	7	2			44

Goals

Player	League	FA Cup	L. Cup	Other	Europe	Total
Young	14	3				17
Crossan	13	1	1			15
Pardoe	9	1	2			12
Summerbee	8	2				10
Doyle	7	1				8
Murray	7		1			8
Bell	4					4
Connor	3					3
Brand	2					2
Gray	1					1
Kennedy	1					1
Oakes	1					1
Sear	1					1
Opposition o.g.	5	1	1			7
Totals	76	9	5			90

1965-66

DIVISION 2

	P	W	D	L	F	A	W	D	L	F	A	Pts
Manchester C	42	14	7	0	40	14	8	8	5	36	30	59
Southampton	42	13	4	4	51	25	9	6	6	34	31	54
Coventry C	42	14	5	2	54	31	6	8	7	19	22	53
Huddersfield T	42	12	7	2	35	12	7	6	8	27	24	51
Bristol C	42	9	10	2	27	15	8	7	6	36	33	51
Wolves	42	15	4	2	52	18	5	6	10	35	43	50
Rotherham U	42	12	6	3	48	29	4	8	9	27	45	46
Derby Co	42	13	2	6	48	31	3	9	9	23	37	43
Bolton W	42	12	2	7	43	25	4	7	10	19	34	41
Birmingham C	42	10	6	5	41	29	6	3	12	29	46	41
Crystal P	42	11	7	3	29	16	3	6	12	18	36	41
Portsmouth	42	13	4	4	47	26	3	4	14	27	52	40
Norwich C	42	8	7	6	33	27	4	8	9	19	25	39
Carlisle U	42	16	2	3	43	19	1	3	17	17	44	39
Ipswich T	42	12	6	3	38	23	3	3	15	20	43	39
Charlton A	42	10	6	5	39	29	2	8	11	22	41	38
Preston NE	42	7	10	4	37	23	4	5	12	25	47	37
Plymouth A	42	7	8	6	37	26	5	5	11	17	37	37
Bury	42	12	5	4	45	25	2	2	17	17	51	35
Cardiff C	42	10	3	8	37	35	2	7	12	34	56	34
Middlesbrough	42	8	8	5	36	28	2	5	14	22	58	33
Leyton O	42	3	9	9	19	36	2	4	15	19	44	23

1966-67

Appearances (substitute appearances in brackets)

Player	League	FA Cup	L. Cup	Other	Europe	Total
Bell	42	6	2			50
Book	41	6	2			49
Brand	3	1				4
Cheetham	1(1)		1(1)			2(2)
Coleman	9					9
Connor	20(4)	3				23(4)
Crossan	38	6	1			45
Dowd	25	1	2			28
Doyle	14(2)	5				19(2)
Gray	2(1)					2(1)
Heslop	37	4	2			43
Hince	1					1
Horne	29(1)	6	2			37(1)
Jones	4(1)					4(1)
Kennedy	20(1)	2	1			23(1)
Murray	10		1(1)			11(1)
Oakes	39	6	2			47
Ogley	17	5				22
Pardoe	40	6	2			48
Summerbee	32	4	2			38
Young	38	5	2			45

Goals

Player	League	FA Cup	L. Cup	Other	Europe	Total
Bell	12	1	1			14
Crossan	8	1				9
Summerbee	4	2	1			7
Young	4	2	1			7
Pardoe	2	1	1			4
Murray	2		1			3
Hince	2					2
Jones	2					2
Oakes	2					2
Coleman	1					1
Connor	1					1
Doyle		1				1
Gray	1					1
Kennedy	1					1
Opposition o.g.	1	2				3
Totals	43	10	5			58

1966-67

DIVISION 1

	P	W	D	L	F	A	W	D	L	F	A	Pts
Manchester U	42	17	4	0	51	13	7	8	6	33	32	60
Nottingham F	42	16	4	1	41	13	7	6	8	23	28	56
Tottenham H	42	15	3	3	44	21	9	5	7	27	27	56
Leeds U	42	15	4	2	41	17	7	7	7	21	25	55
Liverpool	42	12	7	2	36	17	7	6	8	28	30	51
Everton	42	11	4	6	39	22	8	6	7	26	24	48
Arsenal	42	11	6	4	32	20	5	8	8	26	27	46
Leicester C	42	12	4	5	47	28	6	4	11	31	43	44
Chelsea	42	7	9	5	33	29	8	5	8	34	33	44
Sheffield U	42	11	5	5	34	22	5	5	11	18	37	42
Sheffield W	42	9	7	5	39	19	5	6	10	17	28	41
Stoke C	42	11	5	5	40	21	6	2	13	23	37	41
WBA	42	11	1	9	40	28	5	6	10	37	45	39
Burnley	42	11	4	6	43	28	4	5	12	23	48	39
Manchester C	42	8	9	4	27	25	4	6	11	16	27	39
West Ham U	42	8	6	7	40	31	6	2	13	40	53	36
Sunderland	42	12	3	6	39	26	2	5	14	19	46	36
Fulham	42	8	7	6	49	34	3	5	13	22	49	34
Southampton	42	10	3	8	49	41	4	3	14	25	51	34
Newcastle U	42	9	5	7	24	27	3	4	14	15	54	33
Aston Villa	42	7	5	9	30	33	4	2	15	24	52	29
Blackpool	42	1	5	15	18	36	5	4	12	23	40	21

1967-68

Appearances (substitute appearances in brackets)

Player	League	FA Cup	L. Cup	Other	Europe	Total
Bell	35	4	4			43
Book	42	4	4			50
Bowles	4		0(1)			4(1)
Cheetham	2(1)					2(1)
Clay	1(1)					1(1)
Coleman	38	4	4			46
Connor	10(3)	0(1)	0(1)			10(5)
Corrigan			2			2
Dowd	7		2			9
Doyle	37(1)	4	3			44(1)
Heslop	41	4	4			49
Hince	6		4			10
Horne	4(1)		1			5(1)
Jones	2					2
Kennedy	4(2)					4(2)
Lee	31	4				35
Mulhearn	33	4				37
Oakes	41	4	4			49
Ogley	2					2
Pardoe	41	4	4			49
Summerbee	41	4	4			49
Young	40	4	4			48

Goals

Player	League	FA Cup	L. Cup	Other	Europe	Total
Young	19	1	1			21
Summerbee	14	4	2			20
Lee	16	1				17
Bell	14	2	1			17
Coleman	8	1				9
Doyle	5					5
Bowles	2		2			4
Oakes	2		1			3
Book	1		1			2
Heslop	1	1				2
Hince	2					2
Connor	1					1
Opposition o.g.	1		1			2
Totals	86	10	9			105

1967-68

DIVISION 1

	P	W	D	L	F	A	W	D	L	F	A	Pts
Manchester C	42	17	2	2	52	16	9	4	8	34	27	58
Manchester U	42	15	2	4	49	21	9	6	6	40	34	56
Liverpool	42	17	2	2	51	17	5	9	7	20	23	55
Leeds U	42	17	3	1	49	14	5	6	10	22	27	53
Everton	42	18	1	2	43	13	5	5	11	24	27	52
Chelsea	42	11	7	3	34	25	7	5	9	28	43	48
Tottenham H	42	11	7	3	44	20	8	2	11	26	39	47
WBA	42	12	4	5	45	25	5	8	8	30	37	46
Arsenal	42	12	6	3	37	23	5	4	12	23	33	44
Newcastle U	42	12	7	2	38	20	1	8	12	16	47	41
Nottingham F	42	11	6	4	34	22	3	5	13	18	42	39
West Ham U	42	8	5	8	43	30	6	5	10	30	39	38
Leicester C	42	7	7	7	37	34	6	5	10	27	35	38
Burnley	42	12	7	2	38	16	2	3	16	26	55	38
Sunderland	42	8	7	6	28	28	5	4	12	23	33	37
Southampton	42	9	8	4	37	31	4	3	14	29	52	37
Wolves	42	10	4	7	45	36	4	4	13	21	39	36
Stoke C	42	10	3	8	30	29	4	4	13	20	44	35
Sheffield W	42	6	10	5	32	24	5	2	14	19	39	34
Coventry C	42	8	5	8	32	32	1	10	10	19	39	33
Sheffield U	42	7	4	10	25	31	4	6	11	24	39	32
Fulham	42	6	4	11	27	41	4	3	14	29	57	27

1968-69

Appearances (substitute appearances in brackets)

Player	League	FA Cup	L. Cup	Other	Europe	Total
Bell	39	5	3	1	2	50
Book	15	6				21
Booth	28	7	1			36
Bowles	1(1)		0(1)			1(2)
Bowyer	3(3)					3(3)
Coleman	30(1)	6	3		2	42(1)
Connor	20(1)	1	3	1	1	26(1)
Corrigan	4					4
Dowd	27	7				34
Doyle	40	7	3	1	2	53
Glennon	0(1)					0(1)
Heslop	15(1)		2	1	2	20(1)
Kennedy	10		1		1	12
Lee	37	7	3	1	2	50
Mann	7(1)	1				8(1)
Mulhearn	11		3	1	2	17
Mundy	1(1)					1(1)
Oakes	39	7	3	1	2	52
Owen	16(4)	3	1	1		21(4)
Pardoe	39	7	2	1	2	51
Summerbee	39	6	3	1	2	51
Towers	1					1
Young	40	7	2	1	2	52

Goals

Lee	12	4		2		18
Young	14	2		1		17
Bell	14		1			15
Summerbee	6		2			8
Coleman	3	2			1	6
Owen	3	1		2		6
Doyle	5					5
Booth	1	1				2
Bowyer	1					1
Connor	1					1
Pardoe	1					1
Opposition o.g.	3		1	1		5
Totals	64	10	4	6	1	85

1968-69

DIVISION 1

	P	W	D	L	F	A	W	D	L	F	A	Pts
Leeds U	42	18	3	0	41	9	9	10	2	25	17	67
Liverpool	42	16	4	1	36	10	9	7	5	27	14	61
Everton	42	14	5	2	43	10	7	10	4	34	26	57
Arsenal	42	12	6	3	31	12	10	6	5	25	15	56
Chelsea	42	11	7	3	40	24	9	3	9	33	29	50
Tottenham H	42	10	8	3	39	22	4	9	8	22	29	45
Southampton	42	13	5	3	41	21	3	8	10	16	27	45
West Ham U	42	10	8	3	47	22	3	10	8	19	28	44
Newcastle U	42	12	7	2	40	20	3	7	11	21	35	44
WBA	42	11	7	3	43	26	5	4	12	21	41	43
Manchester U	42	13	5	3	38	18	2	7	12	19	35	42
Ipswich T	42	10	4	7	32	26	5	7	9	27	34	41
Manchester C	42	13	6	2	49	20	2	4	15	15	35	40
Burnley	42	11	6	4	36	25	4	3	14	19	57	39
Sheffield W	42	7	9	5	27	26	3	7	11	14	28	36
Wolves	42	7	10	4	26	22	3	5	13	15	36	35
Sunderland	42	10	6	5	28	18	1	6	14	15	49	34
Nottingham F	42	6	6	9	17	22	4	7	10	28	35	33
Stoke C	42	9	7	5	24	24	0	8	13	16	39	33
Coventry C	42	8	6	7	32	22	2	5	14	14	42	31
Leicester C	42	8	8	5	27	24	1	4	16	12	44	30
QPR	42	4	7	10	20	33	0	3	18	19	62	18

1969-70

Appearances (substitute appearances in brackets)

Player	League	FA Cup	L. Cup	Other	Europe	Total
Bell	31	2	6	1	9	49
Book	38	2	7	1	9	57
Booth	41	2	6	1	9	59
Bowles	10(1)		1			11(1)
Bowyer	33(1)	2	6(1)		4(1)	45(3)
Carrodus	6				0(1)	6(1)
Coleman	5		0(1)	1		6(1)
Connor	8(1)		2			10(1)
Corrigan	34	1	7	1	8	51
Donachie	1(2)					1(2)
Dowd	2					2
Doyle	41	2	7	1	9	60
Glennon	3				0(1)	3(1)
Heslop	6(1)		2		2(3)	10(4)
Jeffries	4(3)				2	6(3)
Lee	36	2	7	1	9	55
Mann	9		1		2	12
Mulhearn	6	1			1	8
Mundy	1					1
Oakes	40	2	7	1	9	59
Owen	2					2
Pardoe	38	2	6	1	9	56
Summerbee	32(1)	2	7	1	7	49(1)
Towers	6(1)	0(1)			2(1)	8(3)
Young	29	2	5	1	8	45

Goals

Lee	13		3		6	22
Bell	11		5	1	5	22
Bowyer	12		2		1	15
Young	6	1	1		4	12
Doyle	4		2		1	7
Summerbee	3		2		1	6
Oakes	3		1		1	5
Towers	1				1	2
Booth					1	1
Pardoe			1			1
Opposition o.g.	2				1	3
Totals	55	1	17	1	22	96

1969-70

DIVISION 1

	P	W	D	L	F	A	W	D	L	F	A	Pts
Everton	42	17	3	1	46	19	12	5	4	26	15	66
Leeds U	42	15	4	2	50	19	6	11	4	34	30	57
Chelsea	42	13	7	1	36	18	8	6	7	34	32	55
Derby Co	42	15	3	3	45	14	7	6	8	19	23	53
Liverpool	42	10	7	4	34	20	10	4	7	31	22	51
Coventry C	42	9	6	6	35	28	10	5	6	23	20	49
Newcastle U	42	14	2	5	42	16	3	11	7	15	19	47
Manchester U	42	8	9	4	37	27	6	8	7	29	34	45
Stoke C	42	10	7	4	31	23	5	8	8	25	29	45
Manchester C	42	8	6	7	25	22	8	5	8	30	26	43
Tottenham H	42	11	2	8	27	21	6	7	8	27	34	43
Arsenal	42	7	10	4	29	23	5	8	8	22	26	42
Wolves	42	8	8	5	30	23	4	8	9	25	34	40
Burnley	42	7	7	7	33	29	5	8	8	23	32	39
Nottingham F	42	8	9	4	28	28	2	9	10	22	43	38
WBA	42	10	6	5	39	25	4	3	14	19	41	37
West Ham U	42	8	8	5	28	21	4	4	13	23	39	36
Ipswich T	42	9	5	7	23	20	1	6	14	17	43	31
Southampton	42	3	12	6	24	27	3	5	13	22	40	29
Crystal P	42	5	6	10	20	36	1	9	11	14	32	27
Sunderland	42	4	11	6	17	24	2	3	16	13	44	26
Sheffield W	42	6	5	10	23	27	2	4	15	17	44	25

1970-71

Appearances (substitute appearances in brackets)

Player	League	FA Cup	L. Cup	Other	Europe	Total
Bell	34	3	1	2	7	47
Book	33(1)	3	1	2	6	45(1)
Booth	26	3	1	1	6	37
Bowyer	6(3)	2	0(1)		1(2)	9(6)
Brennan	0(2)					0(2)
Carrodus	5(1)	0(1)				5(2)
Carter	4(1)				0(1)	4(2)
Connor	11(1)				4	15(1)
Corrigan	33	3	1	2	6	45
Donachie	11				3(1)	14(1)
Doyle	37	3	1	2	7	50
Healey	9				3	12
Heslop	19(1)	2		1	3	25(1)
Hill	20(3)			1	4	25(3)
Jeffries	18(2)	2			6	26(2)
Johnson	4(1)				2	6(1)
Lee	38	2	1	2	9	52
Mann	16(2)	3			1(1)	20(3)
Mellor	5(1)				1	6(1)
Oakes	30	3	1	2	4	40
Pardoe	19		1	2	4	26
Summerbee	26	2	1	1(1)	6	36(1)
Towers	33(1)		1	2	9	45(1)
White	1					1
Young	24	2(1)	1	2	7	36(1)

Goals

	League	FA Cup	L. Cup	Other	Europe	Total
Lee	14		1	1	4	20
Bell	13	4			2	19
Doyle	5				1	6
Summerbee	4					4
Book	2					2
Booth	1				1	2
Hill	2					2
Mellor	1				1	2
Young	1				1	2
Bowyer		1				1
Carter	1					1
Heslop				1		1
Oakes	1					1
Opposition o.g.	2					2
Totals	47	5	1	2	10	65

1970-71

DIVISION 1

	P	W	D	L	F	A	W	D	L	F	A	Pts
Arsenal	42	18	3	0	41	6	11	4	6	30	23	65
Leeds U	42	16	2	3	40	12	11	8	2	32	18	64
Tottenham H	42	11	5	5	33	19	8	9	4	21	14	52
Wolves	42	13	3	5	33	22	9	5	7	31	32	52
Liverpool	42	11	10	0	30	10	6	7	8	12	14	51
Chelsea	42	12	6	3	34	21	6	9	6	18	21	51
Southampton	42	12	5	4	35	15	5	7	9	21	29	46
Manchester U	42	9	6	6	29	24	7	5	9	36	42	43
Derby Co	42	9	5	7	32	26	7	5	9	24	28	42
Coventry C	42	12	4	5	24	12	4	6	11	13	26	42
Manchester C	42	7	9	5	30	22	5	8	8	17	20	41
Newcastle U	42	9	9	3	27	16	5	4	12	17	30	41
Stoke C	42	10	7	4	28	11	2	6	13	16	37	37
Everton	42	10	7	4	32	16	2	6	13	22	44	37
Huddersfield T	42	7	8	6	19	16	4	6	11	21	33	36
Nottingham F	42	9	4	8	29	26	5	4	12	13	35	36
WBA	42	9	8	4	34	25	1	7	13	24	50	35
Crystal P	42	9	5	7	24	24	3	6	12	15	33	35
Ipswich T	42	9	4	8	28	22	3	6	12	14	26	34
West Ham U	42	6	8	7	28	30	4	6	11	19	30	34
Burnley	42	4	8	9	20	31	3	5	13	9	32	27
Blackpool	42	3	9	9	22	31	1	6	14	12	35	23

1971-72

Appearances (substitute appearances in brackets)

Player	League	FA Cup	L. Cup	Other	Europe	Total
Bell	33	2	1			36
Book	40	2	2	1		45
Booth	40	2	2	1		45
Brennan				2		2
Carter	0(1)			1		1(1)
Connor	8			1		9
Corrigan	35	2	2	0(1)		39(1)
Davies	40	2	2	1		45
Donachie	35(2)	2	2	2		41(2)
Doyle	41	2	2	1		46
Hanvey				1		1
Healey	7			2		9
Henson	0(1)			1		1(1)
Heslop	7		1			8
Hill	4(2)		1	1		6(2)
Jeffries	9(3)		1(1)	2		12(4)
Johnson	0(1)			1		1(1)
Lee	42	2	2	0(1)		46(1)
Marsh	7(1)					7(1)
Mellor	21(1)		1	1		23(1)
Oakes	31(1)	2				33(1)
Summerbee	40	2	2	1		45
Towers	19(2)	2	1	2		24(2)
Young	3(2)					3(2)

Goals

Lee	33	1	1			35
Bell	12		2			14
Davies	8		1			9
Booth	4					4
Marsh	4					4
Mellor	3			1		4
Summerbee	3					3
Towers	3					3
Doyle	1			1		2
Opposition o.g.	2					2
Book	1					1
Carter	1					1
Connor	1					1
Hill	1					1
Totals	77	1	4	2		84

1971-72

DIVISION 1

	P	W	D	L	F	A	W	D	L	F	A	Pts
Derby Co	42	16	4	1	43	10	8	6	7	26	23	58
Leeds U	42	17	4	0	54	10	7	5	9	19	21	57
Liverpool	42	17	3	1	48	16	7	6	8	16	14	57
Manchester C	42	16	3	2	48	15	7	8	6	29	30	57
Arsenal	42	15	2	4	36	13	7	6	8	22	27	52
Tottenham H	42	16	3	2	45	13	3	10	8	18	29	51
Chelsea	42	12	7	2	41	20	6	5	10	17	29	48
Manchester U	42	13	2	6	39	26	6	8	7	30	35	48
Wolves	42	10	7	4	35	23	8	4	9	30	34	47
Sheffield U	42	10	8	3	39	26	7	4	10	22	34	46
Newcastle U	42	10	6	5	30	18	5	5	11	19	34	41
Leicester C	42	9	6	6	18	11	4	7	10	23	35	39
Ipswich T	42	7	8	6	19	19	4	8	9	20	34	38
West Ham U	42	10	6	5	31	19	2	6	13	16	32	36
Everton	42	8	9	4	28	17	1	8	11	9	31	36
WBA	42	6	7	8	22	23	6	4	11	20	31	35
Stoke C	42	6	10	5	26	25	4	5	12	13	31	35
Coventry C	42	7	10	4	27	23	2	5	14	17	44	33
Southampton	42	8	5	8	31	28	4	2	15	21	52	31
Crystal P	42	4	8	9	26	31	4	5	12	13	34	29
Nottingham F	42	6	4	11	25	29	2	5	14	22	52	25
Huddersfield T	42	4	7	10	12	22	2	6	13	15	37	25

Summary 1965-72

Appearances (substitute appearances in brackets)

Player	League	FA Cup	L. Cup	Other	Europe	Total
Bacuzzi, Dave	15(1)		1			16(1)
Bell, Colin	225	22	17	4	18	286
Book, Tony	209(1)	23	16	4	15	267(1)
Booth, Tommy	135	14	10	3	15	177
Bowles, Stan	15(2)		1(2)			16(4)
Bowyer, Ian	42(8)	4	6(2)		5(3)	57(13)
Brand, Ralph	20	1				21
Brennan, Mike	0(2)			2		2(2)
Carrodus, Frank	11(1)	0(1)			0(1)	11(3)
Carter, Steve	4(2)		1		0(1)	5(3)
Cheetham, Roy	15(5)	2	2(1)			19(6)
Clay, John	1(1)					1(1)
Coleman, Tony	82(1)	10	7(1)	1	2	102(2)
Connor, Dave	106(11)	12(1)	5(1)	2	5	130(13)
Corrigan, Joe	106	6	12	3(1)	14	141(1)
Crossan, Johnny	78	14	2			94
Davies, Wyn	40	2	2	1		45
Donachie, Willie	47(4)	2	2	2	3(1)	56(5)
Dowd, Harry	99	16	5			120
Doyle, Mike	229(4)	30	16	5	18	298(4)
Glennon, Chris	3(1)				0(1)	3(2)
Gomersall, Vic	1					1
Gray, Matt	5(4)		1			6(4)
Hanvey, Keith			1			1
Healey, Ronnie	16			2	3	21
Henson, Phil	0(1)			1		1(1)
Heslop, George	159(3)	18	12	2	7(3)	198/(6)
Hill, Freddie	24(5)		1	2	4	31(5)
Hince, Paul	7		4			11
Horne, Stan	48(2)	11	4			63(2)
Jeffries, Derek	31(8)	2	1(1)	2	8	44(9)
Johnson, Jeff	4(2)			1	2	7(2)
Jones, Chris	6(1)					6(1)
Kennedy, Bobby	69(3)	10	4		1	84(3)
Lee, Francis	184	17	13	4(1)	20	238(1)
Mann, Arthur	32(3)	4	1		3(1)	40(4)
Marsh, Rodney	7(1)					7(1)
Mellor, Ian	26(2)		1	1	1	29(2)
Mulhearn, Ken	50	5	3	1	3	62
Mundy, Jimmy	2(1)					2(1)
Murray, Jimmy	21		2(1)			23(1)
Oakes, Alan	261(1)	32	19	4	15	331(1)
Ogley, Alan	23	5	1			29
Owen, Bobby	18(4)	3	1	1		23(4)
Pardoe, Glyn	217(1)	27	17	4	15	280(1)

Sear, Cliff	19	3	2		24	
Summerbee, Mike	252(1)	28	21	4(1)	15	320(2)
Towers, Tony	59(4)	2(1)	2	4	11(1)	78(6)
White, Howard	1					1
Wood, Alf	1(1)		1			2(1)
Young, Neil	209(2)	27(1)	16	4	17	273(3)
Games played	294	32	21	6	20	373
Won	126	16	12	1	12	167
Drawn	85	10	3	2	3	103
Lost	83	6	6	3	5	103
Goals for	448	46	45	11	33	583
Goals against	329	23	28	10	15	405

51 players used

Summary 1965-72

Goals

Player	League	FA Cup	L. Cup	Other	Europe	Total
Lee, Francis	88	6	5	3	10	112
Bell, Colin	80	7	10	1	7	105
Young, Neil	58	9	3	1	5	76
Summerbee, Mike	42	8	7		1	58
Doyle, Mike	27	2	2	1	2	34
Crossan, Johnny	21	3	1			25
Opposition o.g.	16	2	3	1	1	23
Bowyer, Ian	13	1	2		1	17
Pardoe, Glyn	12	1	4			17
Coleman, Tony	12	3			1	16
Murray, Jimmy	9	1	2			12
Oakes, Alan	9		2		1	12
Booth, Tommy	6	1			2	9
Davies, Wyn	8		1			9
Connor, Dave	7					7
Owen, Bobby	3	1		2		6
Mellor, Ian	4			1	1	6
Book, Tony	4		1			5
Towers, Tony	4				1	5
Bowles, Stan	2		2			4
Hince, Paul	4					4
Marsh, Rodney	4					4
Heslop, George	1	1		1		3
Hill, Freddie	3					3
Brand, Ralph	2					2
Carter, Steve	2					2
Gray, Matt	2					2
Jones, Chris	2					2
Kennedy, Bobby	2					2
Sear, Cliff	1					1
Totals	448	46	45	11	33	583